D1271205

Constitutional Cultures

Constitutional Cultures

The Mentality and Consequences of Judicial Review

Robert F. Nagel

UNIVERSITY OF CALIFORNIA PRESS
Berkeley · *Los Angeles* · *London*

University of California Press
Berkeley and Los Angeles, California

University of California Press, Ltd.
London, England

© 1989 by
The Regents of the University of California

Library of Congress Cataloging-in-Publication Data

Nagel, Robert F.
    Constitutional cultures.

    Includes index.
    1. Judicial review—United States.   2. United
States—Constitutional law—Interpretation and
construction.   I. Title.
KF4575.N34   1989   342.73'02   88-20915
                       347.3022
ISBN 0-520-06375-9 (alk. paper)

Printed in the United States of America
1   2   3   4   5   6   7   8   9

For Pru

Between these alternatives there is no middle ground. The constitution is either a superior, paramount law, unchangeable by ordinary means, or it is on a level with ordinary legislative acts.

John Marshall in *Marbury v. Madison* (1803)

Behind all the theoretical talk of government and legitimacy, behind the systems and projects, behind even the forms of government itself, there is a culture, a living organization of mankind, upon which all the talk of system and mechanism depends, both for its intelligibility and for its effects. . . . In all its complexity and interconnectedness it is our substantive and actual constitution.

James B. White in *When Words Lose Their Meaning* (1984)

Contents

Acknowledgments

I began the essays that comprise this book many years ago. At each stage, many people—too many to be listed here—provided criticisms, suggestions, and other assistance. I trust that each knows how grateful I am. I also appreciate the contributions of participants in colloquia at Northwestern University Law School, Michigan Law School, and (on several occasions) the University of Colorado School of Law. I was fortunate to visit at Cornell Law School in 1980–81 and at Michigan Law School in the summer of 1984; the interest of members of those faculties encouraged me to proceed.

Versions of these essays have been published previously as follows: chapter 2 in NOMOS XXV, LIBERAL DEMOCRACY (J. Pennock and J. Chapman, eds., 1983); chapter 3 in 69 Cornell Law Review (1984) and in 75 California Law Review (1987); chapter 4 in the Supreme Court Review (1981); chapter 5 in 82 Yale Law Journal (1972); chapter 6 in 127 University of Pennsylvania Law Review (1979) and 4 Constitutional Commentary (1986); and chapter 7 in 84 Michigan Law Review (1985). In addition, some passages are drawn from writings published in 7 Harvard Journal of Law and Public Policy (1984), and 84 Columbia Law Review (1984). Material in chapters 2, 4, and 5 is published here with the kind permission of New York University, the University of Chicago, and the Yale Law Journal, respectively.

The University of Colorado law faculty is fortunate to have a highly professional secretarial staff. I thank Marge Brunner, Anne Guthrie, Marcia Murphy, and Kay Wilkie for their hard work and good cheer.

Academic colleagues, friends from the practicing bar, and my parents and brothers contributed in important ways to the ideas in this book. Many who helped must have viewed some of the turns in my thinking with dismay, but their generosity never diminished.

Boulder, Colorado

CHAPTER I

What About *Brown?*

The meaning of the Constitution of the United States, of course, emerges from the adversarial arguments and judicial opinions that make up the legal culture. It is less commonly appreciated that the Constitution is also expressed in the institutions, behaviors, and understandings that form the general political culture. In the chapters that follow I urge that judicial interpretations should be viewed not only in the conventional way, as efforts to extract meaning from the document, but also as embodiments of the intellectual culture of lawyers and judges—embodiments, that is, of certain analytic and communicative styles. I urge, moreover, that for reasons that are intrinsic to adjudication, this legal constitution is inferior in important ways to the political constitution and that excessive reliance on judicial review is undermining both fidelity to constitutional principles and the general health of the political culture.

This book does not attempt anything so conclusive as a theory of judicial review. I aim only to emphasize some undervalued angles from which to view the work of the courts. A challenge to the normal perspectives on judicial review is, I think, timely. Despite all the vigorous academic and political debate about constitutional interpretation, there is widespread underlying agreement that the judiciary should be the predominant protector of constitutional values. In the past few decades, judicial power has come to be not only morally significant but routine.

Today federal courts control more important public decisions and institutions in more detail and for more extended periods than at any time in our history.[1] Constitutional interpretations have important influence over a vast range of policies, including those relating to marriage, parent-child relations, abortion, zoning, public administration, police practices, aid to private education, commercial advertising, defamation, criminal penalties, aliens, women, jury selection, voting, affirmative action, and state taxation. There is no way to be sure how many school districts are significantly controlled by federal judges, but a reasonable estimate would put the figure at more than six hundred. In the few years since the theory of a "conditions of confinement" lawsuit was first created, judges have ordered pervasive prison reforms in more than thirty states and suits are pending in others. There have been decrees affecting some 270 local jails, with hundreds of cases pending. Mental health systems and public housing have been under judicial control in some states, and of course the judiciary has been responsible for numerous legislative apportionment plans. There have been decrees that govern welfare programs, and the courts are now beginning to restructure state and local personnel policies in an effort to dismantle patronage systems.

This unprecedented use of judicial power is not a response to specific and limited necessity or emergency. The power is exercised in every state and on a wide variety of social issues. Moreover, there is considerable potential for growth of judicial involvement in the governmental process. Even a relatively "conservative" Supreme Court seems transfixed; recent decisions, such as those dealing with the legislative veto and political gerrymandering, illustrate the Court's continuing insistence that almost no public issue should be excluded from judicial oversight.[2] Fertile minds in academia and the practicing bar are always at work generating legal theories that would "reinvigorate" provisions, like the clause prohibiting impairment of contracts or the clause guaranteeing the states a republican form of government, that had previously been relatively quiescent.[3] Heavy reliance on the judiciary—in various ideological directions—is fast becoming an ingrained part of the American system; already it is difficult for many, whether in or out of the academy, even to imagine any alternative.

There are enough theories of judicial review. All are animated by the conviction that aggressive judicial enforcement of the Constitution is valuable and in need of legitimation. The parade of theories, each one brilliantly argued and each one profoundly unsatisfactory, itself attests to the need to reconsider the usefulness of judicial review and to try to imagine political life without our current level of dependence on it.[4]

This book suggests that one main enemy of the constitutional order, whether conceived of as a public morality or a political theory, is the routinization of judicial power. The judiciary's frequent intervention in ordinary political affairs works against both the preservation and the healthy growth of our constitutional traditions. Excessively concerned about tangible accomplishment, courts close themselves off from the wisdom available in the political constitution and undermine long-term support for basic principles. I maintain that this is so more than we like to admit even in those areas, such as freedom of speech, where judicial power is usually thought most appropriate. When controlling behavior is less important than shaping attitudes, preoccupation with social control can also lead to judicial abdication. This, too, can impoverish public understandings, and I use federalism to illustrate this possibility.

Courts, then, should attempt less. They should seldom hold the acts of other branches and levels of government to be unconstitutional. The judiciary's power to invalidate the decisions of other institutions should be reserved for those special occasions when some aberrant governmental action is emphatically inconsistent with constitutional theory, text, and public understanding as expressed in prolonged practice. Even this modest role may be asking too much, for, as much of this book explains, a supportive function is incompatible with the way modern judges think and communicate. Nevertheless, it is under these circumstances, if at all, that the decisions of the courts can faithfully articulate constitutional values and reinforce the political culture to protect those values. This viewpoint reduces the pressure that has pushed constitutional theorizing to esoteric and ultimately disappointing extremes. If judicial power is much less essential or even desirable than we have come to think in recent years, retrenchment is called for rather than justification; we need a sense of direction more than a theory.

If the issue of judicial review were fresh, it would hardly be grounds for resisting the perspective offered here that it entailed a relatively modest judicial role. The startling and curious idea would be the one to which we have become accustomed. It would seem downright implausible that the limited number and range of provisions in the Constitution could be persuasively connected—even by the elaborate scaffolding of judicial doctrine—to the resolution of the myriad highly specific political and social issues to which constitutional law is now applied. It would seem magical or superstitious to consult a short, old legal document for conclusive wisdom on the appropriate dynamics of family life, or on the proper way to suspend a public school student, or on the correct relationship between the Congress and the executive agencies administering the welfare state.[5] If the issue were fresh, it would seem so much simpler and more direct for courts to admit that the Constitution either does not bear at all, or bears only in complex and indeterminate ways, on most specific public issues.

Although the current exalted place of the Court's constitutional pronouncements is relatively recent, the issue is not fresh. Reliance on judicial review has varied from one historical period to another, but *Brown v. Board of Education,* the school desegregation case of 1954, was the fulcrum on which the world of judicial review was made to move decisively. The tolerance among otherwise sophisticated people for exceedingly implausible interpretive functions is traceable to *Brown.*[6] The moral force of that decision stands in the way of any judicial role restrained enough to be coordinate with a realistic assessment of legal interpretation. If the courts were to invalidate legislative or executive acts only rarely and only when the judiciary's decisions were supported by plain meaning confirmed by widespread public understanding, then the possibility of important moral decisions might be jeopardized. It is natural to resist any view that threatens the Court's politically potent and morally exciting role. If I am, then, to ask for an open mind on the perspectives offered in the following pages, the reader is entitled at the outset to know, "What about *Brown?*"

It is an answer, but not a satisfactory answer, to match against the Court's moral successes, such as *Brown,* its moral disasters, such as *Dred Scott.* While the full historical ledger is sobering, mixed results will not dissuade anyone caught up in the drama of the Court's modern record or anyone captured by the lure of the possible. However, to acknowledge the inescapable virtue of a few cases like *Brown* is not to concede that extraordinary cases ought to set the outer limits of *normal* judicial decision making. Too much constitutional theory is fixated on the landmark cases; not enough attention is paid to the character and consequences of the ordinary, pervasive application of constitutional decisions. As a matter of logic, any governmental structure, even one where decisions are made by the roll of the dice or the whim of a tyrant, can occasionally produce a profoundly good decision. And, as a matter of process, the routinization of judicial power (as the following chapters argue) eventually undermines the moral and communicative power of decisions like *Brown.*

Still, what about the original desegregation decision itself? Because that decision departed from powerful evidence regarding the intended consequences of the equal protection clause and because it rested on dubious and transient social scientific findings, it has been exceedingly difficult to assimilate into normal justificatory standards. The perspective on judicial review offered in the remainder of this book is more compatible with *Brown* than are those normal standards. The Court's conclusion that official separation of the races in the public schools casts a stigma of inferiority on minority children was in fact rooted in widely shared understandings. Its realistic conclusion was a blessed relief from the fiction—always more believable to those immersed in legal interpretations than to ordinary people—that separate facilities could somehow be equal.[7] Statutory school segregation was a regional aberration within the national culture. *Brown* confirmed and enforced the understanding of "equal protection of the laws" held and practiced by the dominant national culture.

The prevalence of nondiscriminatory educational laws in most of the country, of course, did not assure the rightness of *Brown*. Consensus and practice are not the same as either legality or morality. But they do afford important bases for judgment. It was not rigorous examination of the text of the Constitution or studious contemplation of moral philosophy that led the Justices who voted for *Brown* to comprehend the injustice of school segregation. It was not by reading or dreaming that they knew racial integration to be possible. Our political life had made available to the Justices a body of common experience about both segregation and integration. In the context of this experience, racial exclusion unmistakably involved acute insult and profound political injustice; in light of this experience, nondiscriminatory attendance policies stood, not as imaginable, but as familiar alternatives. Everyday perceptions grounded *Brown* in a morality that was both powerful and widely understandable.

No theory of judicial review is offered here and certainly no theory that can fully legitimize *Brown,* but in important respects the decision is consistent with what is recommended here. In its result and in at least some of its reasoning, *Brown* drew from the substance of general experience and submitted to the discipline of common language. As slight as this claim may seem, it is, as I intend to demonstrate, far more than can be said of the bulk of the Court's work.

CHAPTER 2

Interpretation and Importance

Judicial enforcement of the Constitution has become increasingly pervasive and ambitious in recent decades, but the power itself goes back at least to 1803, when the Court decided *Marbury v. Madison*. Beginning with that decision, the moral and legal authority of judicial review has been justified in part on the grounds that constitutional principles were "designed to be permanent . . . unchangeable by ordinary means."[1] Variations on this theme continue to play an important part in constitutional theory. Alexander Bickel wrote that enforcement of constitutional principles by the courts "may meet a need for continuity and harmony in our values."[2] Henry M. Hart, Jr., sought justification for judicial review in the need for "articulating and developing impersonal and durable principles."[3] The persistent tendency to base constitutional interpretation, at least in part, on the intent of the framers also assumes the feasibility of permanent meaning for constitutional provisions. It is possible to imagine a variety of functions for a written constitution, but any theory that did not allow for durability would hardly be recognizable as "constitutional."

Although much of the legitimacy of constitutional law continues to depend on the possibility of enduring meaning, the suggestion that important constitutional provisions can have relatively plain, stable meaning would be met with widespread skepticism among constitutional scholars. Armed with sophisticated understanding about the inherent inaccuracies of written communication and about the demands created by social change, most legal scholars would regard it as naive to suggest that constitutional principles could have, or should have, consistent meaning through the centuries.

Durable meaning may be more desirable and feasible than is commonly thought. In the first section of this chapter, I suggest that skepticism on this point can be traced to the pervasive influence of the legal profession on how we think about the Constitution. The second section describes those parts of the Constitution that have had relatively constant meaning and that have been fairly consistently realized. I then explore the relationship between heavy reliance on interpretation and the preconditions for durable meaning. I conclude that to an unexpected extent judicial restraint may be necessary to a stable constitutional order.

The Interpreted Constitution

The legal profession monopolizes the opportunity both to present arguments to courts and to render authoritative interpretations. Lawyers therefore affect not only what the Constitution is, as a practical matter, but also how it is thought about and understood. Our conception of the Constitution has been shaped by their instincts and intellectual habits.

Legal training emphasizes argumentative skills. These skills require acute sensitivity to the potential for intellectual uncertainty. Does a provision have a plain, established meaning that is adverse to your client's interests? Perhaps its meaning can be nudged off that fixed point if the provision is read together with surrounding provisions; or, if those provisions do not help, perhaps in the light of other cases, or with the perspective of the most recent sociological data, or in the context of some notion of moral philosophy. Does the history of the provision appear to support the established meaning? Parse the speeches of those who favored that meaning to show that they did not have in mind precisely your client's circumstance. Find the quotation from the atypical framer. Contrast circumstances at the time of the provision's adoption with current conditions.

Despite the common public perception of lawyers, such argumentation is not necessarily sophistic. Effective legal argument can be penetrating: it finds ambiguities because a careful reading demonstrates that the text is less clear than first appeared, and it locates uncertainties in historical intent because history is rich and complex. Indeed, intellectual sophistication is the main ally of those who see the Constitution as a "living document," flexible enough to be useful in modern conditions.[4] But, convincing or not in a particular instance, the lawyers' craft is argument and their milieu is unsettled meaning.

Like veteran police officers who cannot find innocence in their crime-filled world, lawyers almost never see meaning as simple or clear. It is something to be argued about and, ultimately, may seem to be no more than the momentary outcome of argumentation. In short, legal thinking builds upon and accentuates contemporary tendencies toward relativism and solipsism. Oddly, then, those most entrusted with the meaning of our fundamental document are by training, role, and instinct inclined to think that it is difficult to discover meaning. Hence one of the most obvious, but least considered, consequences of lawyers' influence on our understanding of the Constitution is the widespread assumption that interpretation is crucially important.

Because our conception of the Constitution is so shaped by argument about its meaning, interpretation seems indispensable. The most familiar content of the Constitution is simply a series of judicial interpretations. The power of judicial review, often described as the very centerpiece of the constitutional system, was, of course, created out of complex arguments about the nature and purposes of constitutional government, as well as from more conventional textual analyses.[5] Validation of broad national powers was accomplished by structural and contextual arguments that gave the words "necessary and proper" in article I, section 8 the sense of "convenient."[6] The most commonly praised aspect of the Constitution—protection of individuals' rights against state and local governments—is the product of an interpretive device by which most of the Bill of Rights is deemed "incorporated" into the fourteenth amendment.[7] The "constitution" that is popularly discussed today consists of powerful reasons why the requirement of "equal protection of the laws," which was surely aimed at racial discrimination, does not actually prohibit many significant racial inequalities.[8] The same requirement is also represented by analyses about whether exclusion of women from draft registration (a matter the framers never dreamed they were addressing) can actually meet the "tests" of an "important state interest" and a "substantial relationship" between that interest and the means chosen for its accomplishment.[9] And so on. A relatively short document has come to be represented by hundreds of volumes of judicial interpretation that purport to set forth prudential and moral principles relevant to almost any public issue. Legal scholars summarize byzantine doctrines of "constitutional law" in elaborate and heavy treatises.[10] The law journals swell with ideas for variations on the complex explanatory and interpretative structures that have come to be the Constitution: "A 'New' Fourteenth Amendment: The Decline of State Action, Fundamental Rights, and Suspect Classification . . ."; "Due Process as a Management Tool in Schools and Prisons"; "The Newsman's Qualified Privilege: An Analytical Approach"; "A 'Birth Right': Home Births, Midwives, and the Right to Privacy."[11]

Absorption in recondite interpretation tends to legitimize the primacy of the judiciary in constitutional matters because judges are considered expert in the intellectual tasks associated with legal exegesis. This expertise—skill at assessing evidence about historical intent, at textual analysis, at harmonizing various provisions and cases, at clear and reasoned explanation—is thought to be a qualification for accurate and consistent interpretation. Public respect for judicial methods, therefore, tends to reconcile the fact of pervasive interpretation with the ideal of enduring constitutional principles. Ordinarily, judicial interpretations are viewed as marginal shifts in meaning that merely adapt consistent underlying principles to new circumstances. This view dramatically understates the extent of change brought about by interpretation. Its currency suggests that uncertainty and interpretative variation in constitutional meaning have come to be largely taken for granted and is, in this sense, a testament to the influence of the legal profession. The simple fact is that the lawyers have steadily and fundamentally altered the Constitution.[12]

Major organizational principles come and go. The rule that legislative bodies may not unduly delegate their authority to appointed agencies was an important, effective principle for a few years.[13] Hornbooks now describe it as a dead doctrine.[14] But judges and scholars hint the rule may reappear in some new form in the future.[15] For many years the power to regulate commerce among the states was defined narrowly so as not to displace the police powers reserved to the states by the tenth amendment.[16] Then this provision, requiring that unenumerated powers be reserved to the states, became a "mere truism" that did not affect the definition of "commerce."[17] For more than 150 years, according to the doctrine of judicial review, the Supreme Court was the ultimate interpreter of the Constitution. In 1966, while evaluating a statute that prohibited certain English literacy requirements for voting, the Court discovered that Congress had broad power to define "equal protection" under the fourteenth amendment.[18] More recently, the Court has again denied that Congress shares interpretative authority with the judiciary.[19] For decades the power of judicial review was limited by the separation of powers, which was thought to prevent the judicial department from operating prisons or designing reapportionment plans.[20] Now, judicial power frequently reaches both of these matters.

Explanatory doctrines appear and then fade away. The Constitution prohibited "irrebutable presumptions" for a while because they deprived individuals of governmental benefits on the basis of group membership, but that rule is now discredited.[21] Legislative classifications that left illegitimate children at a disadvantage had to be justified under a "strict scrutiny" standard; then "mere rationality" would do; then "strict scrutiny" again; then yet a third standard was created.[22] Indeed, constitutional rights themselves exist and then do not. The rights to contract and to hold property were used to void a range of state regulations, especially those designed to improve conditions of labor, but both are now out of favor and (at least for the moment) are not significantly enforced.[23] Wholly new rights appear, like the right to contraceptives and abortion.[24] Some rights, like the right to have illegally seized evidence excluded at a trial, are nonexistent, then exist, then mysteriously exist though not necessarily as a part of the Constitution itself.[25]

The meaning of other rights changes fundamentally. For some 136 years the Bill of Rights applied only against the national government, but since 1925 some of these rights at various times have begun to apply against state governments.[26] The prohibition against the establishment of religion did not prohibit voluntary prayers in public schools until 1962.[27] Patronage systems began to violate the first amendment in 1976.[28] For most of our history, reasonably vigorous public debate somehow coexisted with traditional defamation rules, but in 1964 it was discovered that the first amendment required significant alterations in these rules in order to foster vigorous public debate.[29] Although since the fourteenth century the word "jury" probably had meant a deliberative body of twelve members and although that was the "usual" expectation of the framers of the sixth amendment, in 1970 the word was reshaped to include groups of only six.[30]

Judicial changes in constitutional meaning have not been confined to recent years or to Courts influenced by the bracing jurisprudence of legal realism. In 1829 the Constitution permitted states to regulate their internal affairs even if the effect was to obstruct interstate commerce, so long as the state rule did not conflict with any congressional statute.[31] By 1851, however, the Court had discovered in the grant of authority *to*

Congress to regulate commerce a basis for *courts* to invalidate state laws inconsistent with judicial views of properly unimpeded commercial activity.[32] Before 1918 the Constitution allowed the national government to prohibit interstate shipment of goods considered by Congress to have harmful effects; however, in that year a conservative and formalistic Court was able to explain that the Constitution prohibited exclusion from interstate commerce of goods produced by child labor.[33]

Specifics cannot capture the scope of the alterations accomplished by interpretation over the years. A document that was originally grounded on the importance of personal industry and private property has been interpreted to emphasize self-expression and sexual freedom.[34] A document carefully designed to constrain strong national power and to protect valued local authority now permits almost limitless national power and regards local authority with suspicion.[35] And (as I show in chapter 4) a political theory that originally appraised individual rights with some caution and emphasized the distribution of power through the principles of federalism and separation of powers has become a theory that views organizational principles skeptically and overwhelmingly emphasizes the protection of individual rights.

Whether particular changes were justifiable or not, it is surely true that durable, "permanent" meaning has not been afforded by judicial expertise. But why, after all, should the judiciary seem a likely institution for preserving stable meaning? The skills and instincts associated with the legal profession are not those of a scholar. Despite sober demeanors and rigorous training, judges do not approximate truth in the manner of the detached scientist or scholar. They identify and exploit ambiguity and uncertainty.[36] Moreover, the process of adjudication is invoked only when a legal principle is, according to someone's lights, not working. Thus judges stand at the spot in the governmental system where constitutional malfunctions are most certain to appear and where the need for revision will seem most apparent. Interpretation itself is a process that is necessary only when established understandings are challenged, when some change in accepted meaning is called for. Put plainly, the special function of the judiciary is to change constitutional meaning.

All this, of course, is widely understood but is usually phrased differently: the Constitution "adapts," "grows," "is kept up to date," and "lives." So great is the influence of the legal profession on attitudes toward the Constitution that what is surprising is not the role of judicial interpretation in altering "permanent" constitutional principles but the contrasting notion that the Constitution might have plain, durable content. But if meaning is not confused with interpretation, many constitutional provisions have had remarkably stable meaning.

The Uninterpreted Constitution

Much of the Constitution draws its meaning from practice rather than from interpretation.[37] This occurs most clearly when the judiciary, for one reason or another, refrains from exercising any significant enforcement role with respect to a provision. For example, the Court early determined that the guarantee to each state of a "republican form of government" in article IV, section 4 was to be enforced by the legislative branch; since then the Court has made little serious effort to interpret the clause.[38] Nevertheless, with the exception of a few isolated episodes—when the nation was new, and when military governments ruled in the South during the period of Reconstruction—the norm throughout our history has been for every state to have a republican form of government. This fact is in vivid contrast to the frequency with which such judicially enforced requirements as free speech or integrated schooling are apparently violated.[39]

The meaning of "republican form of government" immanent in this long practice is not the kind of meaning lawyers are comfortable with or much interested in. Although its core can be summarized—some division of the government into separate branches, substantial accountability to the electorate, the impartial application of the laws—the idea is not fully formalized, articulated, or closed. It is a recognition based on everyday experience. Different people might assign somewhat different intellectual content to the same institutional patterns, and it is not clear how much of the pattern is mandatory. The continuation of the political practices that embody republican government suggests that most people would be surprised and affronted by any dramatic shift away from the established pattern and would either oppose a change or move quickly to reestablish the norm. This is probably because most people approve of the core meaning. But some are not aware of assigning any meaning to the practices at all. Some who generally tolerate them might raise objections to specific aspects, such as the limited scope and equality of suffrage. And some might in the abstract disapprove of the whole idea. Republican forms are allowed to continue partly because of habit, familiarity, and a sense of normalcy.[40] In sum, the sort of meaning that emerges from behavior is readily distinguishable from precise legal rules, but this does not make it any the less real.[41]

Much that is important in the constitutional system rests on the operation of provisions that gain their content from long usage rather than from legal construction. Some of these uninterpreted provisions are fundamental to orderly, accountable government. Congress "assembles" every year as the Constitution requires.[42] Despite the temptation of power, presidents routinely relinquish office when their constitutional terms expire. The provisions for replacement of a president after death or during periods of incapacity have never been abused.[43] The rules controlling impeachment and removal of civil officers have rarely been used and have never led to removal for purely partisan reasons.[44] Procedures for amending the Constitution have been followed some twenty-six times without judicial intervention.

Some of the uninterpreted Constitution is less fundamental but would still seem important if we were not able to take it for granted. With the remotely possible exception of the formation of West Virginia, territorial integrity of the states has been respected, as article IV, section 3 requires. Soldiers have not been quartered in private homes. A census has been conducted every ten years, as required by article I, section 1, without the aid of the Supreme Court. All the presidents have been older than thirty-five. Although the difference between a "treaty," which requires ratification by the Senate, and an "executive agreement," which does not, has never been formalized by the Court, the ratification provisions of article II, section 1 have never fallen into disuse.[45] The import of "advice and consent" was determined by the behavior of George Washington and the subsequent presidents who followed his example.[46]

Some of the uninterpreted provisions deal with relatively esoteric matters but are, on a moment's reflection, of obvious significance. No Supreme Court decision gives an authoritative construction of the ninth amendment's reservation of unenumerated rights to the people, but that provision has been spectacularly realized in the pervasive appeal to the language of rights in political debate.[47] The judiciary has never restricted the plenary authority of Congress to create and restrict the jurisdiction of the lower federal courts, yet the power has not been used to frustrate the enforcement of constitutional rights. Although there have been many abortive proposals to retaliate against unpopular Supreme Court decisions by use of the congressional power to make exceptions to the Court's jurisdiction, only once in nearly two hundred years has this power been found to have been used so as to interfere with the independent judiciary.[48] That single incident occurred in the turbulent period following the Civil War and involved an issue (the restoration of captured property to rebels who had received presidential pardons) that was extraordinarily provocative. Whatever consensus or inhibition prevents alterations in some practices is often subject to challenge. But the Constitution represented by all of these practices has been remarkably durable.

Constitutional principles can also emerge from practice when judicial interpretations do not supply specific meaning but merely ratify the validity of past practices. The constitutional process by which Congress enacts legislation has largely been defined in this way. For example, the Court has defined a "revenue bill," which under article I, section 7 must originate in the House, in conformity with legislative practice.[49] Similarly, the definition of a quorum for purposes of enacting legislation, the number of votes required to override a veto, the formalities of the presidential signature, and the intricacies of the use of the veto power have all been determined by judicial validation of political practice.[50]

Finally, meaning arises from practice when provisions get only part of their substance from judicial interpretation, so that practice can independently supply additional significance. The breadth of congressional power under the commerce clause has varied with the vicissitudes of judicial doctrine. But as Herbert Wechsler has noted, the basic principle of enumerated powers—that national regulation is exceptional and must be specially justified, while state regulation is the norm—is embedded in the political process.[51] Moreover, it has not taken judicial opinions to prevent the adoption of a national religion or classical bills of attainder, or the use of dismemberment and other tortures as punishments. Overwhelming agreement about the meaning of the Constitution prevents such actions, and this agreement reflects and is reflected in prolonged behavior.

In short, although much scholarly and popular attention is focused on the complexities and surprises of constitutional interpretation, much of the constitutional order is consistently realized and derived from practice. To the extent that such meaning is conventionally recognized, it tends to be considered exceptional and dependent on the special character of certain provisions.

It is sometimes thought, for example, that durable meaning is possible when provisions are highly specific and sustained agreement about them is therefore likely. The requirement that a president be at least thirty-five years of age or the definition of the four-year term of office can be contrasted with larger concepts like due process of law, which "gather meaning from experience."[52] However, if sustained consensus were a function of specificity, one would not expect to find so many general provisions among those that have exhibited consistency in practice: the guarantee of a republican form of government, the definition of high crimes and misdemeanors, the reservation to the people of unenumerated rights, and so on. Moreover, it is largely a matter of choice whether to perceive a provision as simple and specific or as complex and general. The phrase "due process of law" probably had quite a definite meaning to the framers, who used it to refer to certain familiar judicial procedures.[53] The term now seems expansive because we have become accustomed to using it in many other ways.

Likewise, although we do not argue about the definition of a four-year presidential term, argument is certainly possible. Similarly "narrow" terms have generated considerable uncertainty—for instance, the definition of a majority for purposes of defining a quorum, or the definition of the "ten days" in article I, section 7 during which the president can veto a bill.[54] Might a four-year term be extended in an emergency? Might electoral fraud, economic chaos, or military danger constitute such an emergency? If such arguments seem farfetched, consider that economic emergency figured in the Court's validation of the Minnesota Mortgage Moratorium Law of 1933, which violated the established (and historically correct) meaning of the impairment of contracts clause, and that military emergency influenced the Court's approval of the internment of Japanese-Americans during World War II.[55] Certainly, there is widespread agreement that the definition of a four-year term ought not be disputed, but that agreement cannot be satisfactorily explained simply on the basis of the specificity of the word "four."

It is also sometimes proposed that relatively fixed content is possible when terms are organizational, when they refer to "governing institutions" rather than to substance.[56] This suggestion is in part a variation on the argument based on specificity, for organizational terms such as "election," "advice and consent," or "assemble" might be thought somehow more specific than substantive provisions such as the equal protection clause; organizational words might therefore be more capable of generating sustained agreement. But, again, the extent to which such terms might seem specific is more a function of tacit consensus than intrinsic specificity. Although history might well support an interpretation of "advice and consent" that required formal, personal consultation with the Senate, this would seem unnatural in light of long practice to the contrary.[57] The requirement that Congress "assemble" could be interpreted to require increased access by the public. But congressional practices regarding executive sessions are sufficiently entrenched and acceptable to make the proposal seem improbable.[58] Moreover, some of the provisions that have not been subject to interpretation, such as "high crimes and misdemeanors" and the prohibition against quartering soldiers, are substantive. And many terms that have prompted considerable argumentation and have undergone large changes in meaning are organizational—for example, the tenth amendment's reference to "reserved powers" and the phrase "legislative powers" in article I.[59] In any event, the line between substantive and organizational is far from clear. The census provides the basis for apportionment and might be thought organizational, but, if improperly conducted, a census might be thought to violate individual substantive rights.[60] The selection of jurors is plainly part of the process of arranging an important decision-making structure, yet the method of selection can violate the substantive rights of criminal defendants.[61]

Finally, it might be said that durable meaning is possible when all real content is lacking. For example, many of the uninterpreted provisions merely lodge decision-making authority in some institution other than the federal judiciary. The ninth amendment at least validates the propriety of invoking unenumerated rights in state and local forums. Everyone can agree with that since the nature of the rights remains undefined. It also might be that the Court has approved many practices regarding the process of legislating because the Constitution largely entrusts the definition of those procedures to each House.[62] In the same way, control over constitutional amendments and impeachment is left to the Congress. Apparently stable meanings for these provisions are easy, it might be thought, since the Constitution merely requires that the relevant decisions be made by the appropriate institution. However, these practices have remained within—and have helped to define—accepted constitutional limits. The absence of judicial interpretation of these provisions has as much to do with effective consensus about content as with any textual requirement of judicial abstinence. Article I, section 5 vests the power to judge the qualifications of its members in the House of Representatives, but in 1969 the Supreme Court invalidated the exclusion of Adam Clayton Powell on the ground that the House had established improper criteria for exclusion.[63] The Court's decision stated: "In order to determine the scope of any 'textual commitment' under Article I, section 5, we necessarily must determine the meaning of the phrase to 'be the Judge of the Qualifications of its own Members.'"[64] In short, the grounds for exclusion from the House were subject to judicial interpretation because the House had acted on the basis of a meaning of the word "qualification" about which there could be disagreement. Analogously, if the House were to impeach a judge (or even a president) on the basis of race, the Court might well intervene. Impeachment, then, has been exempt from judicial interpretation because the House has acted within accepted limits, not simply because the matter is textually committed to it rather than to the judiciary.

A variation on the notion that the uninterpreted provisions lack content is that practice can reflect a consistent "meaning" only when that meaning is amorphous. As I have noted, the understandings that emerge from practice are often not fixed or precise. But meaning need not be formalized to be real. It remains both true and important that effective agreement has consistently existed to the effect that presidents are not removed from office over policy differences, that state governments are organized around basic democratic principles, that Congress "assembles" every year, and so on. As these examples suggest, however, it is true that uninterpreted meaning is usually basic meaning—unsurprising and unexceptional. But that the meaning that emerges from practice should seem obvious merely underlines the extent to which tacit agreement about such meaning is widely shared and firmly established. If constitutional meaning is to be durable, it must seem to be plain to those who are governed by it. Perhaps uninterpreted meaning is both obvious and relatively stable, not because of the special characteristics of certain provisions, but because of the special capacity of practice to sustain effective consensus.

Some Reasons for Durability

The Constitution was written down so that its words would provide reasonably certain and permanent constraints.[65] In turn, we treat it as a legal instrument, to be given written definition by judges, in order to bind. This faith in law is not, of course, wholly misplaced. Our operative assumption is that legal interpretations—that mass of new and often peripheral applications—will help to clarify and protect core constitutional values. The political editorial is ultimately safer, we hope, because the judiciary grapples with the question of whether "freedom of speech" applies to commercial advertising; perhaps the fair trial may even be somehow marginally more secure because the Court decides whether to include a student's brief conversation with the school principal within the

meaning of "due process of law." There is surely some basis for this belief
that legal constructions preserve underlying principles. We are, however,
overrelying on the relationship. Words constrain when they are understood, and practice has important and unappreciated advantages over interpretation for sustaining the sense of shared agreement that can eventually make a particular meaning seem plain or inevitable. These include
informality, generality, and caution.

Informality

The meaning that emerges from practice is implicit, more a matter of
behavior and habit than of verbalization. Congress simply "assembles"
every year without considering the meaning of the word; presidents are
not declared "unable to discharge the powers and duties of [the] office,"
although no one has stated a rule that the incapacity must be extraordinary; the difference between a treaty and an executive agreement is not
formally articulated, but treaties continue to be sent to the Senate for
ratification.

As novelists tell us with regard to social relations, much can be tolerated if left unspoken that might destroy if spoken.[66] Articulation sharp-
ens and focuses attention. It raises the stakes and provokes argument. Individuals who could not agree that three distinct branches are necessary
for a republican form of government might nevertheless find acceptable
the practice of organizing state governments around three branches. A
representative might consistently vote only for narrow impeachment
resolutions but still hold to the expansive view that high crimes and misdemeanors are whatever the Congress says they are. If experienced, the
infrequency of impeachments might be quite tolerable even when, if con-
ceptualized and treated as a principle, it would be unacceptable.

Intellectual informality means that less is being decided and thus increases the chance for agreement. A legislator might believe, for example,
that the president has no power as commander in chief to seize private
property in peacetime without congressional authorization. Yet the same
legislator might accede to a particular seizure for immediate practical reasons if his behavior were not viewed as a concession binding in future
cases.[67] Similarly, it would be easy to gain agreement not to remove a
president from office for a relatively minor incapacity if such a decision
were not thought to have any implications for a later, potentially more
serious, incapacity. The limited, indefinite quality of informal meaning
increases the likelihood that stable practices can develop.

Legal meaning, on the other hand, is verbal meaning. It is formalized in written opinions, specified in holdings, and systematized in explanatory doctrines. Losers are identified and suffer reduced stature. Thus interpretive meaning is hard but brittle. Every decision provokes a new argument, as those who stand to lose attempt to reverse or narrow its scope. The Supreme Court's famous abortion decision, for example, fiercely embittered the losers and raised the controversy to new levels of visibility. The reach of the Court's decision has been tested in every way—skillfully drawn homicide statutes, onerous reporting requirements, parental and spousal consent statutes, and funding restrictions. As a consequence, the Court's own formulation of the constitutional interests involved has begun to shift significantly.[68] And for the first time serious congressional attention has begun to focus on whether the fetus might be defined as a person for purposes of protection under the due process clause.[69] Stable meaning does not easily become established at such levels of visibility and controversy.

Explanatory doctrines and other judicial norms that favor consistency (such as respect for precedent) can also destabilize consensus. These doctrines tie the decisive moral victory of the winning side to a potentially large number of other situations and thus elicit disagreement. In 1979, for example, the Court held that members of the public had no right to attend pretrial hearings in criminal cases.[70] In practice, criminal trials had been open to the public throughout American history and as far back as "the days before the Norman Conquest."[71] It was debatable, however, whether this long practice had been a function of the public's right or the accused's. In its decision the Court explicitly settled this issue by holding that the right was that of the accused. This holding, as well as other aspects of the Court's reasoning and language, strongly suggested that not only public pretrial hearings but also the well-established institution of public trials might be subject to waiver by the defendant. The apparent implication that the press might be excluded from criminal trials provoked harsh public reaction.[72] In 1980 the Court "clarified" its earlier decision by holding that trials, as opposed to pretrial hearings, must be open to the public.[73] This second opinion added a new specification: judges could still close trials if they made a finding of "an overriding interest" in closure. This new decision promises copious new opportunities for interpretive controversy. It will be necessary to examine what circumstances might give rise to such overriding interests and what other sorts of governmental proceedings must, by analogy, be kept open to the public. Within the space of a few months, then, judicial interpretation had succeeded in jeopardizing the long-established institution of public trials, reversing itself, and throwing open a host of new questions that would require resolution. Somehow from the days of the Norman Conquest until 1979, the practice of holding public trials had been secure. Perhaps this was in part because the theoretical bases and precise ramifications of the practice had remained somewhat obscure and ambiguous; perhaps in part it was because whatever exceptions had occurred were of low visibility and were not rationalized.

Generality

To the extent that it is verbalized, the meaning that emerges from practice tends to be general, a characteristic that helps to sustain broad agreement. That presidents are not impeached for policy disagreements does not settle the difficult question of how to distinguish such disagreements from the failure faithfully to execute the law. Nor does agreement on the general practice have any necessary implications for the dispute about whether "high crimes and misdemeanors" must be felonies. Similarly, the core of "republican form of government" is very general and does not settle many specific questions. For example, does issuance of advisory opinions by state courts so violate principles of separation of powers that it contravenes basic requirements of republican government? But by permitting variations on the periphery, practice allows continuing agreement on the general form of republican government. Because the meaning inherent in the practice settles so little, many can abide it.

In contrast, interpretation concentrates attention on specific issues. Judicial elaboration takes place in the context of a concrete controversy. The demands of legal advocacy make it probable that cases with extraordinary facts will be chosen as the occasion for decision.[74] The same demands require that arguments be uncompromising. Moral issues are put in a highly specific perspective, and principles are tested to their limit. If it is agreed that slavery is immoral, courts will be asked whether unpaid labor in mental hospitals is treatment or "slavery." If most can agree that legal discrimination on the basis of race is wrong, courts will have to decide whether the same considerations require the prohibition of gender distinctions. As the litigation process accentuates uncertainties at the periphery, the inhibition against disputing even core meanings begins to weaken. For example, the principle of enumerated powers was pushed to its limit in the period before 1937 when the Court tried to distinguish the national power over commerce from such "local" concerns as manufacturing.[75] In reaction it became common for serious observers to argue that federalism was an outdated principle,[76] and, indeed, eventually the Court largely eviscerated the tenth amendment. Similarly, "due process" safeguards at trial have become so elaborate as to prompt serious and widespread reconsideration of the value of even basic aspects of the adversary process.[77] The right against compulsory self-incrimination has been taken to prohibit police from engaging in what many would see as merely informal conversations with suspects. These decisions have opened public discussion of the wisdom of the fifth amendment itself.[78] If, as now seems likely, the Court will increasingly use the principle of separation of powers to invalidate practical efforts to cope with the complexities of modern governance, that principle will once again be subject to intellectual—and eventually public—disfavor.[79]

Caution

Much of the social consensus that permits durable, "plain" meaning is not necessarily substantive. Rather, it can be agreement that certain issues ought not to be contested. One basis for such an inhibition is a shared sense that a matter is too important, too unpredictable, or too complicated to be made uncertain. To adopt an expansive meaning for "high crimes and misdemeanors," for example, would expose everyone to grave risks by making the occupancy of high office precarious. Similarly, Congress's refusal, thus far, to defeat the enforcement of certain constitutional rights by manipulating the jurisdiction of lower federal courts is partly explainable because of the seriousness and unpredictability of the consequences of jeopardizing important judicial machinery. Organizational terms may generally tend to be exempted from interpretation because they define the mechanisms by which all disputes are settled; effective consensus about them is achieved, then, because of widespread acknowledgment that such basic terms ought not to be unsettled for fear that the capacity for dispute resolution will itself break down. Such inhibitions rest in part on a long-term view that is willing to forgo principles for a pragmatic sense of caution.

Judicial interpretation occurs in an atmosphere that tends to minimize fears about unsettling meaning. Lawsuits are framed and decided within the confining perspective of a single case and in the absolute language of rights. The finding of a legal violation "entitles" the victim to relief; the loser takes on the aspect of an offender whose interests and difficulties become correspondingly less worthy of concern. In providing legal content, the court is simply doing its duty. Any harm or uncertainty created by an interpretation is merely a necessary by-product of the imperative process of defining and protecting rights. Secondary and long-run consequences are of less importance than the immediate protection of the aggrieved party. Indeed, there is something generally comforting about the piecemeal process of adjudication—future uncertainties can always be settled in due time by new authoritative interpretations. The full import of adopting the "one man/one vote" principle or of extending free speech rights to school children or of introducing procedural due process into the authoritarian world of prison administration or of opening government decision making to the public's "right to know"—all surely will require limitations and modifications, but these (it is thought) can be worked out in future cases. In legal argument the concept of endless uncertainty is made a cliché, "the slippery slope argument," and is routinely raised and as routinely dismissed.

In short, many of the attributes of judicial interpretation that most suggest stability and consistency—the formality, the emphasis on timeless principles and rights, the narrow attention to one small case at a time—in fact work to make disagreement and instability the norm. Of course, the judiciary is not the only (or even the major) cause of American contentiousness, and heavy reliance on judicial interpretations of the Constitution is partly a result, not a cause, of the lack of political and social cohesion. But the solution has intrinsic characteristics that exacerbate the problem. To the extent that durable constitutional meaning is a reflection of social consensus, the process of judicial interpretation is in many ways at war with the ideal of enduring constitutional principles.

Judicial Restraint and Constitutionalism

To say that practice has advantages for sustaining a working consensus about constitutional meaning is not to suggest that all uninterpreted meaning necessarily will be permanent. The negotiated distribution of power between the executive and legislative branches, for example, has shifted dramatically over the years and with it the effective meaning of the principle of separation of powers. Nor do I wish to deny that when changes in practices begin seriously to defeat a constitutional value, judicial interpretation can sometimes educate, restrain, and stabilize. What of importance, then, follows from the perspective urged in the preceding sections?

It follows, first, that the judiciary ought not be in constant confrontation with society. Since the desegregation decision in 1954, it has become increasingly common to see the federal courts locked in prolonged political combat over such matters as achieving racial balance in the public schools, improving mental hospitals, and reapportioning legislative districts.[80] Decisions that dramatically alter social and political institutions—for example, the matter-of-fact invalidation of local patronage systems as violations of the first amendment[81]—have become commonplace. Moreover, influential theories about the function of judicial review depict the judiciary as properly a lonely institution continuously engaged in a struggle to keep the political branches true to the Constitution. As Ronald Dworkin would have it:

> Different institutions do have different constituencies when, for example, labor or trade or welfare issues are involved, and the nation often divides sectionally on such issues. But this is not generally the case when individual constitutional rights, like the rights of accused criminals, are at issue. It has been typical of these disputes that the interests of those in political control of the various institutions of the government have been both homogenous and hostile.[82]

Such views require the frequent exercise of judicial power to restrain other institutions, because those institutions are thought to have no disposition to honor constitutional rights.[83] The belief that the judiciary should routinely confront and reshape society is, I believe, a function of narrowed perception. If the practices that give meaning to the Constitution are acknowledged, the capacity of the nonjudicial institutions to sustain constitutional standards need not be viewed so pessimistically. It was, for example, public opinion and a censure vote in the legislative branch, not judicial intervention, that stopped Senator Joseph McCarthy's threat to first amendment freedoms. It was public indignation at Franklin Roosevelt's court-packing plan that protected the independence of the judiciary. Even the illustration Dworkin uses, the rights of accused criminals, ignores the fact that in the famous *Miranda* decision, the Court ordered only the warnings that were already standard procedure among agents of the executive branch of the national government.[84]

Perhaps more important, the confrontation model ignores the constitutional costs of a routinely pugnacious judiciary. Much of the conflict, resistance, and instability that is evidenced in modern constitutional litigation is simply a predictable consequence of overemphasis on interpretation as the exclusive source of constitutional meaning. Stable realization of constitutional principles depends upon preserving the kind of tacit agreement that interpretation itself tends to break down.

Second, it follows from the perspective proposed here that legalistic standards for evaluating judicial opinions are too limited. These standards emphasize the internal quality of the explanations offered. Because it is assumed that constitutional meaning should be provided almost entirely by the intellectual exercise of interpretation, emphasis centers on such matters as the deftness with which doctrine is used or the quality of the moral discourse. Indeed, since the function of the interpreted Constitution is primarily to restrain nonjudicial behavior, which is assumed often to be a consequence of wayward moods and passions, popular disagreement has sometimes become almost a sign of proper, even heroic, use of interpretive authority. Thus, *Brown v. Board of Education* is actually a small embarrassment to Dworkin, who has to describe it as an exceptional use of judicial power in that it sustained and strengthened a latent national consensus on the impropriety of racial segregation.[85]

If public practices are not viewed as being separate from, and antithetical to, constitutional meaning, the capacity of a decision to confirm and to build popular consensus and understanding can be properly valued. But such a broadening of the standards used to evaluate judicial opinions would require some subordination of legal standards and legal power. It is not, of course, predominantly the craftsmanship of an opinion that wins popular acceptance. The communicative force of a decision depends on its timing, its consequences, and the persuasive power of the language in the opinion; the "normative premise . . . in the ruling itself"[86] either conforms to the public's understanding of the constitutional values or it does not. Moreover, common sense and history suggest that occasions when the Court can expect to impose or help build a new consensus are probably few.[87] And, as suggested by the discussion in the preceding section, even in those few circumstances the reliance on judicial interpretation may eventually undercut the newly formed consensus, just as the past twenty years of twisting school desegregation decisions may be undercutting the consensus on racial desegregation that the Court helped to build in *Brown*.[88] Thus, a more usual role for the courts would be to restrain departures from a core of settled meaning—settled both by the clear sense and history of the Constitution and by apparent public understandings. Such decisions, by appealing to an existing sense of constitutional meaning, can be effective and stabilizing. But this view of the judicial function does not require routine exercise of judicial power, since most modern issues are not clearly settled by constitutional text and history and since departures from established understandings and practices would, by definition, tend to be aberrational.

A third implication is that judicial deference is an appropriate way to sustain the constitutional system. The more common viewpoint is that, since the meaning of the Constitution is declared and preserved only by the courts, any restraint in interpreting and enforcing the Constitution is a dereliction of the duty to uphold the Constitution. For example, Bickel's well-known proposal that courts should sometimes use technical legal devices to avoid or postpone constitutional decisions was attacked as profoundly anticonstitutional.[89] In fact, Bickel himself accepted the premise of such attacks and defended judicial deference and avoidance on pragmatic, rather than constitutional, grounds.[90]

But the various mechanisms that allow for judicial deference—humility and caution in the declaration of potentially far-reaching new constitutional principles, respect for the customs and mores of the times, consideration for the judgments of the other branches and levels of government, and sometimes avoidance of decisions on the merits altogether—all have one characteristic in common: they implicitly or explicitly share responsibility for giving meaning to the Constitution. To that extent, lawyers and their interpretative habits are rendered less influential in determining constitutional content. Meaning can then be influenced in part by other values and norms, including those that are formed by reference to established practices. Deference and avoidance, then, are not necessarily an abandonment of the responsibility to enforce constitutional values. They are the major way that courts, controlled as they are by legal norms, can acknowledge and give effect to the various sources of those values. Deference and avoidance are necessarily anticonstitutional only to the extent that lawyers' thinking monopolizes constitutional meaning.

I am recommending that the idea of judicial restraint be reexamined and reemphasized. The essence of restraint is the admission that the Constitution does not apply to many public issues or, at least, that it does not apply in any determinative way. This acknowledgment conflicts with functions that are understandably difficult for judges to yield. It conflicts with the strongly felt duty to assure continuing fidelity to constitutional norms. However, I have suggested that an unchecked urge to enforce those norms through adjudication may in fact undermine the capacity for durable constitutional government.

Restraint is also inconsistent with the courts' capacity to initiate reform and to control immediate political outcomes. Moral growth and social improvement may be important purposes of constitutional adjudication, and, in any event, they are powerfully appealing functions for any decision maker. Nevertheless, I shall be arguing that routine judicial efforts to perform these functions weaken the capacity of the political culture to develop moral understandings and to initiate wise change. Whether the Constitution is conceived as an enduring framework or as progressive change within that framework, lawyers' aggressive instinct for interpretation ought not be permitted to displace the generous understanding that the Constitution belongs to all of us. It can, I think, be safer with us than is commonly believed.

CHAPTER 3

Judicial Review in Free Speech Cases

The right of free speech presents a severe challenge to the claim, just advanced, that judicial review is largely unnecessary and destabilizing. Here, as much as in any area of constitutional law, the Court's role is widely believed to be essential for achieving profoundly important objectives; moreover, the distinctive characteristics of the judiciary are thought to provide special qualifications for the task. The purpose of this chapter is to suggest that the assumptions behind these beliefs are unproven and often doubtful.

A close association between courts and freedom of speech has not always seemed obvious. Neither the federal nor the state courts were significant protectors of free speech prior to 1919, when Justices Oliver Wendell Holmes and Louis Brandeis dissented in *Abrams v. United States*.[1] Despite periods of harsh suppression, the courts made no important attempts to enforce the right either at the end of the eighteenth century or throughout the nineteenth.[2] In the decades preceding World War I, the Supreme Court assumed that speech could be restricted if its content had a "bad tendency" and rejected virtually every free speech claim made during that period.[3] One scholar has even characterized first amendment case law prior to 1919 as a "tradition of [judicial] hostility."[4]

The transformation of the legal meaning of "the freedom of speech" that has gradually taken place since World War I is remarkable. The first amendment now prohibits patronage dismissals and severely limits campaign finance regulations; it protects much of the expression that once was subject to regulation as obscenity and defamation; it applies to billboards, nude dancing, jacket patches, and license plates; it protects school children, prisoners, and corporations.[5] In short, "the freedom of speech" has become a pervasive and complicated regulatory scheme frequently violated by the legislative and executive branches and industriously enforced by the judiciary.

Scholars have provided much of the theoretical underpinning for this elaborate edifice of judicial protection.[6] Both academics and judges intend these protections to create a society in which information is plentiful and vigorous dissent is tolerated. In the following section, I sketch out this consensus on the ambitious purposes of free speech law. I then argue that, given the nature of the judicial process, it is implausible that judicial review can be expected to promote such systemic objectives. Despite their efforts and good intentions, much of what judges do in the guise of protecting speech is likely to be dysfunctional and certainly diverts their attention from other important, if less grandiose, considerations.

The Systemic Objectives of Judicial Review

The dominant consensus that has prevailed for the past sixty years holds that the adjudication of individual cases can promote the level and quality of public debate. It assumes that courts can and should consciously design first amendment doctrines to achieve this objective. This view so pervades current thinking that its ambitiousness may not be appreciated at first.

The impulse underlying the modern judiciary's energetic efforts to enforce the first amendment is the desire to create a tolerant, open society. This purpose dates from Justice Holmes's dissent in *Abrams,* in which he proposed a tightened clear and present danger test on the grounds that the theory of the Constitution requires "free trade in ideas."[7] Under that theory, the judicial function is to help create an open "market" for ideas, which, in turn, requires nothing less than courts which will "be eternally vigilant against attempts to check the expression of opinions that we loathe and believe to be fraught with death."[8]

Courts have indeed been vigilant in the pursuit of systemic objectives in the years since *Abrams.* The Supreme Court sharply restricted traditional defamation rules because "debate on public issues should be uninhibited, robust, and wide-open."[9] It announced a "right of access" to criminal trials, asserting that the first amendment prohibits the "government from limiting the stock of information from which members of the public may draw" and suggesting that without the right of access "freedom of the press could be eviscerated."[10] The Court stated that patronage is "inimical to the process which undergirds our system of government" because, by burdening belief and association, it undermines the "competition in ideas and governmental policies [that] is at the core of our electoral process."[11]

The Court has remained vigilant in seeking to shape a system of open public discussion even when it has rejected free speech claims. It approved compelled disclosure of news sources to grand juries on the grounds that disclosure would not lead to "significant constriction of the flow of news to the public."[12] Before loosening the constraints on obscenity prosecutions, the Court assured itself that suppression of depictions of "hard-core" sexual conduct would not limit "expression of serious literary, artistic, political, or scientific ideas."[13] In short, the Court has designed first amendment rules to guard against the "standardization of ideas either by legislatures, courts, or dominant political or community groups."[14]

Despite the portentous tone of Supreme Court opinions, it is not self-evident that significant threats to an open society were present in any of the cases brought before the Court, or that the legal rules adopted by the Court in those cases could have had any useful systemic consequences even if such threats had been present. Judicial review cannot be expected to have any important impact on many of the major causes of intolerance and censorship. Studies of periods of severe suppression demonstrate that the etiology of intolerance is exceedingly complex and variable.[15] Informed speculation suggests that a wide range of factors coalesce to determine the amount of tolerance or intolerance, including educational levels, methods of child-rearing, economic conditions, international politics, institutional rivalries combined with prolonged political frustration involving a major party, national character, insecurities caused by flux in social status, and even the weather.[16] Adjudication is an unlikely mechanism for controlling such large and complex factors. As Judge Learned Hand understood, the causes of intolerance and censorship—as well as the cures—lie far beyond the sound and fury of particular cases.[17] Upon what, then, is the judiciary's ambitious role based?

The answer, in large measure, is faith. Zechariah Chafee's influential article "Freedom of Speech in War Time" (1919) and the criticism it spawned illustrate how limited the inquiry has been into the feasibility of an extensive role for the courts in promoting freedom of speech. The article suggested that the "clear and present danger" test might become the appropriate "boundary line of free speech" even though the Court had first employed it in *Schenck v. United States* to uphold a conviction under the Espionage Act.[18] Chafee argued that the purpose of the first amendment—to promote the widest possible discussion of public matters—could be properly reconciled with the interest in public safety by allowing the restriction of speech only when "safety is really imperiled."[19] The judiciary, Chafee concluded, should enforce a "broad test of certain danger."[20] Some of Chafee's critics questioned his assertion that the framers had envisioned such a general purpose for the first amendment.[21] Others attacked his decidedly optimistic understanding of the meaning of the phrase "clear and present danger" and the case law that had preceded it.[22] But neither Chafee nor his critics seriously examined the argument's fundamental premise that adjudication can, if properly performed, be expected to protect the free exchange of ideas significantly.

At the time Chafee wrote, this premise might not have appeared as unassailable as it does today; until then, the Supreme Court had contributed almost nothing to the protection of vigorous public debate. Yet Chafee began his article by attributing wide significance to the legal analysis that his article would develop: "It is becoming increasingly important to determine the true limits of freedom of expression, so that speakers and writers may know how much they can properly say, and governments may be sure how much they can lawfully and wisely suppress."[23] After stressing the importance of ascertaining the parameters of the freedom of expression, Chafee acknowledged that the first amendment serves other purposes than delineating the legal boundaries that circumscribe protected expression. He recognized that the Bill of Rights is also "an exhortation and a guide. . . . It is a declaration of national policy in favor of the public discussion of all public questions."[24] The first amendment is important, Chafee asserted, for inculcating a sensitivity—"a constant regard" for free speech—in all public officials.[25]

Why assume, as Chafee did, that the development of legal rules to enforce the first amendment will be compatible with the kind of general understanding of free speech that enhances public discussion? Chafee admitted that legal reasoning had failed to define clear, useful limits to the freedom of speech, yet he minimized the importance of the judiciary's discouraging record, claiming that the cases had been "too few, too varied in their character, and often too easily solved, to develop any definite boundary between lawful and unlawful speech."[26] He believed that, if afforded the right cases, the courts could develop "a rational principle" or "test" that would "solve" the problem of freedom of speech.[27]

Somewhat wistfully conceding that the correct solution would lack the precision of that hoary restriction on conveying estates in land, the Rule in Shelley's Case, Chafee clearly viewed the protection of free speech as an intellectual problem;[28] his argument rested on the belief that first amendment issues are therefore amenable to traditional judicial techniques. The use of these techniques, he assumed, would not only protect "free speech" in specific cases, but would also accommodate, or at least not undermine, other factors that also serve to enhance public debate, such as the attitudes and understandings of nonjudicial public officers. The structure of Chafee's argument allowed for an invincible optimism; because he perceived free speech questions as intellectual problems, he could disregard the record of ineffective or misguided decisions. It is always possible that a newly proposed principle or test will be an improvement over the existing ones. Thus, Chafee needed only to propose a new rule to ward off any inclination to doubt the efficacy of the judicial enterprise.

To a remarkable degree, this structure—and its limitations—has characterized first amendment commentary since Chafee's time. Consider, for example, Thomas Emerson's *The System of Freedom of Expression*. As Chafee did, Emerson acknowledges that free speech requires nonjudicial supports:

> Obviously, the success of any society in maintaining freedom of expression hinges upon many different considerations. Some degree of fundamental consensus . . . is essential. . . . Economic institutions and economic conditions, the degree of security or insecurity from external threats, political traditions and institutions, systems of education, methods and media for forming public opinion, public attitudes and philosophy, and many other factors play a vital part.[29]

In asserting that judicial protections can complement these other forms of protection, Emerson, like Chafee, does not rely on past experience; he acknowledges that major first amendment doctrines "have proved inadequate, particularly in periods of tension, to support a vigorous system of freedom of expression."[30] Nonetheless, continuing the tradition of optimism begun by Chafee, Emerson asserts that legal doctrines can be formulated that have "an overall unity of purpose and operation"[31] with the other protections for free speech. Apparently less formalistic than Chafee, Emerson defines the problem of deciding what speech to protect as a broad question about interrelated social functions. He makes no references to the Rule in Shelley's Case. He even briefly admits that legal doctrines can be depended upon too heavily.[32] Nonetheless, he dismisses the issue of the efficacy of judicial review as a fait accompli:

In the United States today we have come to depend upon legal institutions and legal doctrines as a major technique for maintaining our system of free expression. We have developed and refined this technique more than has any other country. . . . Hence, while the other factors should not be slighted, an analysis of the legal supports for freedom of expression is a first and funda-mental step.[33]

Emerson attempts to support this conclusion with a series of unex-amined assertions regarding the utility of judicial review: (1) the judi-ciary's prestige can "legitimiz[e] and harmonize" the principle of free speech; (2) legal rules can provide the clarity and certainty that the sys-tem requires; (3) judges understand the need for the subordination of immediate self-interest and thus can provide principled, rather than ad hoc, protection; (4) judges appreciate the "sophisticated" idea of free speech and can teach that idea to the general public; (5) adjudication provides opportunity for the necessary flexibility and growth. In what is now a familiar litany, Emerson argues that judges are competent to per-form these functions because they are independent of the other branches of government, politically insulated, well trained, and inclined to use legal procedures.[34]

Although Emerson's discussion moves a step beyond Chafee's, his cen-tral propositions constitute more an expression of faith in the legal pro-cess and in judges than an analysis. Emerson can be content with dog-matic assertions belied by his own summary of the judiciary's record because he believes, as did Chafee, in the bright hope of a better intellec-tual solution. And although Emerson's proposal for solving first amend-ment issues is perhaps more sophisticated than Chafee's "broad test of social danger," ultimately it is also conceptualistic. Emerson writes that "in constructing specific legal doctrines which . . . will govern concrete issues, the main function of the courts is not to balance the interest in freedom of expression against other social interests but to define . . . 'ex-pression,' 'abridge,' and 'law.'"[35]

The tradition begun by Chafee and elaborated by Emerson has spawned a broad, and somewhat odd, consensus. This consensus fre-quently, and sometimes severely, criticizes the Court's first amendment decisions but never questions the possible utility of the enterprise on which the judiciary has embarked. Alexander Meiklejohn, for example, castigates Holmes for having employed the clear and present danger test, the same test that Chafee thought had "solved" the problem of free-dom of speech. Meiklejohn argues that the test was disastrous to "our understanding of self-government"—it was a virtual "annulment of the

First Amendment."[36] He also criticizes another of our most eminent jurists, Justice Felix Frankfurter, for sapping "the very foundations of our American political freedom."[37] Nevertheless, Meiklejohn, confident of the potential efficacy of the analytical principles he proposes, adheres to the view that the "Supreme Court . . . is and must be one of our most effective teachers."[38]

Similarly, in 1976 Walter Berns disparaged the Court's free speech record, asserting that it was incompatible with "a decent self-governing country of the sort the Founders hoped for."[39] He excoriated the Court's self-professed inability to distinguish between vulgarity and important speech.[40] Yet Berns also places his hope in the institution of judicial review: "Of course there will be cases where the power to judge speech by its substance will be abused, but the answer to this is Supreme Court review."[41] Berns urges that if the Court would only return to respect for the framers' design, the judiciary could still promote public understanding of the kinds of decent public debate that undergird the political system.[42]

No commentator better illustrates the power of the modern consensus than Henry Steele Commager. Writing in 1943, he dismissed the argument that the judiciary alone possesses the superior learning and objectivity necessary for constitutional interpretation and thus flatly rejected the view that the courts should play a special role with respect to free speech.[43] Commager concluded, after reviewing the Court's lackluster record, that it had not played a significant role in preventing the federal government from violating the guarantee of free speech.[44]

By 1966, however, Commager too had become a believer. After criticizing prominent tests employed by the Court in first amendment analysis, Commager nevertheless asserted that "the Law . . . [is] by [its] nature . . . not only dedicated to freedom but pervaded by it."[45] And what of his earlier view that free speech depended upon popular understanding of, and respect for, the Constitution? Commager now echoed Chafee, asserting that courts can play "an active, even a decisive, part in the preservation of liberty" by expounding the law.[46] Yet Commager, like those before him, failed to explain how the courts could perform this educating function while so inclined to employ misguided constitutional doctrines.

The structure of Chafee's argument has proved virtually irresistible. Nearly everywhere criticism of the judicial product is found together with faith in the judicial process. In 1968, for example, Samuel Krislov described forty years of judicial interpretations as "inadequate," but concluded nonetheless that "the Court is as uniquely fitted to articulate the values of expression as it is to defend them."[47] Martin Shapiro, writing in 1966, criticized the major judicial first amendment doctrines; yet, he too asserted that the Court could inject into the political system an appreciation for the idea of tolerance.[48] In 1971 Robert Bork found most of the Court's important free speech decisions unjustifiable, yet would have assigned to the courts the job of protecting the "freedom to discuss government and its policies."[49] Even the two most prominent and profound skeptics of the efficacy of judicial review retained some hope in that institution for free speech issues. Justice Robert Jackson conceded that the Court could possibly play a useful role in "cultivating public attitudes."[50] And Learned Hand thought it obvious that "legislatures are more likely than courts to repress what ought to be free."[51]

In short, although participants in the modern consensus may differ on the precise scope of the judiciary's function in first amendment cases, the dominating idea in modern free speech theory and practice is that judges should shape the content of legal rules in a manner that enhances such systemic objectives as vigorous or useful public debate.[52] This recommendation, although at first intuitively simple and appealing, is actually a complicated judgment that the benefits of judicial review, as measured by free speech values, will outweigh the costs as measured by the same values.

An intricate mix of assumptions and beliefs underlies this judgment. First, it is usually thought that the nonjudicial supports for free speech values are brittle and of questionable utility, so that little will be lost by judicial efforts to protect free speech values and much might be gained. Second, it is thought that legal rules can coexist with and supplement the nonjudicial supports, especially by enriching the public understanding and appreciation of the value of free speech. This assumption, of course, presupposes that judges can devise such rules, a belief that rests upon two further assumptions: (1) that the creation and implementation of legal rules that enhance systemic objectives are consistent with other judicial objectives, such as doing justice between the parties, and (2) that systemic free speech issues can be resolved by the methods of legal analysis. Third, it is frequently asserted that judges are inclined to protect free speech or, at least, are more inclined to do so than other officials.

Although "virtually everyone agrees that the courts should be heavily involved in reviewing impediments to free speech,"[53] the widespread belief that judges are personally and institutionally competent to resolve free speech questions is usually expressed in conjunction with serious criticisms of the courts' actual performance. Aside from conclusory affirmations about the virtues of political insulation, commentators pay almost no attention to the possibility, certainly suggested by the barrage of criticism, that both judges and adjudication are unsuited for the broad task being urged upon them.[54] It is past time to consider this possibility.

The Inadequacy of Nonjudicial Supports: Reaction and Overreaction

It may seem too obvious to warrant discussion that if instances of unconstitutional suppression are discovered, the general level of public discussion is in jeopardy. It is only natural, then, that judges who are frequently exposed to claims of illegal suppression will think that more is at stake in a given case than the correction of a particular injustice. Emerson has offered the most vivid account of the generalized importance of correcting individual instances of suppression. Writing in 1970 of "the powerful forces that impel men towards the elimination of unorthodox expression," Emerson asserted that "most men have a strong inclination, for rational or irrational reasons, to suppress opposition."[55] He spoke of government censors with "excessive zeal" and "ulterior purposes," and of the limitations placed on free speech in "atmosphere[s] of public fear and hysteria."[56] Emerson portrayed the courts as a wall standing against the flood of repression; every restrictive act is significant, for "the limitations imposed on discussion . . . tend readily and quickly to destroy the whole structure of free expression."[57] Hence, in his view, "the issue at stake is nothing less than the maintenance of the democratic process."[58]

Such assertions are, no doubt, invigorating for the self-image of judges. Although it would be foolish to deny that Emerson's pessimistic view might sometimes be justified, it would be equally foolish to suppose that Emerson's forebodings are an inevitable description of reality. Indeed, because he failed to provide a single example of the destruction of a whole system of free expression after the imposition of a few limitations upon discussion, Emerson's purpose was probably more rhetorical than descriptive or historical.[59] The image he created of a fragile right existing in a threatening world elevated the importance of the judicial role he proposed while obscuring its risks. In effect, Emerson suggested that there is nothing to lose by aggressive judicial efforts to protect the freedom of speech.

If, however, the urge to speak out is under certain conditions powerful and self-sufficient, the connection between the protection of speech in individual cases and the systemic enhancement of free expression is more problematic. Because individual instances of suppression can generate forceful countermeasures and evasions, judicial efforts to enhance the general level of public discussion may be unnecessary. Moreover, much might be lost by judicial effort under such circumstances. Emerson's proposed rules, for example, provide the broadest possible protections and the narrowest exceptions.[60] His prescription would overprotect speech; it requires protection in the particular instance regardless of the foolishness of the consequences.[61] If not for the brooding threat of the imminent collapse of the whole system of free expression, the infliction on society of the costs of Emerson's rules would be plainly disproportionate and unnecessary. And by undermining the public's patience with the idea of free speech, overprotecting speech would jeopardize important nonjudicial supports for tolerance.

History provides striking examples of the resilience of freedom of expression and the occasional futility of suppression. Newspaper editors arrested and prosecuted by the military during the Civil War sometimes found their papers more popular after their prosecution because of the notoriety they had gained.[62] The aftermath of the prosecution and conviction of Eugene Debs for some of his ideas provides a further example:

> Two days after the Supreme Court decision, [Debs] called Lenin and Trotsky the "foremost statesmen of the age" and . . . denounced the Supreme Court justices as "begowned, bewhiskered, bepowdered old fossils." Two weeks later, when the mayor of Toledo refused Socialists admission to Memorial Hall to hear Debs . . . , 5000 of his followers stormed the building, broke doors and windows, and shouted "To hell with the mayor." . . . [Later] his cell in the Atlanta penitentiary became the virtual headquarters of the Socialist party.[63]

Civil libertarians emphasize that loyalty oaths usually catch principled constitutionalists rather than radicals.[64] The use of trespass laws against sit-ins, police attacks on marchers, the prohibition of draft-card burning, and other similar efforts at suppression often invite expression by publicizing it and by investing it with moral significance.[65]

Not only are isolated efforts at suppression often ineffective, but even systematic waves of suppression often vanish suddenly, jarring the democratic system but not destroying it. Jefferson's election to the presidency, which was assisted by public reaction against the prosecutions under the Sedition Act of 1798, abruptly quelled the suppressions of that period.[66] The use of a wide array of censoring devices during the Civil War failed to constrict the publication of dissenting, even traitorous, views and information, including detailed reporting about military plans.[67] The notorious red scare of 1919 essentially dissipated by 1920 after its excesses induced opposition among moderate Republicans.[68] Senator McCarthy's prominence and power, which had become significant by 1950, ended in 1954 after he was censured by the Senate.[69] In short, none of our most serious periods of repression was influenced significantly by judicial enforcement of the first amendment, yet each ended well short of destroying the system of free expression.[70]

The limited effectiveness of efforts at suppression does not, of course, require the courts to approve of them. But neither should the courts formulate rules based upon an exaggerated sense of the stakes. If conditions might exist under which a society could slide from one isolated instance of suppression to the next toward the general extinction of free expression, the relevant inquiry is into the nature of those conditions. Once they are described, it might be possible to determine whether judicial efforts to resolve individual cases can ever counteract such conditions and, also, whether such efforts may sometimes inadvertently contribute to those conditions.

A milder version of Emerson's pessimism has influenced the development of first amendment law. The Court has imposed restrictions on the government's regulatory power in important areas, such as defamation and patronage, on the largely unsubstantiated assumption that those regulatory powers pose a significant risk to the formation and publication of ideas and ultimately to the political system itself.[71] The Court has inferred the risk from the existence of sanctions without serious attention to the possibility that the urge to speak might be vigorous enough to survive the sanctions. Because the Court has largely assumed that the sanctions posed grave risks to the system, it has never seriously considered whether its rules might be unnecessary or even dysfunctional. Whatever the risks to the system under special conditions, it is clear that the courts cannot justify a *general* sustained program of judicial protections, such as the one that has evolved since *Abrams,* without undertaking this assessment.

Legal Rules and Nonjudicial Supports

Judicial enforcement of the right to freedom of speech might be modestly justified on the grounds that courts have a duty to apply the law, including the first amendment, when resolving cases. This justification requires no assumptions about the utility of judicial review in promoting an overall system of public debate. There is no reason to think that the judiciary's efforts to do justice in individual cases will necessarily foster the vigor or quality of public discussion generally. If, for example, just application of the laws requires the use of "neutral" constitutional rules, courts presumably could not afford any more protection to civil rights protests by the disenfranchised than they afford to communications by the powerful.[72] If justice requires that courts formulate constitutional doctrines strictly in accordance with the intent of the framers, then perhaps the only permissible legal protections are prohibitions against prior restraints,[73] which, in turn, would leave the courts no choice but to legitimize as "constitutional" the many other forms of censorship. Unless "justice" is defined as achieving the outcome that best promotes free discussion generally, the attempt to do justice in individual cases always entails the risk of unfortunate consequences for the general level of public debate.

Alternatively, judicial enforcement might be justified as a method of enhancing public debate, even if at the expense of such legal values as doing justice between the parties to the dispute. For example, courts might protect civil rights protesters from trespass convictions for staging a sit-in on the plausible theory that such sit-ins effectively generate an important political message.[74] If, however, the only available *legal* explanation for the outcome were an exceedingly unlikely interpretation of a state trespass statute,[75] then the judicial effort to create an appropriate level of public discussion has triumphed at the expense of normal concepts of legal justice. Similarly, a judge might employ an absolutist interpretation of the first amendment, not because such an explanation is historically, textually, or logically convincing, but because the rhetorical emphasis sends out a salutary message about the importance of tolerance.[76] There is no obvious reason to assume that decisions designed to maximize the level and diversity of public debate are also compatible with notions like honesty and impartiality in particular cases.

The Drawbacks of Principle

In at least one important respect, however, the ideals of judicial review and the broad requirements of freedom of expression may be thought to coincide conveniently. The modern first amendment consensus holds at least to some degree that "expression must be protected against governmental curtailment at all points, even where the results of expression may appear to be in conflict with other social interests that the government is charged with safeguarding."[77] This is because the "theory [of free speech] rests upon subordination of immediate interests in favor of long-term benefits . . . [that] can be achieved only through the application of principle."[78] Thus, the habit of intellectual discipline so necessary to the impartial application of the law is asserted to be the judiciary's major qualification for its present role. But even the ideal of disciplined adherence to principle has drawbacks, at least if the goal is to achieve systemic objectives as well as individual justice.

The difficulty is that, by definition, the use of principle requires courts to protect speech even in cases in which the immediate advantages are questionable and the social disadvantages are clear. For example, no court has ever relied on more than its own guess as to whether traditional defamation rules significantly reduced the amount and quality of information published.[79] But the relatively new constitutional doctrine that defamation of public figures exists only with proof of reckless disregard for the truth has created obvious costs for personal privacy and reputation. Similarly, the predominantly Jewish community of Skokie had to permit a Nazi march despite the emotional anguish that such a march would inflict on its residents.[80] A town must make some provisions in its zoning laws for nude dancing establishments despite the ease with which potential customers could satisfy their tastes in surrounding communities and despite the clear damage to the tone of that municipality.[81] Although these examples of principled judicial decision making may be consistent with the idea of free speech in the abstract, it is less clear whether social tensions, and the accompanying urge to suppress speech, are thereby increased or decreased. Is public acceptance and respect for the first amendment increased or decreased by the constant message sent out by principled adjudication? So entrenched is the judicial rule and so identified is the judiciary's methodology with the substance of the first amendment, that such questions are now lightly dismissed as reflecting a misunderstanding of the "sophisticated" theory of free speech.[82] But these questions simply acknowledge the existence of long-term, nonjudicial supports for free speech. It is unlikely that courts can foster public support and appreciation by developing the meaning of the freedom of speech most frequently and authoritatively in contexts in which it appears to be a foolish or costly idea.

The judiciary implicitly acknowledges the dangers of principled decisions by creating exceptions. The Court has modified its general protection of "nonobscene" literature—as that term is artificially defined by the courts—to exempt nonobscene pornography involving children.[83] It has carved out an exception to the rule that the public has a right of access to criminal trials to allow for "compelling circumstances."[84] The existence of such exceptions suggests a second difficulty with principled decision making: every principle implicitly pinpoints where censorship may be legitimate. A principle that forbids prior restraints implies that subsequent restrictions may be permissible. A rule that forbids overly broad statutory language may permit precisely drawn restrictions. Even a blanket principle that all "speech" must be protected irrespective of the social costs directs attention to the possibility of restricting "behavior." Where meaning must be principled (that is, obviously costly) it is only natural that justifications will tend to emphasize the limits to the principle, thereby focusing attention on how speech might be restricted. Therefore, even judicial decisions that protect free speech in the case at hand will often indirectly legitimize and invite suppression more generally.

Without judicial intervention, the scope of the first amendment remains unclear and, for the reasons given in chapter 2, perhaps more secure in the long run. The prolonged disinclination to adopt seditious libel laws[85] may have been due, in part, to the absence of a formal ruling announcing their unconstitutionality. Without a formal ruling, no court focused attention on the costs of a prohibition against seditious libel laws and no court articulated the limits to the prohibition. By the same token, when the political process does suppress speech and no judicial pronouncement is made, the suppression is not rationalized and no formal precedent is established. Without an authoritative judicial declaration, the censorship may be submerged in the public awareness or mislabeled or simply forgotten, permitting a quick return to a norm of relative tolerance. For example, the extralegal quality of many of the military's acts of suppression during the Civil War may well have been linked to their short duration. The courts made no significant attempt to control the military's excesses during the war.[86] Thus, the claim that extreme public exigencies could justify censorship was never addressed, and the public was spared both the implausible conclusion that no amount of emergency can justify suppression and the provocative promulgation of a rule that some amount of emergency can. Instead, the suppressions remained illegitimate and irregular and did not lead to any prolonged, general breakdown of free speech.[87]

Courts, of course, must deal in intellectualized principles. Those who value abstractions feel insecure about relying on informal, inarticulate protections. Yet there is real doubt that courts actually promote free speech by engaging in principled decision making; there is a real possibility that they merely provide an emotional safe-harbor for the educated classes.

The Problem of Indeterminacy

The use of judicial decisions to protect the general level of free speech assumes that an adequate or proper amount of free speech is a condition that can be described and roughly attained. The general presumption is that more information is better than less. Certain types of suppression devices, such as prior restraints and content-discriminatory restrictions, are thought to reduce the amount of free discussion too much. Commentators and courts implicitly conceive of free speech as a "thing" that can be observed, measured, and achieved. Starting from these assumptions, it is but a short step to the conclusion that skillful judicial intervention in discrete cases might improve the overall system.

Legal rules are, however, often inadequate to shape a society having the characteristic of freedom of speech because many different forms of a society are consistent with that principle. The concept of "freedom of speech" is too complicated and indeterminate to be a useful guide in resolving many specific disputes. For example, it is naive to think that a rule that increases the availability of information always promotes free speech. Information must be received, sorted, and stored before it can be utilized. At some level, excessive information may interfere with the capacity to process and utilize information.

Although the Court has recognized this fact, it has failed to acknowledge its broader significance. In *Gibson v. Florida Legislative Investigation Committee,* for instance, the Court prevented a state legislative committee from discovering through examination of membership records whether communists had infiltrated the local chapter of the NAACP. The Court's rationale was that the right to free speech implies a right to associate, which is important for free speech purposes because individuals often learn of and assess information in group discussions.[88] The Court concluded that the right to associate and participate in subsequent discussions could be stifled by exposure of membership lists.[89] Viewed from this perspective, decisions like *Gibson* protect free speech values. This protection, however, is achieved only at the cost of limiting the information available to the public and its representatives. In *Gibson,* the Court did not deny that knowledge of whether communists had infiltrated the NAACP would have been of great importance to the public, to the state legislature, and to the NAACP itself.[90] The information might have been important not only for possible legislation, but also for evaluating both the membership of the NAACP and the messages coming out of the organization.[91] In short, the Court "protected" free speech by denying the public access to important information. Moreover, the Court's reasons for doing so sharply conflicted with traditional first amendment theory. The Court feared that potential exposure of membership lists would burden associational rights because the public might misunderstand or misuse the information.[92] The decision thus rested on the belief that an "open market" of ideas could not be trusted.

In decisions like *Gibson* the Court implicitly recognizes the complexity of the idea of the freedom of speech without acknowledging the corollary proposition that free speech principles can justify either outcome. The NAACP needed privacy to function; the public needed information to assess the NAACP and its activities. One could argue that the first amendment accords priority to the former consideration because associational privacy produces more or better public debate than would disclosure of membership lists. This tangled empirical judgment is, however, an unlikely basis for judicial decision making. Can a court claim to know how much information about private associations a decision like *Gibson* will shield from the public or what that information might be?[93] Can a court know how important the information might turn out to be or even what it might be used for? Understandably the Court in *Gibson* did not rely on these bases, but purported instead to weigh a single first amendment value, association, against the nonconstitutional value of pursuing communists.[94] The Court was able to justify the outcome on first amendment grounds only because it did not acknowledge that the principle of free speech pointed in both directions.

The problem of indeterminacy is common. Forced exposure to political messages on public buses increases the amount of information available to the public, but it also reduces the insulation and selectivity necessary for full utilization of information.[95] By requiring that each side of public issues be covered, the Fairness Doctrine may increase the variety of available messages, but it also prevents broadcasters from exercising full editorial control. Traditional defamation rules may have inhibited the publication of useful information, but the absence of those rules reduces the quality of information published by limiting the availability of a jury's judgment as to the truth or falsity of some accusations. In each of these cases, and in many others, the concept of freedom of speech could be used to justify either outcome. Absent complicated and costly empirical judgments that no court is equipped to make,[96] and that courts seldom seriously purport to make, these cases represent judicial choices between two versions of the same set of values.

Free speech case law, then, amply illustrates the point made in the last chapter that because adjudication requires a winner, it is largely incompatible with acknowledging complexity. Courts often can assert confidently that they are protecting the first amendment only because, in reality, they are simplifying the concept. In the case involving forced exposure to information on a bus, for example, the plurality framed the issue as a conflict between free speech and the state's interest in such matters as protecting its revenue, avoiding "sticky" administrative problems, and reducing unpleasant "blare." [97] In its early consideration of the Fairness Doctrine, the Court emphasized the rights of the viewers rather than those of the broadcasters, whom the Court labeled "mere licensees." [98] In the defamation case, the interests that competed with freedom of speech were the principle that states should define for themselves appropriate liability standards and the interest of private citizens in their reputations. [99] In none of the cases did the Court pose the issue in terms of competing systemic free speech interests.

Such decisions might protect free speech by happenstance, if the implicit empirical judgments prove to be correct. It is difficult, however, to see how those decisions could educate the public about the importance and meaning of the first amendment. In fact, they deprive the public of an understanding of the richness of freedom of speech and obscure its various possibilities and difficulties. Moreover, they deprive many citizens of a sense of a stake in the principle. Although the interests represented by each side in a lawsuit may all be first amendment interests, only one side can emerge from the lawsuit wearing that mantle. The losers are left to wonder if the freedom of speech, as it has been narrowed and simplified by the courts, is as valuable as it is supposed to be.

The Effect of Fancy Talk

The idea that judicial opinions are useful educational devices stems, in part, from admiration for the inspiring rhetoric found in many decisions. The ringing words in some of the dissents of Justices Holmes and Hugo Black, for example, have become part of our political culture. [100] But admiration should not be confused with usefulness; rhetoric, even when memorable, is not always of value for educating the public about complex issues.

Consider, for instance, *Cohen v. California*. [101] The issue in *Cohen* was whether a breach of the peace conviction based on the wearing of a jacket that displayed the words "Fuck the Draft" violated the wearer's freedom of speech. The Court, in a decision notable for the seriousness and care of its analysis, overturned the conviction on the ground that it was based solely on the offensiveness of the message rather than on any conduct.[102] The Court noted that, under existing law, a state may not punish a speaker for the content of a message in the absence of a showing of intent to incite a violation of the law. Because such intent was not present in the case, the Court reasoned that the conviction could only be justified as a regulation of the method of communication rather than the content of communication.[103] The Court then rejected as inapposite a number of permissible grounds for regulating speech: (1) the regulation was not aimed solely at protecting the decorum of a courtroom, (2) the phrase was not erotic, hence, there was no obscenity, and (3) the message was too impersonal to constitute "fighting words." The Court concluded:

> Against this background, the issue flushed by this case stands out in bold relief. It is whether California can excise, as "offensive conduct," one particular scurrilous epithet from the public discourse . . . upon the theory . . . that . . . the States, acting as guardians of public morality, may properly remove this offensive word from the public vocabulary.

Having "flushed" the issue, the Court proclaimed:

> The constitutional right of free expression is powerful medicine in a society as diverse and populous as ours. It is designed and intended to remove governmental restraints from the arena of public discussion . . . in the hope that use of such freedom will ultimately produce a more capable citizenry and more perfect polity and in the belief that no other approach would comport with the premise of individual dignity and choice upon which our political system rests.[104]

Reasoning from such heights, the Court found that under our system of freedom of speech there is necessity for, even virtue in, discord and offensiveness, "verbal cacophony."[105]

My reason for summarizing so much of the *Cohen* opinion is not to criticize the analysis. Indeed, it is vintage first amendment reasoning, familiar and perhaps convincing to any reader of Emerson, who warned that even though suppression may often seem "entirely plausible . . . [and] tolerance a weakness or foolish risk, . . . society must be willing to sacrifice individual and short-term advantage for . . . long-range goals."[106] The *Cohen* opinion is methodical and, in a way, unanswerable.

The dissenters described Cohen's behavior as an "antic" and dismissed the Court's "agonizing over First Amendment values . . . [as] misplaced and unnecessary."[107] Yet, reassuring as it may be to hear a note of common sense amidst first amendment doctrine, this response is too easy. As a judicial opinion, precisely where did the decision go wrong? There is no exception to the first amendment for immature antics; any such exception would, in principle, be highly dangerous. The majority was clearly right to label the words "speech" rather than "conduct" and to distinguish the "offensive speech" cases. Step by step, the majority opinion is correct. It does as much as can be expected from a judicial opinion and provides an excellent example of why the protection of free speech is so widely thought well entrusted to the courts.

The dissent, however, is surely correct in asserting that there is an embarrassing incongruity in the majority's serious tone and lavish attention to the issue, which was, after all, only whether there is a right to deliver a message consisting of three tasteless and almost contentless words by displaying them on an article of clothing. But the dissent is mistaken to suggest that this inappropriate highmindedness is a unique and unfortunate exception. Similar incongruities can be found in any number of cases. The Court, for example, has intoned the grand principles of free speech to protect the right to show nudity on an outdoor movie screen without the disadvantage of having to build a visual barrier, the right to display noncommercial billboards if some commercial billboards are permitted, and the right to put on nude dancing shows as long as there are no representations of "masturbation, excretory functions, and lewd exhibition of genitals."[108]

The problem so graphically illustrated by *Cohen* is endemic to judicial review. It arises because courts necessarily determine the meaning of the first amendment in the context of specific factual disputes. Attempts to apply abstract principles to particularized factual situations necessarily produce some strain, especially when the principles are formulated to achieve long-term objectives that purportedly lie at the foundation of democratic society. The more trivial or outlandish the facts, the greater the strain becomes.

There is substantial evidence demonstrating that although the public approves of civil liberties in the abstract, it generally disapproves of them in concrete situations.[109] Although some regard this as evidence of the public's ignorance,[110] it is a fact that must be contended with in attempting to build popular support for the principle of freedom of speech. Whether or not first amendment theory is correct in positing that any minor deviation from the wall of protection for free speech is potentially dangerous, judicial protection inherently creates problems for public appreciation of the importance of free speech. If judicial protection, as the chief mechanism for giving effective meaning to the first amendment, continuously creates that meaning by attempting to fit specific facts to grand theory, public sympathy for free speech will be jeopardized.

The Court could minimize this difficulty by reserving its power, not for the hardest cases, but for the most obviously important ones. It is not clear, however, that there are many such important cases. Harry Kalven asserted in 1964 that the guarantee of free speech most fundamentally forbids punishment of seditious libel; yet, there have been very few relatively unambiguous opportunities to establish this principle.[111] Thus, a court intent upon teaching this lesson might have to seize upon some approximation of the proper occasion—which Kalven argued was *New York Times Co. v. Sullivan*—but then the lesson received might be ambiguous, arguable, and even lost.[112]

Important occasions for the use of judicial power often turn out to be "hard" cases, a fact that tends to reduce the persuasiveness of the desired lesson. Because the Pentagon Papers case involved an instance of prior restraint on a matter of great importance to political debate, it apparently presented the Court with an opportunity to expound important first amendment principles in a grand setting rather than in the trivial or seamy factual situations common to so much first amendment litigation.[113] The case was important, however, precisely because it raised many difficult, unresolved issues. Should the outcome have been affected by the special need for secrecy in foreign affairs, or by the absence of authorizing legislation, or by the failure of the president to act without the aid of the judiciary?[114] Could publication of the papers lead, as at least one Justice believed, to "the death of soldiers, the destruction of alliances, [and] the greatly increased difficulty of negotiating with our enemies"?[115] Confronted by such questions, the Court understandably sounded no clarion call for freedom of the press.[116] Instead, the several opinions drifted off on such issues as separation of powers and the hurried procedures through which the case had come to the Court.[117] The Court actually resolved the matter in a short opinion that simply held that only compelling circumstances could justify prior restraints.

Even if the Court should convincingly articulate a grand principle on a proper occasion, the dynamics of litigation are such that subsequent cases often dilute the message by stretching principles and rules to their limit. For example, courts may limit the application of the principle that there is a right of public access to criminal trials as they determine what circumstances can justify exceptions to the principle,[118] or they may extend it into dubious, far-fetched settings at the prodding of litigators eager to expose other forums of governmental decision making to public scrutiny.

Consequently, the judiciary's use of elaborate explanations and high-sounding principles to resolve specific cases, including many that are extreme and difficult, erects obstacles to an enhanced public appreciation of free speech. A public exposed to the judiciary's lessons will inevitably ask certain troubled questions. Why, for example, if the first amendment's guarantee of freedom of speech is so important, is it so often invoked to protect seemingly silly, unsavory, or dangerous activities? Why does its application so often seem strained, difficult, and doubtful? Although these may be, as some civil libertarians suggest, unsophisticated questions, they are questions that will arise and ultimately may undermine public support for the idea of free speech. This is a risk, unmeasured and largely unconsidered, of using judicial review to protect the systemic objectives of the first amendment. It would be difficult, but nevertheless important, to determine whether this threat to free speech is greater than that posed by indictments of the sort involved in *Cohen*. Preferring naive confidence to serious assessments of usefulness, however, the courts have for the most part ignored the issue.

The Relevance of Categorization

Cohen illustrates another problem with attempting to use judicial review to enhance the general level of free speech. As a "particularized consideration" for its holding, the Court in *Cohen* said that "the principle contended for by the State seems inherently boundless. How is one to distinguish this from any other offensive word?"[119] This nicely confounds the methods of legal analysis with the systemic requirements of freedom of speech. The search for containable categories is familiar to every first-year law student who has encountered a slippery slope argument. A basic assumption of modern first amendment theory is that the kind of explicit categorization so often used in legal thinking can effectively resolve free speech questions and can provide the bridge that links individual cases to the whole system. Because each case is resolved by reference to principles applicable to whole classes of behavior, the protection afforded in a particular case has more general significance.

> A system of free expression can be successful only when it rests upon the strongest possible commitment to the positive right and the narrowest possible basis for exceptions. And *any such exceptions must be clearcut, precise, and readily controlled*. Otherwise the forces that press toward restriction will break through the openings, and freedom of expression will become the exception and suppression the rule.[120]

Accordingly, first amendment case law is replete with lawyerlike efforts at precise classification: obscene speech, incitement, "fighting words," malicious defamation, and so on. Yet, there are reasons to doubt that categorical clarity actually promotes free expression.

If anything is certain from the development of first amendment law since 1919, it is that categorical solutions can only crudely resolve free speech issues. Chafee and others thought that the concept of "clear and present danger" solved the problem of separating protected from unprotected speech. It is uncertain, however, whether this concept would prohibit the government from trying to prevent remote, but catastrophic, dangers. If it does, the category seems dangerous and unwise.[121] If it does not, this apparently hard category dissolves into highly discretionary judicial assessments of the severity of various possible disasters.[122]

Some have thought it obvious that commercial speech should not be protected by the first amendment.[123] But, if it is permissible to censor commercial information, consumers may be deprived of information that is as important to them as any other category of information.[124] If commercial speech is protected, however, then perhaps billboard regulation must become a subject for first amendment law.[125] Similarly, the first amendment does not protect "obscenity."[126] But, as dissenters never tire of pointing out, the concept of obscenity—like the concept of "offensiveness" under scrutiny in *Cohen*—is potentially boundless; what constitutes obscenity is ultimately a judgment based on personal reaction and taste. Because of these and many other difficulties, first amendment law has been characterized by the proliferation of increasingly complex categories.[127]

The Court's focus in *Cohen* on the question, "How is one to distinguish this from any other offensive word?" is misleading. That question is unimportant from a systemic viewpoint unless it is presumed that free speech will be continuously reduced if distinctions are analytically impossible. According to the modern first amendment consensus, only a society that "understands" that it is dangerous to make such distinctions will adequately protect free speech. Thus, the Court has announced many times that regulations based on content are especially suspect. A town may not apply special restrictions to drive-in movie theaters that display nudity.[128] It is even doubtful whether school boards may consider the appropriateness of the content of the books in school libraries or whether town officials may control the content of the plays put on in a town theater.[129] The Court contends that it is dangerous to attempt to separate truths from falsehoods or useful information from drivel.[130]

Thus, advertisements must receive the same protection as political tracts and nonmalicious defamations the same protection as accurate reporting.

All this assumes that categorization is the only relevant basis for limitation. It may even be true that a court could not explain a decision approving such distinctions without adopting a term that impliedly permitted "boundless" suppressions. But to assume that this difficulty for the judiciary is also a problem for the freedom of speech generally is to assume that there are no nonjudicial restraints on censorship. Lines can be drawn not only by verbal categories, however, but also by the sense of proportion and taste created by acculturation and education. People offended by the wearing of "Fuck the Draft" in public places may not be offended by the same message delivered in a different place or manner. A slippery conceptual slope simply does not mean that every suppression based on a judgment of unsuitability will lead to the stifling of political dissent.

If cultural brakes on suppression do exist, the fundamental concern should be the cultural consequences of resolving so many first amendment issues through legal analysis. Does the predominance of judicial solutions build a culture that values new information and dissent? It is doubtful whether a society that has internalized the level of self-doubt taught by the judiciary could make the kinds of elementary judgments of degree, context, and proportion that make vigorous public debate tolerable or desirable.[131] It is questionable whether such a society could even remember the purposes of vigorous debate, which after all include both responsible self-government and the capacity to form judgments, to make moral and aesthetic discriminations.[132] When judges teach that it is dangerous or inappropriate to make decisions about the kinds of books that should be kept in school libraries or the kinds of plays that should be staged in public theaters, they effectively strip the first amendment of much of its moral utility.[133]

The kinds of distinctions that courts do permit—those hard enough to ensure that all potentially useful ideas will be safe from suppression—are based on abstractions that do not track the more subtle sensibilities taught by the culture. For example, the Court has defined obscenity mechanically and artificially,[134] drawing precisely the kind of "legal" distinction that renders the judiciary's "constitution" foreign to the public. It is a sign of the awkwardness of legal thinking, not of any danger in the culture, that the public might not easily understand the concept of "nonobscene" pornographic pictures of children as defined by the Court.[135] If the only distinctions the Court finds permissible under the Constitution are specialized and nonintuitive, the public will inevitably tend to perceive the first amendment as foolish and undesirable.

In some cases the Court has succumbed to the constant pressure to soften its categories. For instance, the Court now acknowledges a gray area between the obscene and the nonobscene, an area that might be termed "the moderately useless and disgusting."[136] When categories soften and thereby threaten to become "boundless," the Court warns that it will not accept just *any* regulation in the area, but rather will scrutinize the regulation and weigh and balance the competing interests. The resulting judicial decisions may over- or under-protect speech, depending upon one's assessment of the balance struck by the Court. While opinions will differ with respect to any given decision, these techniques will enhance the general level of freedom of expression only if the judges' sensibilities are as good as, or better than, the sensibilities of other potential decision makers, a matter that also deserves more skepticism than it has received. Before turning to that issue, however, specific attention should be given to the most complete and thoughtful recent exploration of the possibility that free speech decisions can have useful cultural consequences.

Decisions as Exemplars of Tolerance

Lee Bollinger proposes that the purpose of free speech law ought to be the cultural validation of that set of intellectual and psychological capacities called tolerance.[137] He argues that judicial protections should be demonstrations to various segments of the public of the useful, but sometimes painful, qualities of that trait. By being balanced, receptive, and restrained in the face of provocation, the Court's opinions can teach by example. Some of the cases criticized in this chapter might be thought to have served this subtle and important function. Understood in the context of Florida politics in the 1960s, *Gibson,* despite its simplification of the free speech issue, might have conveyed the lesson that the urge to condemn the ideas of the NAACP should be held in check. During the Vietnam War, *Cohen,* despite its trivial facts, might have symbolized the possibility of constraining potent hostility against protesters. Such attractive possibilities deserve separate consideration.

The perception of judicial decisions by relevant members of the public is, of course, an empirical matter. Bollinger gives some important reasons to expect that an appropriate lesson is being taught,[138] but his insights strongly suggest that judicial action will have multiple meanings. He points out, for instance, that judicial protection of the Nazis' right to march in Skokie might express not only admirable self-discipline in the face of provocation but also insensitivity or even aggression toward the Jewish residents.[139]

A number of related reasons to expect some dysfunctional messages from the judiciary readily suggest themselves. In any political or cultural period, the urge to suppress, at least as to some salient issue, may be expressed most frequently by an identifiable group—whether defined by class, race, gender, or religion. When this occurs, judicial acts of tolerance will necessarily appear to be directed disproportionately at that group. Thus the appearance of judicial bias might be tied to, or even overwhelm, the lesson in tolerance, especially when the composition of the judiciary is different from that of the intolerant group. Moreover, when courts enjoin the acts of other officials, their decisions have both a restraining and an officious quality. Judicial behavior might therefore be viewed (especially by the competing governmental decision makers) as evidencing arrogance or myopic distrust as much as tolerance.

Finally, because the effect of judicial protection is to prevent the imposition of sanctions, there is also a danger that the salient message will be, not the court's self-restraint, but the speaker's irresponsibility. To teach that speech ought not be punished is, perversely, to teach that it ought not be regarded as a serious act. Much modern public debate does have a carnival cast. Protest marches have become pleasant parades or giant celebrative "events." Acts of defiance have become theatrical. Protesters now sometimes prearrange with the authorities to "breach" a police line symbolically and to be arrested as a kind of show for public consumption.[140] Bollinger reminds us that to suppress is to take speech seriously. The converse can be one of the powerful lessons taught by judicial protections.

Without measuring, it is impossible to know how different publics perceive and sort out the various messages that are implicit in judicial acts of protection. It is tempting, therefore, to emphasize (as I have done in this chapter) the kinds of occasions and explanations that courts utilize and then to make inferences about the lessons likely being taught. The very originality of many of Bollinger's observations about legal theory and doctrine creates some doubt that the language of free speech law can be expected to validate tolerance. To the considerable extent that Bollinger's insights enable us to see free speech issues anew, there is reason to think the case law has been an ineffective teacher.

Consider only one of Bollinger's insights. He makes the surprising, but compelling, proposal that tolerance should include a sympathetic appreciation for intolerance. This is because suppressive acts are communicative acts and can express important beliefs and feelings. This idea is a breakthrough *because* it gets past the lessons that the courts have taught for so long. Bollinger's discussion itself shows that even in its most respected opinions, the Court's position has tended to be that all intolerance is deeply antithetical to democratic values.[141] His somewhat hesitant suggestion that such errors may be a correctable failure of understanding is properly modest.[142] For courts to recognize the close functional and moral relationship between tolerance and intolerance would be at odds with their understandable desire to persuade the public of the necessity for decisions that inflict great costs on prized values like personal reputation and decent political debate. The vindication of tolerance in settings where speech creates extreme harm does, as Bollinger says, have pedagogic advantages, such as high drama and visibility. Unfortunately, it also ensures that free speech will seem extremely costly and possibly unwise, unless the courts can successfully exaggerate the stakes. The price of immoderate lessons is the kind of intellectual obfuscation that Bollinger's book so successfully penetrates.

It is always possible that a particular decision may teach at least some groups an appropriate lesson. But what would it take for judicial decision making generally to exhibit the mix of attributes Bollinger calls "tolerance"? Because tolerance requires a full inquiry into the importance of the urge to suppress, courts would have to take into account large and highly speculative considerations. Bollinger argues that in the *Skokie* case, for instance, the courts should have "seriously" considered the risk that the proposed march might have disrupted "the peaceful coexistence that had tentatively been maintained in the community between Jews, Christians, and blacks."[143] Those who are close to the moods of the populace might be able to assess such possibilities. But there is no obvious reason to expect the relatively insulated judiciary to be able to do so. Such political and cultural understanding, especially if the prospect of "degeneration of relations" is long-term, is not the kind of thing about which legal briefs or authoritative judicial decisions can easily be written.

Because tolerance requires assessment of varied and conflicting factors, Bollinger suggests that courts should employ "conscientiously ambiguous" doctrine, and free speech scholarship should "turn somewhat away from . . . the intricacies of the tests employed in the various areas of First Amendment litigation, and examine more broadly what the impact of the concept seems to be in social thought generally. Free speech is too vital a national symbol to be thought about exclusively in doctrinal terms."[144]

Now, the judiciary's reverence for clarity and its devotion to doctrine cannot easily be cast off. Clarity is an ideal bred early into every law student. Doctrine—those tests that define a "public figure" or "obscenity," and so on—has been the obsession not only of first amendment law but, as described in chapter 7, of almost all constitutional law during the modern period. To significantly reduce the influence of either would require far more than greater understanding of the value at issue in free speech cases. It would require important alterations in patterns of legal thought and in the functions of judicial review. I return to this theme in subsequent chapters; for now it is enough to say that if legal explanations are to be richer and more ambiguous, communicative force will be achieved at the price of predictability and control. Lower courts and other political institutions, while perhaps learning from the example set by the Supreme Court's more expressive opinions, would nevertheless have more discretion in making concrete decisions. After all, the point of a tolerant judicial opinion would be to communicate the fullness and difficulty of a dispute.[145] Without simplistic rules to "censor" what is complex and problematic, decisions would become better partly in that they would leave more autonomy to other decision makers. To the extent that the Court is committed to social control—to building a political system characterized by some ideal amount and mix of information—it will continue to depend on crude clarity.

If free speech decisions are generally to be "a forum for education,"[146] the judiciary will have to subordinate its traditional task of authoritatively terminating disputes. If litigation "provides the framework, the occasion, for the community to think about the things free speech is intended to raise for thought," then, as Bollinger acknowledges, the process must move slowly.[147] Both this ventilation function and the need for high-quality opinion writing are in tension with the amount of work required for an extensive dispute resolution role. Moreover, because courts end disputes by coercing one party or the other, it may be too much to ask that judicial opinions candidly and sympathetically portray all sides of the question. For a judge to do so is to risk throwing the resolution of the case into doubt and thus undermining the authority of the decree and of the court. Judges are perhaps wrong to fear such consequences, but there is ample evidence that they have long done so.[148] Moreover, there is reason to think they will continue to do so as long as one party must be made to lose.

Bollinger acknowledges that tolerance is inconsistent with the adversary nature of the litigation process because that process encourages the "tendency to oversimplify, or, in effect, to censor, the complexity of the problems."[149] He observes that excessive definitiveness—for instance, the false portrayal of the constitutional text as absolute—may result, not from misunderstanding, but from normal judicial ideals such as fidelity to external legal authority and personal disinterest.[150] The central doubt about Bollinger's theory, in short, is how often we can realistically expect the courts, which have deeply ingrained habits and ideals and functions that all involve significant amounts of intolerance, to teach tolerance to the rest of us.

The Inclinations of Judges

The increasingly pervasive role of the courts in promoting freedom of speech depends heavily on the belief that, notwithstanding any drawbacks in the methods of judicial review, judges can be trusted with the first amendment more than other officials.[151] However, the common belief that the training and professionalism of judges actually make them especially attuned to free speech values should not be accepted on faith. Undeniably, judges are more likely than other officials to assume that free speech issues are problems susceptible to "solution" by the traditional methods of legal analysis. In addition, because of their institutional perspectives, judges are likely to assume that free speech requires judicial protection from irrational and uncontrolled forces. But, as I have tried to suggest, these predispositions may reflect professional complacency as much as special competence.

Notwithstanding assertions to the contrary, the actual training and experience of judges are of dubious value in preparing them to understand or protect the freedom of speech. Many judges exhibit extraordinary degrees of intolerance every day in their courtrooms, and virtually all of them exercise broad and abrupt powers of suppression in discharging their duties. It is at best unclear why the normally sedate and highly controlled atmosphere of a courtroom is thought to be a good training ground for appreciating the dynamics of vigorous public debate. In contrast, political involvement and accountability provide much of the experience that one might expect would lead to a useful understanding of the requirements of a system of free speech. It is, of course, political candidates who engage in open political debate. They should understand the needs of political organization and private association because they work in these settings. Indeed, to assume that politicians do not understand or appreciate the needs and values of a system of free expression is to assume that they are blind to the world they inhabit and on which they depend.

The judiciary's record in freedom of expression cases does not evince any special competence or sensitivity for promoting the freedom of speech; indeed, the contrary appears closer to the truth. Some judges have freely used injunctions to censor criticism of their decrees. In an action that is not at all unique, one federal judge protected his school desegregation plan by issuing the following order:

1. All protest areas are hereby abolished;
2. No person shall assemble in or near any public school building not authorized by the school authorities;
3. Persons more than three in number shall not gather or assemble along any bus route in this . . . county while school buses are being operated along them.[152]

Moreover, many judges have blocked access to or publication of news about judicial processes. One study found 63 orders restraining statements by participants in trials and 39 restraints on publication in an eight-year period; between July 1979 and May 1981, some 400 motions to close some part of a criminal proceeding were made, of which 241 were successful.[153] There have been significant episodes in which military officers under the stress of battle have shown considerable restraint in dealing with dissent. During the Civil War, for example, the Military Code prohibited newsmen from communicating with the enemy. Although the prescribed punishments included death and many newsmen apparently did give intelligence to the enemy, courts-martial for these offenses were extremely rare and usually resulted in mere exclusion from the lines of a military command.[154] In contrast, there have been many instances in which judges, removed and safe, have displayed little restraint in punishing speech.[155] Politicians, not judges, have had the major role in terminating each of the most serious periods of repression.[156]

A general assessment of free speech cases is not reassuring. Judicial coolness and even hostility to free speech claims prior to 1919 is well documented.[157] Even since then, much of the admiration for judges as protectors of free speech is predicated upon eloquent dissents,[158] occasioned (it bears mentioning) only because a majority of the Justices have voted to sanction some form of suppression. There are numerous major decisions in which the Court has subordinated free speech values to other social interests; they involve nearly every form of suppression and have issued from both liberal and conservative Courts.[159] Even in the cases that ultimately protect free speech, the Court often achieves the protection by indirection—by statutory construction or by the use of doctrines (such as overbreadth, vagueness, and procedural due process) that focus on the means, rather than the fact, of suppression. These techniques manifest distrust of the other branches and levels of government more clearly than outright approval of the free speech values involved.[160] In the relatively few decisions resting directly on free speech considerations, the Court often hedges its rulings with enough cautions and limitations to call into question the scope of the Court's commitment to free speech.[161]

It is true, however, that the Court has struck down many restrictive laws and practices in the past sixty years; it is to this record that proponents of the modern judicial role point as justification for their high regard for judges as protectors of free speech. Routine judicial policing of the political arena, however, means less than is commonly assumed. Perhaps inevitably, legalistic conceptions of freedom of speech do not conform to common beliefs or intuitions. Judicial rules are complicated and specialized. It is not surprising, therefore, that nonlawyers might find it hard to understand why corporations have first amendment rights or how a person who obtained a job through political patronage is said to be punished if he subsequently loses it for political reasons.[162] Certainly, the legal meanings of terms like "obscenity" and "defamation" no longer track the common understanding of those terms. A system in which judges first erect an unfamiliar body of law whose logic naturally is hard for laymen to grasp and then invalidate numerous acts of the political branches for being incompatible with that law does not necessarily demonstrate any special judicial sensitivity to first amendment values.

Special judicial appreciation for systemic free speech values might be inferred from the presumed success of the modern program of judicial protection. An enormous volume and variety of information is available today. Criticism of government is pervasive. Any schoolchild can obtain revolutionary tracts or scatological pictures. One might suppose that today's booming information markets stand as testament to the Court's efforts over the past six decades to enforce the first amendment.

This inference is, however, far less persuasive than might initially appear. First, the inference depends upon the assumption that the judicial efforts are primarily responsible for the present climate. It is more likely, however, that the current mood was caused by fundamental educational and cultural shifts, some of which might themselves have produced the elaborate enterprise of judicial protection.[163] For example, no Supreme Court decision either legitimized or encouraged early criticism of the war in Vietnam,[164] yet the eventual success of that criticism in discrediting the war may not only have legitimized political dissent generally, but also have emboldened the courts to attempt to protect such dissent.[165] It is as unreasonable to conclude on the basis of timing alone that the Court's efforts at protection caused the present culture of free and open communication as it would be to conclude that the failure of the Court to protect free speech during the Civil War caused the fiery political dissent so common at that time.[166]

Second, the inference papers over important difficulties in defining "success" in promoting first amendment values. The defamation decisions presumably encouraged increased criticism of government officials. But how much of this new information is false? The patronage decisions presumably have at least marginally protected an individual's private decisions regarding political affiliation. But at what cost to party organization and ultimately to political accountability? More information is not necessarily better information.

Finally, even if it were possible to identify reasonably unambiguous areas in which the courts have actually promoted systemic free speech values, it is still too early to declare judicial activity a success. Just as overprotection of states' rights once helped to discredit the principle of federalism,[167] overprotection of the freedom of expression might gradually discredit the value of free speech. Judicial efforts—such as those to protect corporate expenditures, nude dancing, and advertising—erode popular support to the extent they breed resentment and call into question the utility of free speech. A successful system of free speech must be maintained over long periods of time. Success in the short run might be counterproductive in the long run.

Proponents of the judicial role also assert that even if judges do not have special sensitivity to first amendment values, their political insulation means at least that they will have different values and will respond to different pressures than executive and legislative officials. This view emphasizes that judicial review is useful because it injects into public decision making ideas and priorities that otherwise would be short-changed or missing altogether. Because it is undeniably true that politicians are vulnerable to sudden shifts in mood and to occasional dark impulses to suppress, it may be that the judiciary—subject at least to *different* moods and impulses—might, at times, provide a useful brake on the political process.

Political insulation in this sense, however, does not justify a routine or pervasive judicial program of protections of the kind that now exists. Even its relatively slight implications have gone untested. It does not necessarily follow from the supposition that judges react to different pressures that their reactions will be useful. Whether their reactions are useful depends on the nature of the suppressive moods that sweep the political arena. The psychological and social functions of the waves of suppression that arise (often during periods of warfare or economic instability) are complex and mysterious. They feed on personal insecurities and their main effect is sometimes to provide symbolic solidarity and reassurance—the psychological preconditions for tolerance.[168] Accordingly, these moods, if permitted to reach their extreme, sometimes generate their own political checks.[169] When such suppression would otherwise occur if unchecked, the judiciary's success in stopping specific forms of suppression will only cause a relocation of the urge to suppress or postpone the natural termination of the period of censorship. It is surely simplistic to assume that judicial review serves the larger purpose of re-establishing a climate for tolerance merely because judges respond differently than do the other institutions. Before concluding that a particular decision will actually provide long-term, systemic benefits, a court would have to understand many imponderables. Certainly the modern regime of pervasive judicial intervention in the political process is too reflexive to be responsive to its complexity.

Conclusion

In this chapter I have questioned the belief that an extensive, detailed system of judicial protection can be expected to maintain an open system of public debate. At a minimum, the systemic utility of judicial review in free speech cases has been a proposition characterized far too much by convenient assumptions and cheery faith. I suspect that few are willing to take the next step and accept my gloomy view that the Court's program, taken as a whole, has done great damage to the public understanding and appreciation of the principle of free speech by making it seem trivial, foreign, and unnecessarily costly. Probably even fewer will agree that these drawbacks are, for the most part, inherent in the judicial process and can therefore be avoided only by generally avoiding judicial review, not by using more skillfully contrived rules and doctrines. After decades of dependence, it is difficult to imagine *not* depending heavily on the courts to protect free speech.

I do not, however, intend to suggest that the courts can never have an important role to play. Even if I am right in believing that the modern edifice of protections is not justified in systemic terms, careful analysis of many complex factors might, as Bollinger demonstrates, lead a court to enhance the appreciation of free speech values in the political culture, at least on rare occasions.[170] It is also possible that doing justice to individuals may demand frequent judicial protection. Perhaps courts could convincingly explain why this is so if they turned their attention away from systemic objectives and focused instead on political legitimacy and the effects of censorship on the individual.[171] But the propriety of such decisions should be assessed without an exaggerated sense of the stakes. If courts decide cases on such a basis, they should do so admitting their ignorance about the potential systemic consequences of particular decisions; they should do so facing the strong possibility that overall the routine concretion of free speech principles works against the maintenance of a general system of free debate.

CHAPTER 4

Federalism as a Fundamental Value

Standing in dramatic contrast to its irrepressibly vigorous efforts to protect free speech, the modern Court's record of enforcing the principle of federalism is anemic. It was only after almost forty years of sanctioning the growth of congressional power to regulate commerce[1] that the Supreme Court finally—in a single case—defined some limit to the power of the federal government. In *National League of Cities v. Usery,*[2] decided in 1976, the Court held that the extension to most state employees of the wage and hour provisions of the Fair Labor Standards Act was unconstitutional as a violation of the tenth amendment. Although some serious commentary had suggested that the Court's record prior to *Usery* verged on abdication of constitutional responsibilities,[3] *Usery* precipitated criticism that was extraordinary both for its breadth and severity. Justice William Brennan, a respected and unapologetic practitioner of judicial power and imaginative constitutional analysis when the issues involve individuals' rights, labeled the decision "an abstraction without substance" and a "patent usurpation."[4] Three prominent scholars reacted to the decision extremely critically. Laurence Tribe and Frank Michelman, both resourceful at constitutional interpretation, professed themselves totally unable to understand the explanation offered by the Court in *Usery* and proposed that the decision could make sense only as an inchoate statement of a right to the provision of certain state services.[5] Jesse Choper reacted with a forceful argument that, even if *Usery* were constitutionally correct on the merits, the Court should have held such matters to be nonjusticiable in order to save its resources for—that phrase again—the protection of individuals' rights.[6] Many others also criticized *Usery*.[7] Those who were at all supportive of the decision were muted or ambivalent.[8]

For its part, the Court refused in case after case to extend the principles announced in *Usery*[9] and then, only nine years later, overruled the decision itself. In *Garcia v. San Antonio Metropolitan Transit Authority*,[10] the Court confessed its inability to maintain the distinction between "traditional" and "nontraditional" state functions, which had been one of the inquiries suggested in *Usery;* apparently unable to muster any of the optimism that underlies the continual adjustments made in free speech law, the Court did not attempt any modification of the tenth amendment analysis proposed in *Usery* and instead announced that the appropriate forum for establishing the limits of congressional power over the states was the political process rather than the courts.

The harsh reaction to *Usery* is one aspect of a widespread pattern that inverts the priorities of the framers: an obsessive concern for using the Constitution to protect individuals' rights. This fascination with rights reinforces a form of instrumentalism that is too confining to be an adequate way to think about constitutional law. If *Usery* is viewed without these intellectual constraints, a rather plain and defensible explanation for the decision emerges.

I develop this explanation in this chapter, but my major purpose is not to insist that *Usery* was "correct." Like other important decisions, including most notably *Brown v. Board of Education, Usery* is difficult to reconcile with standard legal criteria. It was a departure from some precedent, and it rested on psychological and political judgments that are certainly disputable. Moreover, if applied mechanically as a part of a comprehensive effort by an activist Court to insist on a single version of federalism, *Usery* would have led to improvident and rigid consequences. Like many of the results of the judiciary's program in areas like free speech, these consequences might eventually have undermined the constitutional principle at stake. Nevertheless, I will argue that *Usery* itself was the kind of extraordinary judicial intrusion that can—on rare occasions—call us back to fundamental constitutional understandings.

My purpose, then, is to suggest that the general inability to credit the *Usery* decision demonstrates the extent to which the capacity to appreciate important aspects of constitutional principles is being lost. These aspects have more to do with sentiments and attitudes than with specific institutional arrangements. The capacity to appreciate them is already conspicuously absent among judges and legal commentators; to the extent that the general political culture depends on these sources for an understanding of the Constitution, it is being undermined in the rest of society.

The Preference for Rights over Structure

Modern judicial decisions generally reflect a priority in favor of protecting individuals' rights over the structural principles of federalism and separation of powers. Despite some bold and far-reaching decisions enforcing separation of powers,[11] opinions directly resting on either of these structural principles are rare compared with decisions involving individual rights.[12] Issues of federalism and separation of powers are usually analyzed in terms of nonconstitutional doctrines. For example, they are frequently reduced to matters of statutory construction.[13] The scope of the judicial power over states is often discussed in amorphous, discretionary terms. There are, for instance, only wavering and obscure standards for determining the limits on judicial remedies, the characteristics of those who may sue, the nature of "judicial" questions, and the appropriate degree of comity between the national and state governments.[14] Even when structural principles are treated as fully constitutional matters, their main influence is on the definition of individual rights.[15] Those decisions that do deal unambiguously with structural values for their own sake demonstrate less explanatory creativity than do decisions dealing with rights, a fact that suggests a relative lack of judicial interest in structural matters if not lower quality opinions. Missing from decisions involving structural values are the doctrinal innovations used so often in decisions involving rights. There are no analyses of motive, no dissections of legislative purpose, no demands that less drastic means be used, no tiers of judicial scrutiny.[16] Instead, decisions having to do with structure frequently rest on the baldest forms of "balancing" and on an unconvincing use of such generalities as "undue impairment" of the states' functions or the nature of "legislative" acts.[17] Finally, cases in which rights are articulated are frequently followed by a series of decisions that are designed to "actualize" the original right, and in the process the right is often recast in even more ambitious terms.[18] Important cases that articulate structural values tend quickly to be limited and then largely abandoned.[19]

Modern judges work diligently at redesigning local educational programs and at defining the acceptable number of square feet in a prison cell. They void a multiplicity of laws relating to hair length, sexual preference, and abortion. But they deal rarely and, for the most part, gingerly with the great issues of power distribution that were faced so ambitiously and successfully by the framers.

Academic writing generally reflects the same priority. Scholarly discussion of constitutional structure often falls back on the more familiar issues of individual rights. For example, Charles Black's *Structure and Relationship in Constitutional Law* illuminates the possibilities of argument based on structure only quickly to apply that potential to the definition of individual rights.[20] John Ely's *Democracy and Distrust* emphasizes the central importance of democratic self-government in the constitutional design, but this insight is enlisted chiefly in support of rationalizing the Warren Court's creative definition of individual rights.[21] (The book was then criticized, not for overemphasizing the dependence of democratic processes on individual rights, but for attempting to define rights by reference to considerations other than the needs of individuals.)[22] Many books and articles appear on the injunctive devices that lower federal courts are using against states in an effort to implement individuals' constitutional rights. Much of this commentary seeks to conceptualize individuals' rights and the judicial function in ways that permit significant aspects of self-government to be assumed by the courts for the sake of remaking the world to suit some ideal suggested by values implicit in certain rights.[23] Much of the rest of the commentary emphasizes the practicalities of judicial enforcement and largely assumes that, if courts are able to implement individual rights effectively, implementation must have priority over other values.[24] Those who examine the remedial role of the federal courts as an aspect of constitutional structure are quickly urged to return to the proper business of legal scholars, which is expressly defined as arguing about rights.[25]

Scholarly preoccupation with rights is also evident in the tolerant and highly imaginative approaches frequently taken in the definition of rights. Scholars commonly argue that it ought to be no bar to a constitutional claim that there is ambiguity about whether the framers intended a certain interpretation or that they did not consider a possible interpretation of a constitutional right.[26] The argument is extended in such important areas as school desegregation to include definitions of rights that are rather clearly in conflict with historical intent.[27] It is not uncommon for sophisticated scholars to make unembarrassed arguments for an interpretation of a right based largely on the personal values of the proponent of the right.[28] What more than this can be meant by assertions about "goodness" or "minimal standards of human dignity" or "personhood"?[29] Such argumentation, even if it involves more than private values, demonstrates how wide and free the scope of acceptable constitutional argument about rights is. Indeed, scholarship indulges almost any amount of philosophical or psychological vagueness and complexity when the goal is defining rights. We ponder how "just wants" or the "mediation of liberal conversation" or "equal respect and concern" or the ideas of Roberto Unger might bear on the definition of rights.[30]

In contrast, scholars often exhibit a kind of intellectual crabbedness when structural claims are made. Consider the scholars who were content to rest a defense of expanded institutional rights on an assertion about "fostering minimal standards of dignity." They had just tested federalism and separation of power claims about institutional injunctions by demanding to see evidence that the framers actually foresaw and opposed judicial operation of public institutions.[31] Almost any slight ambiguity about historical intent is urged to help defeat structural claims. One scholar, for example, has argued that the intent of the framers with regard to judicial enforcement of federalism was indecisive because, despite clear statements supporting this judicial responsibility, Federalists at times pointed to other protections for the principle as well.[32] Similarly, arguments based on concepts such as separation of powers or democratic accountability are termed hopelessly indeterminate. The same scholar who demands specificity in the concept of "state sovereignty" would ground interpretations of individual rights on values such as "a meaningful opportunity [for individuals] to realize their humanity."[33]

In short, the hostile reaction to *Usery* is part of a broader pattern: many jurists and scholars tend to envision constitutional values mainly in terms of individuals' rights and to undervalue judicial protection of principles that allocate decision-making responsibilities among governmental units. This tendency may be largely a consequence of the influence of the lawsuit in shaping views of the Constitution. Lawsuits, of course, are discrete arguments, usually involving an individual, and they are often resolved by labeling the interests of one side as "rights"; thus, the lawsuit itself tends to convert even organizational matters into individual concerns.

To see the purposes of judicial review almost entirely in terms of securing individual rights is to invert the priorities of the framers and ultimately to trivialize the Constitution. The framers' political theory was immediately concerned with organization, not individuals. Their most important contributions had to do with principles of power allocation— with the blending and separation of power among the branches of government and with the bold effort to create a strong national government while maintaining strong state governments. This structure itself was to be the great protection of the individual, not the "parchment barriers" that were later (and with modest expectations) added to the document.[34] Even the danger of local majoritarian excess—so frequently cited today as a justification for vigorous protection of individual rights—cannot reconcile the modern emphasis on rights with the priorities of the framers. Although aware of the threat posed by "faction," the Federalists proposed social heterogeneity and layered government as the protection,[35] not the Bill of Rights, which, after all, was originally thought to restrain only the national government.

The modern priority on individuals' rights is striking in light of the common assumption that judicial review allows for some continuity in the articulation of our most basic principles. In adopting a viewpoint and a vocabulary that focuses on individuals, modern judges and scholars have tended to shut themselves off from full participation in the great debates about governmental theory begun by the framers. The writings of Jesse Choper, the bluntest and most extreme critic of judicial enforcement of structural values, provide a more specific understanding of how this participation has been limited.

Naive Instrumentalism and Structure

Although the priority given to judicial protection of rights rather than structure is widespread, the preference is often muted or qualified.[36] In Choper's writings, it is forthright. He argues that the two basic structural principles—the enumeration of a limited number of subjects as proper for congressional legislation and the separation of the national government into three distinct branches—ought to be left to the accommodations made in the political process.[37] Courts should preserve their political "capital" for the protection of individual rights.[38]

Choper argues that a court misallocates its efforts when it attempts to enforce constitutional limitations on congressional power, because the judiciary has no special competence to decide such issues. "The functional, borderline question posed by federalism disputes is one of comparative skill and effectiveness of governmental levels: in a word, an issue of practicability."[39] Judicial attempts to influence such practical decisions are often futile and make the courts unpopular politically—all for no important purpose, since the political branches are able and inclined to preserve an adequate level of power at the state level.[40]

On the other hand, Choper argues that questions of individual substantive rights are matters of "principle"—a term that is not fully explained—on which the courts do have special competence.[41] These matters of principle cannot be entrusted to the majorities in the political process, apparently because it takes judicial skills to determine what they are.[42] Furthermore, federalistic disputes cannot be squeezed into this substantive-rights mold by focusing on the individuals' rights that might be served by decentralization. There is "no solid historical or logical basis" for the "assertion that federalism was meant to protect, or does in fact protect, individual constitutional freedoms."[43] Federalism, Choper asserts, was designed to protect states, not individuals, for the purpose of achieving governmental efficiency in a large, heterogenous land.[44] Insofar as the existence of state power was designed to protect individuals from governmental restrictions on their liberty (in a general sense), such protections are less important than substantive constitutional freedoms because the right "to choose in smaller political units whether and how some activities would be regulated" is "not for the ultimate security of defined liberties."[45] In contrast, "the essence of the individual rights claim is that no organ of government, national or state, may undertake the challenged activity."[46]

Choper is right, of course, that the principle of federalism determines only the level of government that may restrict a liberty. But to the extent that decentralized government permits decisions to be made by local officials who might differ from national decision makers in their accessibility or sensitivity, the principle does serve "the ultimate security of a defined liberty" and is not on this ground inferior to constitutional rights. Choper appears to acknowledge this, although—true to the intellectual habits of the time—he insists on referring to self-determination as a "freedom," as if a principle cannot be taken seriously unless conceived of as attached to individuals.[47] Choper explains the inferior status of the most basic interest served by the principle of federalism with this remark:

> [It is] equally likely that the withdrawal of judicial review will result in more fastidious concern for states' rights by the federal political branches [and] [m]ore important, continuing jurisdiction over states' rights claims can . . . undermine [the Court's] ability to perform the critical task of protecting all individual liberties.[48]

In the end, Choper's argument largely begs the question. Individual rights should be protected in preference to the interest in self-determination because judicial efforts to protect this interest might be unnecessary and might conflict with the "critical" task of protecting individuals' rights. But as Choper acknowledges,[49] judicial protection of any right might reduce congressional concern over the subject. And Choper does not mean that judicial protection of substantive, individual rights—the right to work more than a ten-hour day comes to mind—at times has not significantly reduced the Court's prestige and political power. Nor is an answer to the question supplied by the adjective "critical." Why the protection of rights is more critical than the protection of the principle of federalism was the question at the outset.

Although Choper's specific treatment of the interest in self-determination does not explain the inferior status of structural values, the direction and emphasis throughout his argument is suggestive of an explanation. Consider again Choper's striking and repeated assertion that the interests protected by federalism are "not for the ultimate security of defined liberties."[50] This assertion is not strictly relevant to self-determination because local control is "ultimate" in the sense that no decision maker would be permitted to remove certain decisions from the local level. Nevertheless, requirements as to decision-making processes do not provide any ultimate security with respect to outcomes. Indeed, local decision making can be used to achieve very unfair outcomes—a realization that was of constant concern to the framers.[51] The interest in local decision making might be thought less significant than individuals' constitutional rights to the extent that the protection of rights requires the realization of some substantive vision of a moral world. While it may be a moral good to have some decisions made locally, that value might not seem as important as an absolute constitutional protection that restricts and prescribes outcomes, at least to the extent that the values implicit in such rights are morally compelling.[52] And Choper, of course, does assume that these values are compelling and asserts that their realization serves "the dignity of the individual."[53]

It might be objected that it is possible (if not likely) to approve morally of the decentralization of power to the same extent as one might approve of a world where the values implicit in individual constitutional rights are realized. But can a world of decentralized authority be morally compelling to this degree if no specific version of decision-making allocation is constitutionally mandated? Choper suggests throughout his argument that questions of individual rights have specific intellectual content.[54] Matters of federalism are said not to be matters of principle and, thus, are not subject to specific intellectual elaboration. Federalism is a process that is elaborated by self-interest.[55] The only certainty provided by the tenth amendment is that states must not be totally destroyed or rendered ineffective.[56] An enormous range of power allocations is consistent with the abstract requirement that some degree of state sovereignty be maintained. Hence, Choper and others can argue that the principle is sufficiently devoid of content that it can safely be entrusted to the political process.

Aspects of Choper's argument, then, suggest that the priority of rights over structure rests on a preference for constitutional values that can be concretely implemented.[57] To be implemented, a value must be measurable. To be measurable, it must be determinate and specific. To the extent they are more concrete (a matter I shall return to shortly), rights may generally seem more important than processes. Any specific, morally compelling outcomes that are required by rights can easily seem more important than vague processes. Indeed, the basic premise of Choper's argument—that the courts should allocate their efforts to the areas where they can achieve the greatest payoff—attests to the strong connection between the preference for rights and naive instrumentalism.[58] Under this view, a major criterion for assessing legal rules is their capacity to produce measurable changes in the real world; accordingly, it neglects not only intrinsic values but also those consequential values that are less tangible and, therefore, less easily assessed.

While the other major criticisms of *Usery* are different from Choper's, they generally share this same basic orientation.[59] Tribe and Michelman convert *Usery*—a decision apparently aimed at protecting the organizational principle of state sovereignty—into a decision that would establish an individual right to some level of state services. The daring of this reformulation itself attests to the strength of the instrumentalist urge to speak the language of rights rather than the more abstract language of organization. And, although they deny that their interpretations of *Usery* would justify a court in requiring some specific level of state services,[60] both arguments depend on a judicial determination at some point of an acceptable level of concrete state services. The inclination to use law to achieve tangible changes in the world is reflected in these efforts to define structural values by reference to some level of individual welfare.

The sorts of justifications that Tribe and Michelman offer for rushing past organizational matters to settle on their more farfetched interpretations are also consistent with the kind of instrumentalist orientation underlying Choper's arguments.[61] For example, *Usery* is criticized for not relying on specific evidence as to the effect of the wage and hour provisions on state governments—for not looking to the "actual impact of the regulations."[62] The opinion is criticized for protecting the state as a private agent but not as sovereign lawgiver and enforcer.[63] It is criticized for protecting the government's apparatus but not its policy-making prerogatives.[64] And it is criticized for protecting the exercise of its traditional functions but not the sovereign prerogative to decide what new functions ought to be assumed by the state.[65] In short, as Justice Brennan complained, *Usery* created an "abstraction without substance."[66] Or, as Michelman put it with understated relish, it is "no easy matter to ascribe operational content to that notion [of sovereignty]."[67]

Given the nature of the barrage of academic criticism, it is no surprise that the Court's repudiation of *Usery* was also firmly rooted in crude instrumentalist assumptions. The bulk of the *Garcia* opinion was given over to an unusually detailed criticism of the distinction between traditional and nontraditional state functions. Despite its length, this criticism did not explain the Court's conclusion that *Usery* should be flatly overruled. The *Garcia* decision conceded that there are affirmative constitutional limits on the commerce power and even vaguely suggested a potentially more useful approach to defining those limits;[68] thus the criticism established only that a single sort of judicial inquiry should be discarded. The criticism is, however, revealing of an underlying assumption about the purposes of judicial review. The Court argued in numbing detail that distinctions like those "between licensing drivers and regulating traffic . . . or between operating a highway authority and operating a mental health facility [are] elusive at best."[69] The implicit notion, clearly recognizable from the Court's performance in areas like free speech law, is that the purpose of constitutional doctrine is to shape the world in certain and measurable ways. A constitutional principle must therefore be susceptible to routine and pervasive applications. This naive instrumentalism, in the end, is the basis of *Garcia*. The intellectual effort begun in *Usery* was thought to be unnecessary because the "special and specific position in our constitutional system [of state governments] will be effectively protected by the federal political process."[70] Because the world does not require changing, the Court could see no reason for judicial involvement.

In focusing on the difficulties and needlessness of using judicial doctrine to make the abstract concept of federalism operational, the major criticisms of *Usery* all display the same intellectual orientation. The belief that judicial protection of rights is more valuable than judicial protection

of structural principles may, then, have become widespread because structural values are not easily assimilated into the instrumentalist assumptions that underlie so much of modern legal thought.[71] However, the precise relationship between this operationalism and the critics' common
emphasis on individuals' rights remains somewhat mysterious. Their lack
of enthusiasm for structural values is more understandable than their vigorous commitment to judicial protection of constitutional rights. Why is
it, after all, that the values implicit in constitutional rights are thought of
as being sufficiently specific to fit comfortably with the instrumentalist
demands of the major critics of *Usery*? If it is difficult to identify when a
federal statute interferes with some "essential" level of state functioning,
it is equally difficult to identify when the provision of state services has
dropped below some "minimally adequate level."[72] If a state's "sovereignty" is an abstract idea, so is an individual's "humanity."[73]

A principle like state sovereignty might, however, be thought to be
different from a principle such as free speech in that almost no conceivable statute could impair the value behind the existence of state governments. In contrast, as chapter 3 demonstrates, it has become easy and
customary to think that specific statutes impair the values behind, for example, the first amendment. And it is possible to define the value protected by the tenth amendment in such a way that its impairment by any
one statute is improbable. The Court has, for instance, said that the commerce power may not be used in a way that centralizes all power in the
national government.[74] No statute other than one that abolished the
states could do that. But no conceivable statute threatens the larger purposes behind the first amendment either. Whether these purposes are defined systemically ("the maintenance of open public debate for the sake of
democratic decision making") or personally ("the protection of access to
and use of information for the sake of autonomous individuals"), these
larger values are not threatened by any discrete act. A statute that prohibits the reading of pornographic books in one's home will not destroy
autonomy unless accompanied by a wide array of other restrictions that
destroy other sources of personal autonomy.[75] Even a major instance of
prior restraint over the publication of political news could not by itself
destroy the level of debate generally necessary for the democratic system
to operate.[76] Discrete governmental restrictions may threaten these larger
values cumulatively and in the long run. Rights *can be* made operational,
then, not so much because the values they serve are specific or concrete,
but because they *must be*. Rights must be made operational precisely be-

cause their purposes are remote and general and can be undercut only gradually and insensibly. But that, of course, is also true of the exercise of federal power as it gradually diminishes state sovereignty.

Although rights are not innately more concrete or measurable than structural values, concentration on rights does lead to instrumentalist habits of thought. This is not to say that the broad intellectual movement called instrumentalism grew out of concern about individuals' rights. It is to say that, whatever the derivation of that movement, extreme or "naive" forms of instrumentalism are encouraged by concentration on rights.

This is because noninstrumentalist justifications for decisions that protect rights are never fully satisfactory. Even Judge Hans Linde's well-known effort to emphasize noninstrumental justifications for major Warren era cases demonstrates the difficulty of severing rights from instrumentalism. He asked, "What would be the implications for the Constitution, in its role as primary national symbol, of a decision saying that a bit of organized public prayer never hurt anyone?"[77] This question was designed to suggest that compliance with judicial decrees—concrete alterations of actual behavior—is less important than the sense of understanding and reassurance that the Court's statement of principle creates.[78] As important as this argument is in supplementing the narrow emphasis on the immediate and tangible consequences of decisions,[79] it is not fully satisfying. To the extent that a court can make compelling the normative premise in its decision regarding an individual right, the court has stated reasons for realizing that right in actual situations. Parties who have convincingly been labeled "wronged" may be reassured by their abstract vindication, but they will also want the matter righted. And what is good for one individual is morally compelling for others in analogous situations. Thus, the vindication of a constitutional "right" localizes the moral claim in an individual and thereby creates an inevitable insistence on "actualization."[80] In short, the constant impulse to define rights in measurable ways derives from the fact that, as Choper has emphasized, constitutional rights are individuals' rights. Rights are specified—the percentage of each race that should attend public schools, the extent of acceptable governmental participation in parochial education, the number of square feet required in prison cells—to give some assurance that each individual can receive whatever moral benefit is inherent in the right.

Because structural values need not be immediately localized in individuals, symbolic and educative justifications may be more fully satisfying when applied to matters of government organization than when applied to matters of right. Such justifications, because not linked to concrete alterations of the world, would not be credited or even noticed by those absorbed in matters of individual rights. Such justifications underlie *Usery* and, once appreciated, make it an illustration of potentially valuable use of judicial power.

National League of Cities v. Usery
in Perspective

The Court's decision in *National League of Cities v. Usery* is understandable and admirable once the intellectual habits associated with thinking about constitutional rights are set aside. The Court did not attempt to limit congressional power by a restrictive definition of "commerce among the States." Such a tactic had been employed by the Court prior to 1937 when, for example, it attempted to distinguish such local matters as "manufacturing" from the national concern, "commerce."[81] This approach, like present-day efforts to actualize rights, involved the Court in efforts to create and maintain a concrete, identifiable "constitutional" condition—a condition that then consisted of a "proper" division of substantive areas of regulation between the state and nation. The effort, of course, is now properly discredited. The *Usery* Court, instead, emphasized the abstract concept behind the principle of federalism; it spoke of states as being "coordinate elements" and as needing "separate and independent existence."[82] This language did not require some tangible, static system of power allocation, a fact that was emphasized by the unwillingness of the Court to rest its decision on any specific measurement of the burden imposed on the states by the Fair Labor Standards Act (FLSA).[83] The Court's language was true to the idea of federalism in that it described a process rather than an edifice.[84]

In applying these abstractions to the facts of *Usery*, the Court first distinguished those cases that involved the exercise of federal authority over individuals from those over states "as States."[85] It emphasized the importance of the employment relationship for the effective exercise of state functions and (in general terms) the sorts of burdens created by the FLSA for important programs carried on by state and local governments.[86] It described the burdens as affecting broad areas of governmental activity, including areas where states have traditionally delivered services.[87] These factors, I believe, can be shown to define state sovereignty in a way that is entirely consistent with the Federalists' political theory. Although the Court in *Usery* did not specifically refer to this theory, the main elements of the opinion are protective of the purposes that the framers intended the states to serve in the "federal" system.[88]

Those purposes, although not reducible to anything concrete or measurable, are well known and important. Proponents of the proposed constitution who, like Madison and Hamilton, argued for a strong national government had to answer the fears of those who thought that the new national government would consolidate all power at the national level.[89] The reasons why the anti-Federalists feared this possibility were varied. They feared that regional interests would be undervalued in a legislature so small and so physically remote and, more generally, that the quality of political accountability would suffer because the national leadership would become culturally and psychologically alienated from localities.[90] They argued that national authority would not be sufficiently responsive to elicit voluntary compliance, so that force would become the mechanism of government.[91] They were concerned that the opportunity for participation and identification with government would be too limited, ultimately threatening devotion to liberty itself.[92] Such fears were sufficient to threaten the adoption of the proposed constitution and to force not only the adoption of the first ten amendments, but also the creation of a theory of federalism that explained and justified the proposed system of power allocation.[93]

This theory turned the anti-Federalists' emphasis on the size and heterogeneity of the country into a powerful argument for adopting the Constitution. It was, the Federalists argued, the size and variety within the nation that would reduce the likelihood of overreaching by the national government.[94] Because state governments would remain alternative power centers, the national government would be in constant competition with state governments.[95] This would curtail the tendency of the national government to unresponsiveness and would prevent excessive centralization of power. Thus, the anti-Federalists' argument that state governments were more responsive was turned on its head: the very efficiency and responsiveness of local governments would enable them to act as a "counterpoise" to national authority.[96] The existence of states could, then, make practical what at the time seemed a contradiction in terms—a large country with a strong national government that would not degenerate into a "tyranny."[97]

The theory of the proponents of the new national government, in short, depended on assurances that effective state governments could continue to exist. As modern writers also argue, the states' influence on the national political process was identified as a major protection for state sovereignty, and this influence was thought to depend in part on how the electoral process was organized.[98] However, unlike the modern writers, the Federalists understood and emphasized that influence through electoral politics presupposes that state governments exist as alternative objects of loyalty to the national government.[99] Unless the residents of the states and their political representatives understand that states are entitled to claim governmental prerogatives and unless they perceive states as legitimate, separate governments, there will be no impulse to use political influence to protect the interests of states as governmental entities. It is, as Madison put it, "the existence of subordinate governments *to which the people are attached* [that] forms a barrier against the enterprises of ambition."[100]

The justifications offered in *Usery* for limiting congressional power over commerce are directly relevant to preserving those preconditions necessary for the states to act as a counterpoise to national authority. The factors emphasized by the Court all define state sovereignty in the sense relevant to the Federalists' theory, because they all preserve the capacity of state governments to elicit enough respect and loyalty to act as legitimate competitors to the central government. These sources of legitimacy can be grouped into four categories: symbolic, regulatory, communicative, and organizational. All can be shown to be inherent in the Federalists' theory, and all connect *Usery* to existing case law.[101]

Symbolism as a Source of Legitimacy

The framers of the Constitution were acutely aware of the emotional underpinnings of governmental authority. Madison referred to "that veneration which time bestows on every thing, and without which perhaps the wisest and freest governments would not possess the requisite stability."[102] Similarly, Hamilton spoke of "impressing upon the minds of the people affection, esteem, and reverence towards the government."[103] Supreme Court decisions have reflected the same sensitivity, asserting that the national government could not control the location of a state capital, suggesting that the statehouse would be exempt from federal taxation, and, after some hesitation, protecting state court proceedings from interruptions by federal courts.[104] None of these decisions can be explained on the basis of actual impact on the functioning of states. The business of state government can go on once the capital city has been located, a tax on a state operation might be greater in amount and consequence than a tax on the statehouse, and state courts would not dry up because of occasional interruptions by federal injunctions. All these decisions are explicable only as efforts to protect the symbolism of the states as sovereign governments and, therefore, their capacity to sustain emotional attachments.

The symbolism of a state that is unable to control the wages and hours of its employees is stark. The *Usery* Court's repeated emphasis on the effect of the federal rules on the states, as states, can be understood in this light. The apparatus of government may not be a special aspect of sovereignty in some exalted philosophical sense,[105] but psychologically the apparatus does represent the government's authority to the people. The Court's reliance on the impact of the FLSA on such traditional areas of state control as police and fire protection was also responsive to the requirements of symbolic authority. Again, as *Usery*'s critics maintain, "sovereignty" might be equally involved in innovative functions as in traditional ones, but the longer an area has been subject to state control the more symbolic of state authority that area becomes. Psychologically, a federal burden on a state water-bottling operation, for example, simply does not threaten the legitimacy of a state government in the same way as would federal burdens on public education or police protection.[106]

Regulatory Authority as a Source of Legitimacy

The Federalists understood that any government "must be able to address itself immediately to the hopes and fears of individuals; and to attract to its support those passions which have the strongest influence upon the human heart."[107] They argued repeatedly that states would have a natural advantage over the national government because of "the nature of the objects" of state regulation.[108] States, Hamilton thought, would control the "variety of more minute interests . . . which will form . . . many rivulets of influence running through every part of the society." Not only would state control be pervasive but it would also involve "all those personal interests and familiar concerns to which the sensibility of individuals is more immediately awake."[109]

Madison echoed these arguments and added to them by appealing to a widely held assumption that states could be expected to deliver services effectively.[110] In contrast to all these resources available to state governments, the powers granted the national government were "few and defined."[111] That is, "relating to more general interests, they will be less apt to come home to the feelings of the people; and, in proportion, less likely to inspire an habitual sense of obligation and active sentiment of attachment."[112]

Many of the Federalists' arguments regarding the natural advantages of state power sound quaint today and may have been somewhat disingenuous at the time. Certainly, the Federalists cannot be read as predicting or guaranteeing the primacy of state power.[113] But the underlying idea in these reassurances cannot be dismissed lightly. It is a necessary part of the Federalists' larger theory: to be able to protect themselves in the political process, states would need (and were assured under the proposed Constitution) the capacity to elicit loyalty by providing for the needs of their residents. Consequently, there is nothing improper or unusual in judicial sensitivity to the need to preserve traditional areas of primary control for state authority. Such sensitivity is commonplace in areas like education and family law.[114]

Nevertheless, a fundamental fear of *Usery*'s critics was that the principle of the case could not be restricted to protecting the states' governing apparatus, but would necessarily be extended to protect state control over policies regarding private citizens as well.[115] Why, they asked, is state control over employees more a sovereign matter than state control over citizens? But *Usery* did not require that any particular area of policy necessarily be reserved for state control. The Federalists' reassurances make clear that the basic idea behind enumerating federal powers was to reserve to the states the capacity for a pervasive relationship with their citizenry—to require that federal control over citizens be exceptional and specially justified.[116] The extension of the FLSA to state employees insinuates a federal presence into nearly every activity carried on by the state, which could seriously undermine the role of the states as the governments with broad primary contact with the citizenry.[117]

Moreover, the Court's emphasis on the importance of the services affected by the FLSA extension—"fire prevention, police protection, sanitation, public health"[118]—tracked the framers' assumption that states would control most policies of personal importance to people. And Madison's acknowledgment of the importance to state sovereignty of effective delivery of such services was echoed in the Court's concern that the wage and hour provisions would disrupt what the states had regarded as useful methods of administration. In short, the FLSA was threatening to *all* the elements of what the framers thought were the special characteristics of state regulatory authority. When a single federal statute compromises the states' authority to respond effectively and pervasively to the ordinary concerns of personal importance to the people, the Court was justified in sensing an incompatibility with the assumptions behind the constitutional design.

Communication as a Source of Legitimacy

How did the Federalists think that states might resist encroachments of federal power? One answer was that the states would provide a constant method of measuring whether federal policy had strayed too far from the popular will:

> Either the mode in which the federal government is to be constructed will render it sufficiently dependent on the people, or it will not. On the first supposition, it will be restrained by that dependence from forming schemes obnoxious to their constituents. On the other supposition, it will not possess the confidence of the people, and its schemes of usurpation will be easily defeated by the State governments, who will be supported by the people.[119]

A second sort of answer was that the states would "sound the alarm" and organize resistance both within their respective borders and among the other states. The national government might then be faced with "the disquietude of the people; . . . the frowns of the executive magistracy of the State; the embarrassments created by legislative devices."[120] In the first of these roles, states require a formal capacity to articulate possible alternatives to federal policy. In the second, states require the capacity to express dissatisfaction with the federal policies officially. Such considerations must underlie judicial reluctance to expose official state legislative acts to federal injunctions or to supplant the state appointment process.[121.]

Usery was responsive to the need to protect the capacity of state governments to represent and articulate opposition to federal power. The Court properly noted the special and fundamental character of the power to set wages and hours,[122] for federal control over basic working conditions would be a major way of shifting the loyalty of state employees to the national government. To the extent that opposition to federal policies must be expressed through the state employees who have daily and immediate contact with the citizenry, the capacity for opposition would be compromised. Moreover, the Court's emphasis on the impact of the FLSA on the states, as states, was widely understood to insulate from congressional control such formal elements of governance as the adoption of legislation or the promulgation of regulations.[123] To the extent that *Usery's* principles protected these formal elements of policy articulation, the decision protected the capacity of states—governments rather than individual leaders—to endorse (if not implement) policies that could stand as potential alternatives to national policy.

Organizational Authority as a Source of Legitimacy

The Federalists thought that the states would draw loyalty from the people on the same principle that "a man is more attached to his family than to his neighborhood, to his neighborhood than to the community at large." [124] Physical proximity would be reinforced by immediate opportunities for participation in local government:

> Into the administration of [the governments of the states] a greater number of individuals will expect to rise. From the gift of these a greater number of offices and emoluments will flow. By the superintending care of these, all the more domestic and personal interests of the people will be regulated and provided for. With the affairs of these, the people will be more familiarly and minutely conversant. And with the members of these will a greater proportion of the people have ties of personal acquaintance and friendship, and of family and party attachments; on the side of these, therefore, the popular bias may well be expected most strongly to incline. [125]

The capacity of states to elicit participation in government depends in large part on their authority to organize and control the units of local government. [126] It is by determining the appropriate amount of decentralization over such matters as taxation or public education that states can attempt to match local control to local interest, and the resulting political participation serves to give people a stake in public decisions and a sense of identification with their government. The Court has repeatedly recognized the special importance to state governments of control over such organizational decisions. [127]

The Court in *Usery* was sensitive to the impact of the wage and hour provisions on local participation. It noted, for example, that the provisions would lead to "a significant reduction of traditional volunteer assistance which has been in the past drawn on to complement the operation of many local governmental functions." [128] The decision insulated political subdivisions from the wage and hour provisions on the grounds that these "derive their authority and power from their respective States." [129] At least one critic somehow found this protection of state authority proof that *Usery* was not aimed at protecting "the state as object of political loyalty." [130] The framers understood the sources of loyalty more realistically. In their scheme, it is important that the emotional referent of local governments continue to match their legal referent, so that the states derive full advantage from self-government at the local level. Federal control over wages and hours of employees of political subdivisions could begin to displace to the national government the allegiance and identification of those who are part of local government.

In summary, the Court in *Usery* displayed a sure feel for protecting the "essential role of the States in our federal system of government" as the framers defined that role. Despite the Court's failure to refer specifically to the role of the states as political competitors to the national government, the tracking of the Federalists' theory was not coincidental. The case law that informed and shaped the Court's assumptions about federalism was no doubt influenced by the framers' ideas, and, in any event, the *Usery* Court, like the framers, focused on what is necessary for the states' "separate and independent existence."[131] *Usery* was not incomprehensible to its critics because its holding and explanation were unrelated to the Constitution. It was incomprehensible because of the critics' intellectual habits, which had developed out of long concern for questions of individuals' rights.

Naive Instrumentalism and Public Understanding

The *Usery* Court's account of federalism, although indecipherable to so many jurists and academic experts, is understandable in the language of ordinary political practice. The thinking in the legal culture has been less consistent with the framers' theory than has been our behavior in the political culture. To be sure, relationships between the national and state governments have changed dramatically over the years. The national government has grown in authority and prestige. Nevertheless, states are not administrative departments of the central government. They elect their own leaders, who determine and implement significant policies. It is unthinkable for governors to be appointed by the president or for state legislatures to be dissolved by Congress or for all government workers—those public school teachers, city police officers, and state bureaucrats—to be made federal employees. States, in short, have retained their status as governments. This seems obvious and unexciting only because public expectations are so deeply entrenched. What is taken for granted is what defines the core of our constitutional understandings. The extension of federal wage and hour controls to almost all state and local employees was an important departure from this core. Viewed against the backdrop of settled expectations and practices, it is the sort of political decision that might, when reconsidered in light of a Supreme Court decision, seem deeply aberrational.

My argument has been that *Usery* is understandable in light of the theory that shaped the Constitution and the practices that give it continuing meaning. My argument has not been that the result was ineluctable. The Court, perhaps, could have waited for an even more telling occasion for illustrating the theory of federalism that underlies our political institutions. Although nationalization of regulatory authority usually proceeds partially and incrementally, it is imaginable, for example, that the national government could completely and abruptly displace state authority in an area of crucial importance; it might be that the status of state governments would suffer more in such an episode than from the extension of the Fair Labor Standards Act. Indeed, it is even possible to doubt whether federal control over the incentives and working conditions of state employees will in fact undermine the capacity of states to compete with the national government even in the long run. In the same way that the Court in *New York Times Co. v. Sullivan* might have been wrong to suppose that vigorous political criticism could not coexist with traditional defamation laws, it may be that, despite the FLSA, states can retain sufficient control over and identification with their employees. Such imponderables always surround major judicial decisions and are not the special basis for the extraordinary criticism and eventual repudiation of *Usery*. *Any* single change, whether the nationalization of public education or the coerced location of a state capital, will not by itself transform public perceptions. All that can be said is that *Usery* offered special advantages for richly conveying a central lesson about our constitutional system, a lesson in danger of being slowly submerged by the drift of events.

The idea that decisions can be "correct," in the sense that they will alter political or human arrangements into a constitutionally required form, is generally unrealistic for another reason. Whether concerned with rights or structure, many constitutional provisions reflect ambiguous compromises and suppressed disagreements rather than determinations about some mandated state of affairs. Therefore, constitutional cases often involve questions—such as the proper distribution of power between the national and state governments—that were not resolved in the Constitution, but carried forward. Under these circumstances, it is realistic (and not insignificant) to ask that judicial opinions be true to the terms of the debate that are set out in the Constitution. To demand more is to demand that judges wish away the difficulties and ambiguities communicated in the historical record and in the text itself. It is to insist that judges determine matters that the Constitution leaves open.

In attempting to protect the preconditions for competition between governments, *Usery* was true to the terms of the Constitution's theory; the decision sought to allow for the ongoing resolution of issues of power allocation under conditions where the competitors would each be understood to have governmental status. In this effort to shape attitudes and comprehension, *Usery* was educative and deeply true to the nature of the document. As Tocqueville observed:

> In examining the Constitution of the United States . . . one is startled at the variety of information and the excellence of discretion which it presupposes in the people whom it is meant to govern. The government of the Union depends entirely upon legal fictions; the Union is an ideal nation which only exists in the mind, and whose limits and extent can only be discerned by the understanding.[132]

The Court cannot help to maintain such understandings, any more than it can reinforce public appreciation for freedom of speech, through the prosaic correction of everyday affairs. Resolution of an exceptional case like *Usery*, however, can offer an opportunity for vivid illustration of some basic tenet of the constitutional design.

Unfortunately, judicial review is generally not well suited to this educative task, because the judicial frame of mind is so influenced by the habits associated with its duty to protect rights. These habits emphasize the usefulness of constitutional doctrine for altering behavior in immediate and measurable ways. To the extent that the Court strains to protect structural values in the same systematic way that rights have come to be protected, the results are wooden decisions of the sort that threatened the New Deal before 1937 and that now jeopardize attempts to achieve some political accountability in the modern welfare state.[133] On the other hand, to the extent that structural values can be understood only in terms of intangibles, the result has been (as the modern Court's treatment of the tenth amendment demonstrates) relative lack of judicial interest and, ultimately, abdication.

Although all sorts of constitutional decisions have important educative functions, decisions like *Usery* that protect structure are different from the more familiar efforts of courts to protect rights. Structural principles such as federalism are intended to maintain a rough system of power allocation over long periods of time. There is no analogy to the adjudication of rights where, at some point in time, desegregation must be achieved or enough services must be provided. Structure is a process that is maintained, not achieved. The courts' function in matters of structure is largely to sustain (or at least not undercut) the understandings, the attitudes, and the emotional ties that underlie the system of power allocation. These objectives may be intangible, but they are directly relevant to preserving the constitutional system, since that system presupposes divided loyalties and complex attitudes toward authority. Structural decisions are not necessarily based on the injustice of depriving a single individual of a particular allocation of authority. Hence, the assertion of structural values is not essential in every case where they are potentially implicated; nevertheless, their assertion in especially appropriate cases like *Usery* is important because of the indirect, long-run consequences to the whole political system of ignoring the underpinnings of constitutional structure. These consequences are not adequately described by images of states as "empty vessels" or "gutted shells."[134] Such metaphors are more expressive of the critics' urge to render the issues tangible (and therefore more familiar) than of the values at stake in a dispute about federalism. In the Federalists' scheme, the states were to be maintained partly for their own sakes and partly as a tool for assuring adequate levels of political responsiveness, competition, and participation.[135]

Much of the scholarly and judicial attention to the definition of individual rights is aimed at achieving these same goals by more direct means. Definitions of free speech, equal protection, procedural due process, privacy, and other rights are grounded on the belief that these protections will produce the kind of independent individuals who can participate vigorously in the political process. And it may be that these rights are ultimately important to the potential for self-government. But, quite aside from the familiar charge that enforcement of such rights centralizes too much power at the national level, excessive attention to rights can be a threat to self-government. A subtle conflict exists between rights, taken too seriously, and structure. The frame of mind that is created by concentration on the direct, tangible protection of individuals does not easily appreciate the less determinate requirements of constitutional structure. A judicial system deeply engaged in achieving immediate justice for all individuals will not be sensitive to, or much interested in, the intellectual and emotional preconditions for political competition between sovereigns. The "constitutional law" that develops in such a system will be more attuned to the demands of measurement and the excitement of accomplishment than to the full range of the framers' concerns.

Suppose for a moment that divided and limited loyalties are not as important as the right to contraceptives for preserving the capacity for self-government in the modern world. At least, a decision like *Usery* that presumed there might be some small usefulness in promoting the framers' organizational theory ought not to have been dismissed as *constitutionally* incomprehensible. That the decision was so widely unappreciated and so quickly reversed ought to be unsettling to anyone who is not certain that the framers' structural principles are worthless today.

Conclusion

The tenth amendment is sometimes thought to express either a failed constitutional principle or an outdated one. But in the political culture federalism is successful and important. States as geographic and political governments have existed continuously in the United States from the beginning. Moreover, these governments have, almost without exception, had essentially "republican" characteristics. They have all exercised significant governmental functions, including legislation, administration, and adjudication. They have all been pervasive influences in the lives of their citizenry. In addition to discharging these generalized functions of governments, the states have also continued to perform specialized functions contemplated in the Constitution; for example, they have played a role in amending the Constitution, in electing the president, and so on. The existence of state governments (including their subsidiary units at the municipal level) has provided countless citizens with opportunities to participate directly and meaningfully in the government of their affairs. Federalism is unappreciated partly because in practice it has been such a continuous success that it is taken for granted.

This success, however, has been achieved despite the sorry record of judicial enforcement. This record, which has swung between excessive zeal and confused retreat, is attributable to an intellectual perspective that has developed its special form and dominating force in part because of the Court's efforts to enforce individual rights. A modest, but useful, interpretive function may be possible. This function would require fuller appreciation for the Court's educative function and, therefore, would entail considerably more modesty than exists in our current assumptions about the objectives and frequency of judicial enforcement of constitutional norms. A supportive role would also entail, as I shall now begin to explain, important adjustments both in how judges think and in how they communicate their thinking to the larger culture.

CHAPTER 5

Rationality and Equal Protection

The preceding chapters have questioned our ambitious efforts to use the resolution of specific legal controversies to construct a "constitutional" state of affairs. A basic theme has been that these efforts tend to undermine the public's appreciation of constitutional values. This claim runs counter to some elementary and widely shared understandings about the nature of judicial work. The courts are commonly thought to be especially appropriate for a didactic function. Their traditions and trappings are, after all, intensely cerebral. The appellate brief is a place for penetrating argument; the judicial opinion should be a model of clear exposition and dispassionate analysis. If words can illuminate and instruct, surely the political culture has much to gain from the courts. In the remainder of this book, I examine the Court's use of written explanations more closely. This examination suggests that the promise associated with the judiciary's intellectual methods is unfulfilled. Too often the kinds of reasons that courts give obscure what matters.

My approach in the next three chapters is to explore at increasingly general levels of analysis the methodology of judicial explanation. This chapter investigates the "mere rationality" test, a specific doctrine that is relatively simple and reveals deficiencies that are common, but less easily observed, in other areas of constitutional discourse. In chapter 6, I deal with a set of doctrines that all evidence the intellectual tradition called "rationalism." This type of explanation includes the rationality test but is seen in many other doctrines as well; it is basic and prevalent and so provides a vantage point from which to assess some important consequences of the intellectual habits of our legal culture. The final chapter examines, not doctrines or types of doctrines, but the expository style that the judiciary usually employs when it applies its constitutional tests in the written opinions that are supposed to educate the rest of us. My objective in these remaining essays is not so much to criticize logic or result as to provide three pictures, taken at increasing distances, of the mentality of judicial review.

I begin with a straightforward and frequently used doctrine. Throughout this century, the Supreme Court has repeatedly held that, under the equal protection clause, statutory schemes may treat classes of citizens differently only if the statutory classifications are rationally related to the purpose of the statute.[1]

> The Equal Protection Clause . . . imposes a requirement of some rationality in the nature of the class singled out. To be sure, the constitutional demand is not a demand that a statute necessarily apply equally to all persons. "The Constitution does not require things which are different in fact . . . to be treated in law as though they were the same." . . . But the Equal Protection Clause does require that, in defining a class subject to legislation, the distinctions that are drawn have "some relevance to the purpose for which the classification is made."[2]

In the modern era, when the Court has determined that a "fundamental interest" or a "suspect classification" is involved, it has buttressed the basic requirement of "some rationality" with the additional requirements that the government show a higher degree of rationality as well as a compelling interest to justify the statute.[3] Emphasis on these newer doctrines for a while diverted attention from the traditional minimal equal protection standard.[4] The "mere rationality" test has, however, remained a persistent feature of the Court's jurisprudence. In recent times it has been applied to a broad array of issues; it has been used, for example, to sustain a maximum welfare grant rule, to strike down a statute under which men were preferred to women as administrators of decedents' estates, and to void a law that made it illegal for unmarried persons to obtain contraceptives.[5]

The continuing utilization of the traditional rationality requirement and the partial dependence of the fundamental interest and suspect category doctrines on the basic idea of rationality make it an important doctrine well worth careful analysis.[6] Indeed, in some ways the mere rationality test is paradigmatic. It is an explanation that apparently allows for careful, detached analysis but in fact affords only diversion and misunderstanding. Although this emptiness may be thought traceable in part to considerations specific to the concept of "equal protection,"[7] the Court's use of the test abundantly displays a characteristic of modern constitutional opinions that is, as I show in subsequent chapters, widespread. Here I merely attempt to demonstrate how one simple constitutional doctrine, applied so often and with such elaborate care, serves to mislead rather than to explain.

Rationality and the Definition of Purpose

It is always possible to define the legislative purpose of a statute in such a way that the statutory classification is rationally related to it. This deflating fact was ignored for many years because the commentary on the rationality requirement centered on the issue of classificatory accuracy.[8] Courts and commentators asked whether a statute's classifications included individuals irrelevant to the statutory purpose or whether they excluded people relevant to that purpose.[9] But the question of whether a statute's classifications are precisely related to its purpose does not depend only on the nature of the classifications; it depends also on how the purpose of the statute is defined.[10]

When a statute names a class, that class must share some common characteristic, for that is the definitional attribute of a "class."[11] The nature of the burdens or benefits created by a statute and the nature of the chosen class's commonality will always suggest a statutory purpose—to burden or benefit the common trait shared by members of the identified class. A statute's classifications will be rationally related to such a purpose because the reach of the purpose has been derived from the classifications themselves.[12] Legislative purpose so defined is nearly tautological, but it is also the purpose suggested by the plain terms of a statute. For deciding whether "the distinctions that are drawn [by the statute] have 'some relevance to the purpose for which the classification is made,'" the purpose suggested by the terms of a statute serves as well as any other.[13]

The process of deriving a legislative purpose (and substantiating its rationality) from any statute's terms can be illustrated by an examination of the statute at issue in *Eisenstadt v. Baird,* in which the Supreme Court struck down a Massachusetts law that, among other things, made it a crime for anyone to dispense contraceptives to unmarried persons for the purpose of preventing pregnancy.[14] The statute permitted physicians and pharmacists to dispense contraceptives to married persons for the purpose of preventing pregnancy, and it had been construed to permit anyone to dispense contraceptives to married or unmarried persons for the purpose of preventing disease.[15]

Justice Brennan's plurality opinion tested this statutory scheme against the "some rationality" test, which he formulated in standard terms: "The Equal Protection Clause . . . does . . . deny to States the power to legislate that different treatment be accorded to persons placed by a statute into different classes on the basis of criteria wholly unrelated to the objective of that statute."[16] The specific question posed by the plurality opinion, therefore, was "whether there is some ground of difference that rationally explains the different treatment accorded married and unmarried persons under [the Massachusetts statute]."[17] The plurality determined that the statute was not rationally related to any of the three possible legislative objectives considered.[18]

The first legislative goal considered was the discouragement of premarital sexual activity. The plurality found that the statute had "at best a marginal relation" to this objective because under the statute unmarried persons could obtain contraceptives if they were to be used for the prevention of disease. It was also observed that the statute could not prevent married persons from obtaining contraceptives in order to engage in sexual activity with unmarried persons. Thus, because the statute would eliminate only an insignificant amount of premarital sexual activity, the plurality opinion declared that it could not have been rationally intended to discourage such activity.[19]

The plurality then held the statute not rationally related to the second objective considered: that of regulating the distribution of potentially harmful drugs and devices. It argued that if "there is a need to have a physician prescribe . . . contraceptives, that need is as great for unmarried persons as for married persons."[20] That is, because physicians were not permitted by the statute to prescribe contraceptives to unmarried persons for the prevention of pregnancy, that whole class of persons was excluded from the benign regulatory scheme. Since physicians are presumably as skillful in protecting the health of the unmarried as they are of the married, the plurality concluded that the exclusion of the unmarried from medical supervision indicated that the statute was not rationally related to the goal of regulating the distribution of potentially harmful drugs.[21]

Finally, the plurality found that the statute was not rationally related to the third objective considered, preventing the use of contraceptives, because the terms of the statute did not forbid their use by married persons.[22]

By treating each legislative objective separately, the plurality opinion achieved apparent analytic clarity, but the isolated consideration of each objective was misleading in at least two ways. It enabled the Justices to use statutory terms, which in fact made the statute quite reasonable in relation to one purpose, as evidence that the statute was not rational in relation to a different and irrelevant purpose. For example, consider how the plurality argued that the distinction drawn by the statute between married and unmarried persons was not rational in relation to the public health objective of regulating the distribution of potentially harmful drugs.[23] This distinction was drawn, obviously, because the statute was also designed to discourage in some degree premarital sexual activity by making most kinds of contraceptives harder to get for the unmarried.[24] It is not surprising that the distinction had no clear relationship to another, quite different purpose of the statute, that of seeing that those who could legally get contraceptives got medical supervision as well. If the two purposes are considered together, the distinction between married and unmarried persons is not irrational in relation to the public health objective—it is merely irrelevant.

The "divide and conquer" analytical tactic also permitted a convenient simplification of each purpose, for it is only in the context of the full statutory scheme that full meaning can be given to each legislative objective. For example, when the plurality opinion discussed the third objective (preventing the general use of contraceptives), it asserted that the evil "as perceived by the State" was identical as between the use of contraceptives by married and by unmarried people.[25] The plurality could then argue that exemption of married persons from the prohibition against obtaining a prescription was not rational, for if contraception itself is evil, is it not as evil for married as for unmarried persons? But, if the legislation was also designed to discourage premarital sexual activity, the use of contraceptives by unmarried persons manifestly is not the same evil as is their use by married persons.[26]

These illustrations show that if the plurality had defined the overall legislative purpose as consisting of the partial achievement of several sub-purposes, the determination that the statute was irrational would not have been so easy. The legislature's overall purpose might have been defined as follows: to discourage premarital sex by making contraceptives harder to obtain to the extent that this would not increase the risks of venereal disease; to provide for the medical supervision of the distribution of contraceptives to the extent that this would not increase the availability of contraceptives to the unmarried; and to discourage the use of contraceptives to the extent that this would not interfere with the private behavior of married persons. Unless it is "irrational" per se for a legislature to design a statute to achieve a set of somewhat conflicting policy objectives, the Massachusetts statute met the rationality standard.

This analysis can be put in more general terms: if the statutory purpose is seen as a mix of subpurposes, the classifications can be accurate as to the overall purpose—thereby satisfying the "some rationality" test—while inaccurate as to a subpurpose. The identification of an imprecision (a finding of nonrationality) only means that the purpose of the statute has not yet been fully stated. The more fully stated purpose is not only more complete, it is also a more accurate reflection of the statutory terms.

The *Eisenstadt* opinion does not go through this process of refined speculation about legislative purpose. Indeed, its use of the rationality test is an elaborate exercise in distorting and obscuring the public purpose supposedly being evaluated. Considered together, the majority and dissenting opinions in *Levy v. Louisiana* do go through a process of increasingly accurate speculation as to legislative purpose. The statute considered in *Levy* created a right to sue for wrongful death of a mother; it gave such a right to legitimate children but withheld the right from illegitimate children.[27] The nature of the benefit given suggests one purpose: to compensate children for the loss of their mother resulting from wrongful death.

Justice William Douglas saw no difference between the two sets of children in relation to this purpose: "These children, though illegitimate, were dependent on her; she cared for them and nurtured them; they were indeed hers in the biological and in the spiritual sense; in her death *they suffered wrong in the sense that any dependent would.*"[28] But the statutory classification suggests that compensation for loss was not the only purpose of the statute. Noting that the statute had been construed to distinguish between legitimate and illegitimate children,[29] Justice John Harlan argued:

> If it be conceded, as I assume it is, that the State has power to provide that people who choose to live together should go through the formalities of marriage . . . it is logical to enforce these requirements by declaring that the general class of rights that are dependent upon family relationships shall be accorded only when the formalities . . . of those relationships are present.[30]

Thus, the classificatory distinctions suggest a second purpose: to encourage the formalization of relationships between parents.

Justice Douglas was surely right that the statute is under-inclusive with respect to the first purpose, since some children who suffered the wrong of their mother's death would not be compensated. But it is not under-inclusive with respect to a fuller statement of the purpose: to compensate children for the wrongful death of their mother to the extent that such compensation does not legitimize relationships that have never been legally formalized.

I do not intend the restatement of the statutory terms at issue in *Eisenstadt* and *Levy* to prove that such terms will suggest all of the legislation's purposes. But if a burden or a benefit is placed on a group that shares a trait that can be named, at least one purpose for doing so can always be to burden or benefit those who share the trait. To be sure, it might be an unconstitutional purpose to burden or to benefit a particular group,[31] but the purpose still exists. The rationality test under consideration here does not itself contain standards for labeling certain purposes illegitimate;[32] it merely requires a rational fit between purpose and statutory means.

If all statutes are "tautologically" rational, how is it that the courts have struck down so many under the equal protection rationality test? It is possible that courts have developed principled doctrines to restrict the range of acceptable goals for different types of legislation, so that the rationality test is at least sometimes apposite.[33] I believe, however, that the courts have not developed such doctrines and that the rationality test is always inapposite. I suggest below that in every case in which the Court has construed a statutory goal in such a way that the statutory classification could be found to be not rationally related to the legislative purpose, it would have been equally possible to define the purpose so that the statute could have been found rational. Further, I describe how the courts have sometimes admitted the (necessary) rationality of statutes but have used various doctrines and devices to avoid the conclusion that the statute is therefore constitutional under the rationality test of the equal protection clause.

Just as there may have been urgent reasons for voiding the laws reviewed in *Eisenstadt* and *Levy,* reasons may exist for declaring unconstitutional many of the statutes discussed in the remainder of this chapter. But, despite the judiciary's aspirations to intellectual clarity and integrity, those reasons are not discovered or communicated by the Court's method. The analytic technique so congenial to our judges in equal protection cases is debris that must be cleared away before either they or their audience can understand what is at stake.

Irrationality and the Definition of Purpose

The various methods by which courts have been able to define a statute's purpose so that the classification used in the statute is inappropriate to its purpose[34] are interrelated and usually achieve the same result—nonconsideration of the purpose suggested by the plain terms of the statute. Nevertheless, for purposes of illustration I have divided these methods into three groupings: (1) ignoring a purpose, (2) stating the purpose as a unit rather than as a mix of policies, and (3) manipulating the level of abstraction at which the purpose is defined.

Ignoring a Purpose

On occasion courts have attempted to show that a statute fails the rationality test by listing several purposes that the statute is not designed to achieve. Such enumeration, however, proves nothing about whether there is some other purpose to which the statute is rationally related.

In *City of Cleburne v. Cleburne Living Center*,[35] for example, the Court struck down a requirement that group homes for the retarded get special use permits before locating in areas zoned for apartments, fraternity houses, hospitals, and so on. The Court started by emphatically holding that discriminations against the mentally retarded should be evaluated according to whether they are rationally related to any legitimate governmental interest. It then considered a series of public purposes to which the city's special use requirement was not closely related. If the city, for instance, had been concerned about the size of the homes, it should have required a special permit for all large lodging houses. If it had intended to reduce traffic congestion, the requirement should have applied to all establishments likely to draw traffic. If the purpose had involved fire hazards or public serenity, the rule should have applied to other uses (like fraternity homes) that can involve noise or recklessness. Having demonstrated its interest in purposes that would be appropriate to an ordinance employing a broader classification, surprisingly the Court was unable to find a purpose corresponding to the narrower category "group homes for the retarded." After all, protection against incompatible, value-reducing uses is a fundamental objective of all zoning systems, and the Court itself noted the possibility that the public might hold special animosities and fears toward the retarded.[36] As prejudiced as such attitudes might be, they would affect the value and usefulness of property in the zoned area in unfortunate, but distinctive, ways.

The inability of a court to find an appropriate legislative purpose is no less dubious when it merely posits one purpose for a statute, rather than listing multiple possibilities as the Court did in *Cleburne*. For example, in *Smith v. Cahoon* the Court considered a statute that required a bond of all motored carriers except those transporting agricultural goods.[37] Positing that the purpose of the bonds was the public safety and arguing that agricultural carriers had no characteristics that made their exemption relevant to public safety, the Court struck down the law. If the Court had formulated the purpose of the statute by examining its terms, the purpose might have been to ensure public safety to the extent that no additional burden need be placed on the agriculture industry.

It has been suggested that the Court in *Smith* ignored one of the obvious purposes of the statute because of an implicit rule that when there is consensus concerning the usual aims of certain types of legislation, that consensus will define a statute's purpose to the exclusion of other possible purposes.[38] Whether or not it is a sensible use of the equal protection clause to force the legislature to employ only orthodox means for the achievement of certain ends,[39] it is certainly a fiction to state that the only purpose of the statute was public safety. The very terms of the statute make it plain that one "goal the legislators had in mind" was to favor the agriculture industry.[40]

Framing the Purpose as a Unitary Value

Courts are aware, of course, that legislation is normally contrived to achieve a mix of purposes, with compromise and bargaining among the legislators determining the trade-offs among the competing purposes. In *Massachusetts Board of Retirement v. Murgia*, for example, the Court upheld a requirement that state police officers retire at age fifty, even though some older officers, obviously, remain able to perform their duties.[41] The Court pointed out that the rule was not aimed merely at assuring physical fitness but also at avoiding the expense involved in the individualized testing that would be necessary to identify the fit older officers.

But in many other cases the Court has strangely obscured the fact that statutes are normally designed to achieve a mix of goals. Consider more fully the harms, as listed by the Court in *Cleburne*, that might justify requiring special use permits for group homes for the retarded: traffic congestion, fire hazards, changes in the tone of the neighborhood, population density, dangers to the residents of the home, the possibility of public liability for actions taken by those residents, and so on. Each of these purposes considered alone can be plausibly related to establishments (like nursing homes and fraternities) that were excluded from the requirement. However, as the list of purposes lengthens and as they are considered in combination, the public interest more and more closely tracks the classification chosen by the city. Apartments, for example, bring traffic congestion but not special questions of legal responsibility. Fraternity members create fire hazards but are not as helpless as the retarded. Nursing home residents are helpless but are not visible enough to change the tone of the neighborhood. The Court's conclusion that the special zoning rules for the retarded are irrational was based on viewing the public's purposes woodenly, as items rather than as a whole.

Similarly, when the goals of the wrongful death statute considered in *Levy v. Louisiana* were considered in isolation—either the compensation of children for the wrongful death of their mother or increasing the number of formalized marital relationships—it was plausible to argue that the statute did not achieve its purpose, for some children were never compensated and the causal link between withholding such compensation and increasing the number of formalized relationships is by no means clear.[42] But the full purpose of the statute was a combination of these purposes. The relative mildness and potential ineffectiveness of the incentives indicate that one goal of the legislation was not to guarantee a certain number of formalized marriages, but rather to encourage formalization of relationships in general by fostering a general belief among the citizens that the government does not approve of illegitimate children. And, since illegitimate children were not to be compensated, the other statutory goal was not to compensate all children, at whatever social cost that might involve, but only to do so to the extent that governmental policies would not somehow condone the failure to formalize a marriage. Failure to treat the purpose of the wrongful death statute as a mix of competing policies does make it easier to find "irrationalities" in the statute, but only because the statutory terms are then tested against a simplified statutory goal. Similarly, in *Baird* the Massachusetts statute regulating the distribution of contraceptives could be found rational if tested against a legislative purpose reflecting a complex public policy.[43]

Manipulation of Level of Abstraction

Just as it is always possible for a court to ignore a legislative purpose or to simplify it in such a way that the statute cannot meet the rationality requirement, it is always possible for a court to define the evil or the good at which legislation is aimed so as to make the statutory classifications too broad or too narrow for achieving the purpose thus defined. In *Baird*, for instance, the Court emphasized that the Massachusetts legislature could not reasonably have intended to deter premarital sexual behavior because the exceptions to the statute did permit unmarried persons to obtain contraceptives—for example, when the contraceptives were to be utilized for the prevention of disease.[44] Obviously, the statutory exceptions make the statute "irrational" only if it is assumed that the goal of the legislation was to deter *all* premarital sexual activity. The statute's terms show that the legislation was not designed to deter all premarital sex, but to "discourage" such behavior at least to the extent that the statute's disincentives would not add to a different problem (the spread of venereal disease).[45] The conclusion that the statute was irrational as to the objective of discouraging premarital sex followed inevitably from the Court's decision to judge the statute against a goal far broader than the goal that the statute, on its face, was designed to accomplish.

Manipulation of the level of abstraction at which the government's purpose is defined can lead to conclusions that are startling to the non-legal mind. Two Justices of the Supreme Court (as well as several lower federal judges) actually adopted the view that it is irrational for a public transit authority to exclude from employment anyone using narcotic drugs, defined to include both heroin and methadone.[46] Since methadone is a narcotic with many of the same effects as heroin and is used as a medical substitute for heroin addiction, the policy was obviously aimed at reducing risks to safety and efficiency. Yet, depending on how generally the public purpose is stated, the exclusion of narcotic users can be labeled "irrational." The evils to be prevented can be stated in the following descending order of generality:

1. to decrease those safety risks caused by any personal deficiency that could affect any transit job,

2. to decrease those safety risks caused by any personal deficiency that could affect dangerous transit jobs,

3. to decrease those safety risks caused by any narcotic use that could affect any transit job,

4. to decrease those safety risks caused by narcotic use not medically prescribed that could affect any transit job,

5. to decrease those safety risks caused by narcotic use not medically prescribed that could affect dangerous transit jobs.

The transit authority's employment policy was too narrow to be related to purposes (1) or (2) and too broad for (4) or (5). A majority of the Supreme Court defined the purpose roughly at level (3) and so upheld the policy. However, the dissenting Justices defined the purpose closer to levels (4) and (5) and thus concluded that the policy was irrational.[47] They insisted on a policy under which applicants on long-term methadone maintenance would not be excluded from nondangerous jobs. Because at least some individuals on short-term methadone maintenance programs would perform certain jobs adequately, even this scheme would be irrational if the purpose were defined more narrowly still:

6. to decrease those safety hazards caused by narcotic use that actually leads to inadequate job performance.

The characterization of public purpose can always be altered to make it more or less abstract. The rationality test, therefore, operates like a shell game, with the outcome dependent on the judge's willingness to change the level of generality.

To declare a statute or other policy unconstitutional is a serious step. Misunderstanding the governmental interest does no good for either the judges who make the decision or the public that should be made to understand the decision. The rationality test, however, cannot be used to void legislation unless the government's objective is ignored, simplified, or manipulated.

Admission and Avoidance

It is always possible for a court to define a statute's purpose such that the statute will not meet the rationality requirement. The difficulty with such definitions of purpose, I have argued, is that because they necessarily do not reflect the statutory terms fully, there is always an element of artificiality about a "purpose" thus defined. If a statute's terms are fully reflected in the court's definition of its purpose, however, it is inevitable that the statute will fulfill the rationality requirement. To avoid this dilemma, courts have sometimes acknowledged that the statute is rationally related to a purpose but have still denied that the statute therefore meets the equal protection rationality requirement. The two grounds for this denial to be discussed here are: (1) that the statute is rationally related to an impermissible goal, or (2) that the statute is not rationally related to a mandatory goal. The effect of using either of these arguments is to avoid the significance of the fact that the legislation *is* rationally related to some legislative purpose.

Impermissible Goals

When a statutory goal has been declared impermissible but is not in violation of any explicit constitutional provisions, courts have sometimes left the reasons for labeling the purpose "impermissible" unarticulated or unexplained. This was true, for example, in *United States Department of Agriculture v. Moreno,*[48] a case involving a food stamp rule that excluded from the program households whose members were not all related. The Court noted that this exclusion did not relate to either of the announced purposes of the statute; it did not stimulate the farm economy or help the needy meet their nutritional requirements. Nevertheless, the terms of the exclusion itself suggested a further purpose, which the Court phrased as follows: "[the] amendment was intended to prevent so-called 'hippies' and 'hippie communes' from participating in the food stamp program."[49]

The Court then asserted that "a bare congressional desire to harm a politically unpopular group cannot constitute a *legitimate* governmental interest."[50] There was no explanation for this attractive, but somewhat mysterious, conclusion.[51] At any rate, the fact that the regulation was rationally contrived to achieve an impermissible goal stood, by the majority's analysis, only to condemn it. The dissent, however, phrased the purpose differently: "the basic unit which [Congress] was willing to support with federal funding . . . is some variation on the family as we know it."[52]

Both the majority and dissenting opinions, then, agreed on the purpose, one preferring to describe it as harming hippie communes and the other preferring to describe it as aiding traditional families. Neither formulation is more speculative than the other because each merely states that the burden or benefit will fall on those possessing the traits defining the statutory classification. Each characterization is as accurate as the other because the two goals are reciprocal—it was by disadvantaging the communes that traditional families were to be encouraged. Under either phrasing, the exclusion was rationally related to its purpose.

Moreno demonstrates, then, one difficulty with avoiding the conclusion of constitutionality by the device of labeling one of the goals impermissible: the statutory terms may indicate two (or more) purposes, one arguably impermissible and one arguably permissible, but either capable of making the statutory classification tautologically rational. To strike down such a statute therefore involves an implicit, but far-reaching, principle: a statute rationally related in equal degree to several purposes is unconstitutional if only one of those purposes is impermissible.

It might be objected, however, that the goals in *Moreno* are unusual and that the one objective set of social consequences reflected by a statute's terms can often involve no permissible goals. It might even be that the *Moreno* Court was willing to hold that neither disadvantaging the hippies nor protecting traditional families was a permissible goal. Nevertheless, that single set of social consequences will be related to a more remote set of consequences, and at some point along the range of causality there should be some permissible goal for any conceivable statute. Consider, for example, these two wordings of the purpose behind the statute considered in *Smith v. Cahoon:*

1. The purpose of the exemption for agricultural carriers is to put more money in the pockets of farmers.

2. The purpose of the agricultural exemption is to benefit the American economy by strengthening the agricultural sector.[53]

The second phrasing of legislative purpose is as much a reflection of the statute's terms as is the first, because the method by which the agricultural sector is to be strengthened is by putting more money in the pockets of farmers. Absent some theory of social causality that holds that the agricultural sector cannot be strengthened by putting money in the pockets of farmers or that the American economy cannot be benefited by strengthening the agricultural sector, the second wording is as valid a purpose of the legislation as is the first.[54] Although the narrower wording implies favoritism and therefore might be treated as impermissible, the broader wording is surely a permissible purpose.

To the extent that any statute can be found to be rationally related to some benign goal, the voiding of any statute because it is also rationally related to an impermissible goal cannot be described as an implementation of the traditional equal protection rationality requirement. In such cases the requirement that the statute be rationally related to a legitimate objective has been met and the rationality test only masks the important inquiry into why certain purposes are impermissible. Of course, the statute can be voided *in spite of* the rationality requirement. This result might be explained by reference either to some analysis of legislative motivation or to some implicit or explicit balancing process.

Motivation.   The Court in *Moreno* might have had some way of knowing that the legislators "really" intended to disadvantage hippies rather than help traditional families; and the Court in *Smith v. Cahoon* might have had some way of knowing that the legislators' "real" purpose was to line the pockets of farmers without regard for the welfare of the general economy. Since in each case both the "real," intended goal and the unintended goal are suggested by the same statutory terms and involve the same social or economic consequences, the Court's special knowledge could not have come merely from examining the statute or its consequences. The Court would have had to know or to conjecture what prompted a majority of the legislators to enact the legislation.

A major difficulty with defining "real purpose" as legislative motivation is that the motivations behind voting for a statute are as varied as the possible consequences of the statute's enactment. For example, one piece of legislation might have all the following kinds of consequences: its enactment salves the conscience of one legislator; it brings bribe money to another; it directly benefits the constituency of a third; some of its indirect consequences will benefit the constituency of a fourth, and so on. How is a court to determine which consequences a majority of the legislators had in mind when each legislator might have had several motivations (some overlapping or even conflicting) and no majority had the same set of motivations?[55] It is possible that a legislator might have voted for the food stamp exclusion both because he approved of traditional family life *and* because he harbored hostility to hippie communes. It is also possible that a legislator might be unaware of his hostility to hippies or that he voted without any knowledge of the content of the exclusion at all. At best, the determination of legislative motivation is a tangled empirical problem, necessarily involving the simplification of complex motivational patterns concerning equally complex anticipated social and personal consequences.

Despite these difficulties, some sophisticated arguments have been made that inquiry into legislative motivation is sometimes both necessary and potentially principled.[56] If a historical or empirical inquiry is feasible, the important part of the Court's opinion would be the factual basis for its conclusion about motive. To the extent that such an inquiry is not feasible, characterization of motivation may be a veiled way of articulating normative judgments. In either event, the rationality test is irrelevant to the important considerations in the Court's decision.

Balancing.   Perhaps in *Moreno* or in *Smith v. Cahoon* the Court did understand that the statutes involved had both permissible and impermissible goals and that the fact that some or all of the legislators were motivated by the possibility of reaching impermissible goals could not erase the plain terms of the statute suggesting permissible goals. Under this assumption, the outcomes of those cases might be explained as the result of judicial balancing of the relative importance of the permissible and impermissible goals. For example, the *Moreno* decision might be explained on the principle that the harm done to "hippie communes" outweighed the benefit accorded traditional families. A rule that when two goals are equally related to the statutory terms, an impermissible goal is more salient than a permissible goal could explain why in the Court's view such a statute is "evil." It does not explain why the statute does not fulfill the rationality requirement.[57] Nevertheless, this balancing process can be found in two equal protection doctrines—strict scrutiny and impermissible means.

Strict Scrutiny.   In certain "strict scrutiny" cases, decisions have been fairly explicitly based on the Court's balancing of the relative importance of the statute's permissible and impermissible purposes. The Court has, for example, indicated that the importance to the government of reducing expenditures will not justify a statute that is also rationally contrived to distribute burdens according to "invidious classifications."[58] Similarly, the Court has indicated that when the achievement of a statutory goal entails abridging a "fundamental interest," the statute will be struck down if that goal does not involve a "compelling governmental interest."[59] This set of doctrines enables courts to strike down statutes that are admittedly related rationally to a permissible goal on the grounds that the value of this goal is outweighed by the value of the impermissible goal to which the statute is also related. The rationality requirement is irrelevant to this kind of balancing process since the rationality of the statute as to all goals is conceded, and the decisions turn on a balancing of the importance of the different goals.

Another aspect of the strict scrutiny doctrine is the requirement that, if one of the statutory goals is the burdening of a fundamental interest or a suspect category, the statute must not only further a compelling governmental interest, but its classificatory scheme must also be *necessary* for accomplishing that interest.[60] This requirement is generally taken to mean that the accuracy of the legislative classification will be examined with greater care.[61] There is no reason to suppose, however, that a more careful examination of the statute's classifications should lead to the conclusion that the statute is not rational. A strict scrutiny of the statute should, indeed, suggest classificatory inaccuracies, but, as explained above, the identification of these inaccuracies should only suggest a more refined definition of the statute's purpose.[62]

It might be argued that the rationality requirement, or at least a stringent rationality requirement, can be meaningful when combined with a
determination that one or more statutory goals are impermissible. The
intuitive appeal of this argument lies in the possibility that if one or more
of the statutory goals can be eliminated as impermissible, it should be
possible to find classificatory inaccuracies with regard to the goals that
remain. The Supreme Court used such an approach in *Shapiro v. Thompson*,[63] in which state welfare residency requirements were struck down.
The Court first determined that the goal of discouraging the poor from
changing residence in order to obtain higher welfare benefits was an impermissible one because it was an unconstitutional abridgement of the
right to travel.[64] The Court found "no occasion to ascribe the source of
this right to travel interstate to a particular constitutional provision," but
did insist that the right was fundamental under the Constitution.[65] The
Court then acknowledged that its determination that one statutory goal
was impermissible did not necessarily mean that the statute was not rationally related to the other, permissible goals. Four alternative purposes
were considered: (1) facilitating budget planning, (2) providing an objective test of residency, (3) minimizing the chance of a recipient fraudu-
lently receiving checks from two jurisdictions, and (4) encouraging early
entry into the labor market.[66] The Court dismissed these goals partly on
the grounds that they were not compelling governmental interests, and
insofar as this was the basis of the Court's decision, the holding turned
on a balancing of the importance of goals rather than on an implementation of the rationality requirement.[67] But the Court went further in an
apparent effort to apply the rationality requirement. Having eliminated
the statute's obvious purpose (providing disincentives to migration) as
impermissible, the Court determined that, as to the other goals, the statute's provisions were not rational.[68]

Like the statute in *Moreno*, however, the welfare residency requirement has a permissible goal that is reciprocally related to the impermissible goal. The goal of encouraging early entry into the labor market is
reciprocally related to the goal of discouraging an inward migration of
welfare recipients. There can be little doubt that a year-long delay before
receiving welfare benefits is rationally related to encouraging entry into
the labor market. It is precisely this same threat of delay and the con-
comitant pressure to find work at any personal cost that is the disincen-
tive to migration. Given this causal relationship, it is not clear why the
Court conceded "that the one-year waiting period device is well suited to

discourage the influx of poor families in need of assistance," but denied the rationality of the statute for encouraging early entry into the labor market.[69]

The Court's first phrasing of the goal of encouraging early entry into the labor force was "encouraging new residents to join the labor force promptly." But when holding the statute not rationally related to this goal, the Court rephrased the statute's purpose as being "to encourage employment."[70] With the goal thus reworded, the Court found the statute's classifications under-inclusive because the statute would not function to encourage long-time residents of the state to seek employment. And so in a case combining the strict scrutiny standard with a determination that one statutory goal was impermissible, the Court was able to find the statute not rational only by the device of defining the degree of evil at which the statute was aimed so broadly that the finding of classificatory imprecision, and hence statutory irrationality, necessarily followed.[71] The statutory terms,[72] of course, suggest a narrower purpose to which the statute's classifications were rationally related: to provide an incentive to find jobs for those who encounter extraordinary obstacles (created by the dislocation of moving interstate) in the way of finding work.

My point here is not to criticize the result in *Shapiro;* it is to point out that a combination of the strict scrutiny doctrine with a determination that one statutory purpose is impermissible still does not make the rationality requirement useful. However, if the holding of the Court that the residency requirement was not rationally related to any of the statute's objectives is disregarded as an artifice resulting from the Court's method of formulating the statute's purpose, the holding in *Shapiro* can be viewed as resting only on a balancing process.[73] Thus the rationality requirement was not implemented but was again circumvented.[74]

Impermissible Means. It is sometimes suggested that, although a legitimate legislative purpose exists and although the statutory classifications are rationally related to that purpose, the means chosen are inconsistent with the equal protection clause. In *Reed v. Reed,* for example, a unanimous Court struck down an Idaho law that established a preference for males when two or more individuals (who otherwise qualified under the statute) sought to be appointed the administrator of the same estate.[75] The Court began by invoking the traditional rationality test—the means chosen could not be "wholly unrelated to the objective."[76] The Court then admitted that the statute did achieve one purpose—it eliminated the need for some hearings at which the relative qualifications of competing applicants would be weighed. Having found the statute rationally related to a permissible purpose, the Court did not then validate the statute. Instead, it asserted: "The crucial question, however, is whether the statute advances that objective *in a manner consistent with the command of the Equal Protection Clause.*"[77]

The Court answered its question in the negative, having found that the statute's presumption against women amounted to arbitrary discrimination.[78] The difficulty with this reasoning is that the only definition offered by the Court of "arbitrary discrimination" was the "some rationality" test,[79] which merely requires that the classification be precise with regard to a legitimate purpose. Since the statute was admittedly rationally related to a permissible purpose, in what sense was its discrimination arbitrary?

The only answer supplied by the Court was that there was something arbitrary in the *manner* by which the objective was to be accomplished.[80] The manner in which the permissible objective was to be accomplished was by disadvantaging women in competing for positions as administrators of estates. Assuming that women are generally as capable of acting as administrators of decedents' estates as are men, the statute was not well designed for picking the most competent administrators. With respect to this purpose, the disadvantaging of women could easily be viewed as arbitrary under the rationality requirement. To hold that statutory means are impermissible because they are arbitrary is apparently, then, no more than to hold that the statute is not rationally related to *some* of its purposes. But the rationality requirement does not require that the classificatory distinction be rationally related to all possible legislative purposes.[81] The *Reed* holding, therefore, cannot be explained on the basis of the traditional rationality requirement.

An alternative explanation of *Reed* is that the Court determined that the state's interest in judicial efficiency was less important than the interest of women in equal treatment with respect to the purpose of choosing qualified administrators of decedents' estates. The basis of the decision is thus disguised balancing. The statute did not fall because it could not be shown to be rationally related to a permissible purpose, but because the Court implicitly determined that the interest of women in equal opportunity outweighed a legitimate objective of the statute. The rationality requirement served to give the Court something to discuss other than the significant considerations underlying its decision.

Mandatory Goals

All the admission and avoidance devices described above have a similar drawback. To the extent that they attempt to implement the rationality requirement, they rest on the questionable assumption that if a statute can be shown to be rationally related to an impermissible goal, the statute does not fulfill the rationality requirement. There is another admission and avoidance device—the assigning of a mandatory goal—that does not involve this difficulty.

If a court is ready to assert that any legislation in a certain area must pursue a certain goal or goals, a requirement of rationality can be used to determine whether the statute under consideration does in fact pursue that goal. Because the goal is independently mandated by the Court without reference to the legislatively determined statutory terms, it is not certain that the terms will reflect the mandated purpose. Since to be constitutional the statute must be rationally related to the mandated goal, the fact that the statute may be (almost certainly is) rationally related to other permissible goals is irrelevant.

The reapportionment cases are an example of a field where the Court has explicitly mandated a goal for all legislation. The Court has recognized that reapportionment is an area where the possible legislative purposes are "complex and many-faceted."[82] But whatever purposes a reapportionment statute might be contrived to accomplish, the Court has mandated that all reapportionment plans must pursue at least one basic purpose: "The achieving of fair and effective representation for all citizens is . . . the basic aim of legislative apportionment."[83]

In determining that the goals of reapportionment must include the goal of fair representation for individuals,[84] the Court has said that the source of the mandate is the Court's functional analysis of the requisites of democracy: "As long as ours is a representative form of government, and our legislatures are those instruments of government elected directly by and directly representative of the people, the right to elect legislators in a free and unimpaired fashion is a bedrock of our political system."[85] In a later passage the Court made it clear that the goal of fair representation is an imperative one: "The basic principle of representative government remains, *and must remain* . . . the weight of a citizen's vote cannot be made to depend on where he lives."[86]

The southern school desegregation cases are another example of an area where the courts have established a mandatory goal. Courts have required that whatever the other objectives of public educational policies in the South, they must have the objective of eliminating segregation in public schools.[87] This mandatory goal was originally deduced from a sociopolitical theory stressing the prime importance of education as a function of government and a sociopsychological theory regarding the inherent inequality of state-segregated schools.[88]

Utilization of mandatory goals as adjudicatory standards requires three prerequisites: there must be (1) some generally accepted theory—social, political, legal, etc.—from which the court can credibly deduce the mandatory goal; this goal must be (2) definable in terms of a required burden or benefit; and the goal must (3) define the precise class to whom the benefit must be extended or on whom the burden must be placed. In the area of legislative apportionment, the goal was definable in terms of a benefit (the right to influence the outcome of elections by one vote) and in terms of the class on whom the benefit must be conferred (all eligible voters). In the desegregation cases the goal was defined as a benefit (the right to full educational opportunities) that was to be extended to the class of all citizens, regardless of race.

When a court is able to supply an independent goal that defines both the statutory burden or benefit and the statutory classification, the rationality test is at least relevant to a decision to invalidate legislation. Such invalidation need not rely on the assumption that if a statute is rationally related to an impermissible goal, it is not related to a permissible goal. Instead, the assumption behind the invalidation is that the goal supplied by the social theory is so important that the rational relationship of a statute to a permissible goal is not sufficient to outweigh the lack of a rational relationship to the mandated goal. In essence the mandated goal overbalances all other goals, permissible or impermissible.

Courts generally have not decided cases involving mandatory goals under the banner of the "mere rationality" test. This has been for good reason. In such cases, the persuasiveness of the Court's decisions depends on the power of the moral or political claim that underlies the mandated goal. Any discussion of the irrationality of the statute with respect to other goals would only divert attention from the important determination.

Conclusion

Courts do not in fact use the rationality requirement to strike down statutes, because it is virtually impossible to do so. Instead, courts sometimes ignore the clear import of a statute's terms to formulate a fictional statutory goal to which the terms are not rationally related. Or courts sometimes determine that a statutory goal is impermissible; but because legislative objectives are multifaceted, the finding of one impermissible goal does not mean that the rationality requirement—which requires merely a rational relationship to a permissible goal—cannot still be met. Therefore, courts sometimes question the legislators' motivation, balance the relative merits of competing legislative objectives, or assign mandatory goals. Even if such efforts are convincing, they only explain why the statute is unconstitutional despite the fact that it satisfies the rationality "test."

The disputes that arise under the equal protection clause have to do with matters far more difficult and profound than the rationality of public policies. They involve widely divergent political aspirations and sharp conflicts in moral values. The judiciary's long dependence on the basic rationality test is, therefore, disquieting. Why over so many decades and so many different kinds of issues have our judges held so tenaciously to an intellectual inquiry that leads nowhere? Why do they so repeatedly and earnestly expend their effort applying a "test" that obscures the crucial issues? The answers to such questions begin to emerge from an examination of the kinds of doctrines considered in the next chapter, for the basic rationality test is closely related to a variety of more stringent standards. These doctrines, which implement many provisions besides the equal protection clause, suggest that the mere rationality test is dismayingly persistent because it is part of a deficient intellectual tradition to which the judiciary is captive.

CHAPTER 6

Rationalism in Constitutional Law

The "mere rationality" requirement discussed in the preceding chapter is, of course, only one of many judicial doctrines. These "tests" implement a great variety of constitutional provisions and they can be complicated, yet there is a remarkable similarity running through many of them. Although in one way or another most demand more than the basic equal protection standard, they are strangely reminiscent of that standard. Some of the words keep changing, but the tune continues to sound suspiciously familiar.

A "time, place and manner" restriction on speech, for example, must serve a significant governmental interest. The government may restrict commercial speech if its interest is substantial and if its regulation directly advances that interest. Programs that aid religions must have a secular legislative purpose. To justify discrimination against a "suspect classification," the government must show that its purpose is substantial and that the distinction is necessary for accomplishing that purpose. Gender classifications must serve important objectives and must be substantially related to achievement of those objectives. Abortions may be regulated in the second trimester in ways that are reasonably related to protecting maternal health. Whether administrative procedures comply with due process standards depends in part upon the weight of the government's interest. State regulations that restrict interstate commerce must serve a legitimate local purpose and there must not be alternate means for promoting that purpose. In short, across a surprisingly wide array of subject areas,[1] the Court strikes the same chord again and again: the government must justify its rules by articulating a sufficiently important purpose and by demonstrating that the rule in some degree will actually achieve that purpose.

For the most part the recurrence of the theme of means/ends rationality seems to cause the Justices no embarrassment. Perhaps the appropriateness—indeed, necessity—of demanding this general sort of justification is to them natural and self-evident. Nevertheless, to anyone not inured to the Court's methods, it must be perplexing that constitutional provisions apparently so different substantively should all turn out to have such similar meaning operationally. Indeed, the coincidence is sufficiently striking that the uninitiated might wonder how much the Court's "interpretations" could possibly have to do with the Constitution itself.

Scholars sometimes attempt in sophisticated (and inventive) ways to explain why aspects of the means/ends inquiry are relevant to the substance of particular provisions.[2] Whether or not convincing on their own terms, these explanations do not directly address the questions raised by the coincidence that so many of these particular provisions all turn out to have the same essential meaning. One commentator has bravely faced up to this issue. Cass Sunstein attempts to convert the source of embarrassment into an intellectual asset; the very fact of coincidence, he urges, implies the possibility of "a unitary theory of the Constitution."[3] But why should a constitution, presumably designed for many purposes, be amenable to a single theory? Sunstein's answer is that the framers were broadly influenced by a concern that power be exercised only on the basis of a sense of civic virtue—that is, only on the basis of the common good. Starting from this historical claim, he does not find it surprising that many provisions are concerned with a demonstrable relationship between laws and identifiable public purposes.

The idea that the Court's frequent insistence on means/ends justifications is appropriate to the substance of the Constitution is consoling not only jurisprudentially but also psychologically. The myriad of judicial formulae can be viewed as neutral intellectual tools, subject to conscious control and calibration. To the extent that the typical demand for justification is shown to be inapposite to the substance of a specific provision, doctrine can be modified accordingly; the usual demand can even be omitted in unusual instances.[4] The resulting preoccupation with adjusting doctrine is, then, premised on a bracing conception of the Constitution; rather than a collection of compromises or suppressed disagreements or abstract ideals, its provisions can be thought of as a series of objectives, to which the judiciary's formulae should be reasonably related. Concentration on the design of various means/ends formulations thus permits the satisfaction that comes from a self-contained intellectual system, for the universe of governmental action, including judicial review itself, is to be assessed by a single, overriding criterion.

Although the framers' political theory surely did involve some significant fear of public power being used for private ends, the extent to which the demand for means/ends justifications runs through the Court's doctrines remains troubling. One reason is the variety that at least apparently characterizes much of the Constitution. It is simply implausible that provisions as disparate as that authorizing Congress to regulate interstate commerce (adopted as a central part of the original document in order to strengthen the national government) and that prohibiting Congress from abridging freedom of speech (adopted as an amendment because of fears about the strength of the national government) could be anchored in some single generic value—much less that the same value should reappear decades later under the profoundly different circumstances of the Civil War amendments.[5]

In explaining the similarity in so many of the Court's doctrines, any appeal to the framers' design is further undermined by the range of uses to which those doctrines are put. Nearly any aspect of public policy turns out to be subject to the Court's preferred method of analysis: Should 65-foot "double" trucks be permitted on state highways? Should physicians be required to inform patients about the "detrimental physical and psychological effects of abortions"? May a community decide to keep posters off telephone poles? May aliens be excluded from the civil service? Should it be considered rape for a female to have intercourse with a male under the age of eighteen? Should the air force permit its personnel to wear yarmulkes? May a state prohibit the distribution of pornographic pictures of children? Should a state automatically provide hearings before removing a child from a foster home? May an agricultural fair confine religious solicitation to a fixed location within the fair grounds? The Court has answered all these questions,[6] and a multitude of others, in large part by assessing the extent to which the government is achieving an articulated public policy.

The pervasive application of the Court's methodology suggests something quite different from the measured utilization of an intellectual tool formulated to achieve the framers' purposes. It suggests a compulsive retreat to familiar mental terrain, a habit of thought more controlling than controlled. It suggests, in short, that modern constitutional law is largely the free-floating application of one version of "reason" to public issues.

To this extent, the "constitution" is nothing more than a vision of a virtuous social order that happens to be congenial to a style of intelligence common, not surprisingly, to lawyers.

Rationalism and Its Sources

The recurrent inquiry required by so much of constitutional doctrine has a name and an identifiable place in modern intellectual history. Michael Oakeshott terms the general approach "rationalism." Rational conduct, according to Oakeshott, is "behavior *deliberately* directed to the achievement of a *formulated* purpose and governed solely by that purpose."[7] Oakeshott's account is subtle and can only be sketched here, but his description will be quickly recognizable to anyone conversant with modern constitutional law.

The rationalist values brains; he "has . . . a great belief in training them, and is determined that cleverness shall be encouraged and shall receive its reward of power."[8] The rationalist seeks always to convert moral sensibilities into abstract statements; although he knows that knowledge of this kind can be imperfect and in need of correction, he never doubts the possibility or usefulness of precise formulation.[9] To be sure, "he can imagine a problem which would remain impervious to the onslaught of his own reason. But what he cannot imagine is politics which do not consist in solving problems."[10] Accordingly, the rationalist sees no alternative but to bring "the social, political, legal and institutional inheritance of his society before the tribunal of his intellect."[11]

No one doubts that the methods of rationalism are of some use. Nor is there any doubt that these methods are to some degree appropriate in the enforcement of a Constitution that was itself heavily influenced by precisely this frame of mind. Indeed, so ascendent is rationalism in modern society that a predictable reaction to Oakeshott's description is to ask what alternatives are imaginable for the judiciary or any other conscientious decision maker. Unless the principles embodied in the Constitution are to have no effect or unless they are self-evident and absolute, some method must be used to accommodate governmental action with these basic values. To the modern mind this requires the evaluation of the importance of the policy according to its effectiveness. Rationalism is our methodology for demanding justification. Attempting to supplement rationalism seems almost the equivalent of seeking alternatives to intelligence itself.

Despite its currency, rationalism is not a synonym for justification. It does not exhaust the available methods of moral and intellectual inquiry. It is not the same as insight, creativity, wisdom, vision, instinct, or empathy. Although the Constitution was framed within a rationalist tradition, the design of the document—chiefly, the requirements of electoral accountability and multiple governments—plainly leaves room for the interplay of power exercised on the basis of other types of decision making. The anti-Federalists' major contribution to the Constitution, discussed in detail in chapter 4, was to insist on assurances that the new national government would not be excessively powerful or culturally remote; they demanded that the opportunity for active participation and identification with government be preserved.[12] In response, the Federalists emphasized the variety of opportunities for organization and influence that a large and politically layered nation would provide.[13] Those who created the Constitution understood that power should often be responsive to self-interest and felt preferences—"to the hopes and fears of individuals."[14]

Given the range of legitimate bases contemplated in the Constitution for the exercise of power, why has the demand for rationalism become pervasive? The simplest explanation begins with the fact that courts so commonly state constitutional values with glorious abstraction. If a value is sufficiently abstract, it will necessarily seem to have broad relevance to human affairs, important or petty. The more abstract the value, then, the more issues—from truck lengths to abortions—will be brought before the tribunal of the rationalist's intellect. And in large measure, constitutional interpretation has come to be the identification of a trace of some grand value in a particular provision and then the explosion of the meaning of that provision so that it stands for the grand value itself.

The Court, for example, has said, "If the right of privacy means anything, it is the right of the *individual,* married or single, to be free from unwarranted governmental intrusions into matters so fundamentally affecting a person as the decision whether to bear or beget a child."[15] The equal protection clause invalidates laws that perpetuate "stereotyped view[s]" of men and women.[16] The free speech clause is aimed at insuring that public debate is "uninhibited, robust, and wide-open," and ultimately it protects "the premise of individual dignity and choice upon which our political system rests."[17]

In its drive to find ever more expansive values in the Constitution, the Court has not been off on a frolic of its own. It is deeply enmeshed in a general intellectual fashion. Scholars have described the purposes of free speech as including "individual self-realization" and "moral growth."[18] The lowly impairment of contracts clause has been said to be a limitation on "rent-seeking factions" and is thus "an essential part of our basic constitutional scheme of limited government."[19] One scholar described the purposes of procedural due process as maintaining "personal dignity and autonomy" and minimizing "subservience and helplessness."[20] Perhaps setting a record even in this highly competitive area, he described the purpose of the right of association as "facilitating the emergence of relationships that meet the human need for closeness, trust, and love . . . without which there can be no hope of solving the persistent problem of autonomy and community."[21]

Constitutional values are stated at exalted levels of abstraction partly because modern sophistication, having liberated judges from the confines of text and history, has liberated constitutional values from specificity as well. The exalted nature of the values is also a corollary to assumptions about constitutionalism itself: the Constitution necessarily must address the most serious public concerns and must achieve a result that can be seen as virtuous in order to be worthy of its fundamental status. Any imperfections or limitations in the document must be remedied by interpretation. The idea that the fundamental law must be omnipresently virtuous is itself one aspect of the method of thinking that has become so confounded with the Constitution. The essence of rationalism, said Oakeshott, is "the imposition of a uniform condition of perfection upon human conduct."[22] To the kind of mind that believes autonomy and community constitute a "problem" that can be "solved," anything is possible; to such a mind even the great dilemmas (although annoyingly persistent) can be expected to yield eventually to proper analysis. "The odd generation of rationalism in politics is by sovereign power out of romanticism."[23]

The coexistence within the constitutional design of rationalism with other forms of decision making is precarious. The Court's resort to the methods of rationalism not only has been but can be expected to be reflexive and arrogantly expansive. It is important, therefore, to consider how other aspects of the constitutional system are jeopardized by excessive reliance on this single strain in the framers' thought.

Rationalism and Public Values

Although rationalism is no doubt compatible with aspects of the framers' thinking and with traditional judicial methods, an unconfined demand for rationalism in government is not desirable or realistic in a democracy. Treating social choices as a series of intellectual problems is reassuring to many in the educated classes, but it also tends to denigrate important values and to stunt moral and political discourse. At a time when it is increasingly fashionable to rationalize the scope of the Court's power on the basis of the capacity of judges to contribute to public dialogue,[24] it is grimly ironic that the predominant judicial approach is a prescription for avoidance, misunderstanding, and obduracy.

The Demand for Independent Articulation

Because rationalism emphasizes the conscious evaluation of whether a policy will achieve its objective, policies for which such analysis is unnecessary are unappreciated. If a governmental decision is based on a value that cannot usefully be articulated independently of the decision itself, the exercise of matching means to ends is disappointingly unnecessary. When a policy implements personal taste, for example, the objective is indistinguishable from the policy. In such cases, litigants, having anticipated the intellectual predilections of the Court or having internalized them, desperately generate separate objectives. The resulting assessment of the values at stake is often wildly inaccurate. For example, in requiring visual barriers around drive-in movie theaters that show films displaying nudity, a community is plainly expressing a taste as to the kinds of images that will dominate its night sky.[25] This preference, like a preference for quiet parks or for the grandeur of tall buildings, is part of a locality's self-definition. It is a statement best understood on its own terms, not as a proxy for some ulterior purpose. Nevertheless, the Court's evaluation of the barrier requirement solemnly emphasized the low probability that nearby drivers, distracted by some sudden vision on the horizon, might run off the road. In its relentless search for external justifications, the Court was too grave to pause for the comic aspects of its own discussion. The foolishness of the community's asserted justification, however, did not demonstrate that the policy was "wrong," but only that its defenders had been driven to silliness by the Court's demand for derivative justifications.

This problem is not limited, as is sometimes thought, to aesthetics. In the critical evaluation of any value choice, there is virtue in clarity and directness. Public choices must be confronted as assertions of identity and aspiration, as direct embodiments of value.[26] Finding a connection between an independently stated objective and a "rational" policy yields a satisfying sense of reasonableness, but the policy is not intrinsically better than one that is justified on its own terms. The reason for favoring the independent objective, after all, is also a matter of preference. At any rate, to the extent that constitutional rationalism forces communities to explain their decisions in terms of relatively remote relationships between policies and objectives, absurd purposes are postulated and important values are unfairly trivialized.

The Demand for Simplicity

Rationalism searches for conclusive answers to questions and "consequently the question must be formulated in such a way that it admits of such an answer."[27] If the values behind a rule are too subtle, intuitive, or varied for easy articulation and measurement, the rationalist will tend to ignore or simplify them. The process of simplification, plentifully illustrated by the Court's "minimum rationality" analysis, described in chapter 5, is endemic throughout constitutional adjudication.[28] Like a cracked mirror, the Court reflects back to the public a weirdly distorted view of its laws and policies.

For instance, when the Court upheld a statutory rape statute under which only men could be criminally liable,[29] the justification accepted by the Justices was that, since only women can become pregnant, the discrimination against males was related to the purpose of preventing teenage pregnancy. The opinion at least appeared, then, to rest on sober empiricism. But what of the possible bases for the discrimination that are not related so neatly to physiology? After all, sexual activity has long been believed to have different moral or psychological implications for girls than for boys. It is one thing to deplore double standards and quite another to dismiss the beliefs on which they are based merely because they cannot be proven as easily as the fact that only females can become pregnant. Yet the Court passed quickly over such matters with a brief allusion in the text and a defensive footnote about chastity,[30] returning with relief to the question of where the risk of pregnancy falls. That the constitutionality of this statute could have been argued and decided on such grounds is dismaying. Criminal penalties are, after all, a draconian method of enforcing the objective of planned parenthood. A society that leaps to this defense of itself is pitiable. Even more dismaying is the fact that the serious grounds for the statutory distinction were avoided because of the understanding, shared by all parties, that within the rationalistic culture of the courts those grounds would inevitably seem frivolous.

Complicated, vague, or sentiment-based objectives are not necessarily inferior bases for public policy. Many of the most important interests are pursued indirectly and partially. Constitutional rationalism tends to deprecate, ignore, or distort such values. One effect is that the society being judged is less likely to understand or appreciate its own purposes. Eventually those being judged change themselves to suit the standards of the judge. For instance, even among groups that should know better, there is a stubborn effort to justify suppressing certain types of erotica by linking them with sexual crimes.[31] This effort submerges less definite, but no less important, issues, such as the possibly debasing effects of pornography on attitudes toward sex and the self-image of women. To the extent that anticipated legal arguments affect public discussion of such issues, the Court's strangely distorted reflections become, of all things, accurate.

The Demand for Validation

The process of "rational" policy formation requires that alternate means be compared and that policies be justified as achieving some preferred mix of the relevant values. Therefore, courts not only formulate purposes to permit potential validation; they also often insist that evidence of the efficacy of a policy actually be furnished. The requirement of a "close fit" between ends and means is only one form of the demand for validation. The requirement that a rule be the "least restrictive alternative" for achieving a governmental objective permits courts to speculate whether (and how effectively) a different policy might achieve the same social goal.

These demands—that decisions be justified by proof of their consequences or by proof that the same consequences could not be achieved some other way—are sometimes appropriate, but they are not as neutral as they sound. They disadvantage decisions with effects that are difficult to isolate and identify. Important social decisions cannot be limited to those areas for which information is readily available and susceptible to conclusive analysis. Indeed, the more important the policy, the more likely it is that it will have far-reaching impacts that are difficult to measure. In such areas, decision makers typically must act in the absence of full information. This phenomenon is equally applicable to judicial decision making. In *Craig v. Boren,* the Court demanded hard statistics on the relative frequency of drunken driving by males and females in order to determine whether a gender-based statute on the sale of beer was justified; its own approach in sex discrimination cases, however, is based on the profoundly speculative (although fashionable) position that generally there is in fact little congruence between gender and legitimate legislative purposes.[32]

Similarly, when courts seek to determine whether alternative means

exist for the achievement of governmental objectives, the potentially unlimited number of policy alternatives and consequences renders full information prohibitively expensive. When they engage in such analysis, therefore, courts do not demand actual proof that other policies can achieve
the desired goal; instead, they rely on judicial notice and speculation.[33]
The difference between courts and other decision makers in this regard is
that courts often are no longer involved in the controversy when information about the effects of their policies does begin to become available;
or, if still involved, courts have special reasons for being unreceptive to
the new information.[34] At any rate, requiring a close empirical "fit" between policy and objective could subvert highly important judicial policies, just as it subverts important legislative policies. On precisely those
issues where participants in the political process might well consider innovative or risky measures, constitutional rationalism is disabling.

The demand for empirical validation is debilitating to the political
process in another way. It skews dialogue away from aspiration. Implicitly it legitimizes a dull and limited view of public policy as being
nothing more than a grappling with the present. In *Craig,* for instance,
the Court conceived the legislative determination as being only that
young females are more likely than males to be responsible drinkers. Like
many public decisions, however, the statutory distinction was also an af-
firmation, whether or not benighted, about a suitable or desirable future.
The statute was part of a complex web of legal determinations cumulatively representing judgments about appropriate roles within the family
and relations between the sexes. An aspect of the statute's function was to
create a reality where young women saw themselves, consistently with
the hopes of their political community, as careful and mature. Now, it
may well be that this effort to shape the future was unwise or even deeply
unfair.[35] Perhaps the creation of a reality where men and women were
equally responsible at all ages would be better. But it is certain that the
reason for preferring the latter vision will not be found by examining the
data on roadside sobriety tests. Neither those who oppose nor those who
support gender differentiation are adequately served by a judicial decision that elides their desire to shape the future. To conceive the issues this
way degrades the equal protection clause and retards public understanding of the subtlety and power of public decision making.

The Demand for Intention

A controversial, but tenacious, aspect of modern constitutional law is
the idea that the Court should credit only the "actual" legislative pur-

pose, not purposes supplied with the benefit of hindsight.[36] Although somehow associated in legal minds with a tough realism, the proposal is impractical. There are many sound reasons for embarking on an activity before finally formulating an objective. Because the potential consequences of an important program are often unlimited, decision makers lack the resources to gather or evaluate all the relevant information.[37] Accordingly, it may be desirable to begin a tentative program and to reformulate incrementally both the objectives and the means chosen for their achievement in light of actual experience. The reformulated objectives can differ dramatically from the original, tentative objective.[38] Thus, constitutionalism that requires a decision maker to identify consequences (and relate them to an articulated value) before acting can result in the abandonment of potentially useful activity.

The utility of experimentation is sufficiently obvious that the recurrent judicial insistence on the original articulation of purpose is comprehensible only as an expression of the assumptions of rationalism. The fundamental objective of rationalism is not a rule that is (or turns out to be) wise or fair; the objective is the rational formulation of policy. If the value was not articulated *before* the policy was adopted, conscious analysis could not have been employed in formulating the policy.

One view of morality holds that moral values cannot be known independently of the activities to which they refer, for "the objects of our desires are known to us in the activity of seeking them."[39] Even if public values sometimes can be adequately stated prior to implementation, it is nevertheless clear that important values can also be discovered during the performance of an activity. Constitutional rationalism disfavors such values and frustrates policies that are no less important for having been justified by experience. The Court's approach belittles political dialogue and participation, for those processes depend on trusting and honoring the reactions of the public to the experience of being governed. The dignity and importance of political involvement does not consist in the formulation of neat intellectual solutions. It consists in trying, failing, and learning.

The Demand for Originality

In significant parts of constitutional law the identification of "archaic and stereotypic notions"[40] is a prelude to invalidation. This is to say that courts often operate under the assumption that beliefs that originate in tradition (and thus have the advantage of being time-tested) are impermissible bases for public policy, unless they can be justified by some rational standard extrinsic to the tradition. The foundation for this hostility to customary attitudes is that traditional policies are seen as being reflexive rather than the products of conscious thought. Therefore, while courts can, and sometimes do, test means against ends that represent old practices or values,[41] rationalism generates pressure against doing so, for the rationalist must always ask whether those purposes have been validated by recent deliberation. Customary beliefs are by their nature collective and experiential. The older and more deeply embedded a value, the less likely it is to carry the aura that surrounds a solution created by individual mental effort. "Like a foreigner or a man out of his social class, [the rationalist] is bewildered by a tradition . . . of which he knows only the surface. . . . And he conceives a contempt for what he does not understand."[42] The "irrational" quality of reliance on traditional values is so intolerable to the constitutional rationalist that the absence of social change is itself sometimes evidence that the political system is malfunctioning.[43]

Not surprisingly, the felt interests of those who hold affection for tradition are systematically (although, of course, not always) slighted by constitutional rationalists. In *Moreno,* the case involving the exclusion of "hippie communes" from the food stamp program, the Court, in effect, declared it *impermissible* for a government to distribute resources so as to encourage traditional family life.[44] No explanation was thought necessary for the conclusion that a disinclination to subsidize unconventional lifestyles is constitutionally improper. Also notable have been the Court's assertions that neither a fetus's father nor a pregnant girl's parents have any interest in the abortion decision that is distinct from the interest of the state itself.[45] Even when history and tradition are invoked as bases for constitutional interpretations, it is not unusual for the result to be the creation of new areas of insulation from long-established public regulatory authority over matters such as marriage and child-rearing.[46] Frequently judicial disapproval of tradition is only implicit, as when the Court cannot bring itself—perhaps because of embarrassment—to state forthrightly or seriously the old-fashioned basis for some statute. Rules that required pregnant school teachers to leave their jobs when they began to "show" had long antecedents in squeamish (but complicated) attitudes toward the physical aspects of pregnancy; in fact at times it has been customary for women to remove themselves from society during a long period of "confinement."[47] Nevertheless, the Court's stonefaced analysis of a school's pregnancy policy centered on the "modern" justification to the effect that pregnancy might render a teacher incapable of performing her duties.[48]

As the example of pregnancy policies no doubt suggests, customary ways of thinking should not always prevail in the political process. Traditions, needless to say, can be outmoded or repressive. However, to the extent that the Constitution is seen as requiring a continuing presumptive hostility to the past, the courts will prevent people from building a coherent knowledge and sense of morality. Even the fact that prudish attitudes about pregnancy have become outdated is something that needs to be brought out, tested, and legitimated through the kind of political debate that is avoided by adjudication. To the extent that adjudication does contribute to political dialogue, the need for change cannot be fully understood if the Court is itself too squeamish about our history to portray sensitively what it is that we are changing *from*.

It should be equally obvious (although to the rationalist it is not) that traditional ways of thinking are not inherently pernicious. It is possible for a person to resist change for no reason other than appreciation of the present;[49] for such a person, to attempt to perpetuate habitual assumptions is not somehow illegitimate, but a normal effort to protect perceived self-interest. That representative government might reflect such preferences is no more objectionable than a majoritarian preference for discovering the consequences of change.

Habitual denigration of traditional values carries the risk that certain groups will come to see the Constitution as an alien document, used by segments of the educated classes to belittle and undermine their ways of life. Political tolerance and participation presupposes self-respect and self-confidence. If accumulated experiences and perceptions—a person's background and identity—are distrusted in public decision making, an important source of political vitality is threatened.

Rationalism and the Legislative Process

The wide range of issues to which the standards of constitutional rationalism are now routinely applied has troubling implications, not only for political discourse generally, but also for the legislative process itself. The danger is that, because of the prestige of constitutional law and its constant use, legislators will begin to think like judges.

Because it is the failure of legislators to act "rationally" that triggers and controls active constitutional scrutiny, it is no wonder that the judiciary has had to be so busy tidying up government. Legislators do not always know or articulate moral objectives before enacting programs and frequently rationalize them to their constituents only afterwards. When legislators do announce values before adopting programs, the announced values are often either concocted or, at least, subject to being altered to reflect subsequent experience with the policy. They attempt to accommodate complex and hopelessly conflicting values in the same policy. After announcing grand objectives, they quickly alter or renounce these goals in subsequent legislation. They respond to wildly irrational arguments and even to power unadorned by intellectual argumentation. No legislator hears from or knows of all the affected interests before a decision. Legislators cannot possess in advance full information about the consequences of a decision, and they do not necessarily pay any attention to the information they do have. Compared to the detached, careful evaluation of briefs and evidence in light of an explicit, consistent set of legal values that is the ideal of the judicial process, the legislative process is a nightmare of irrational decision making.

Legislative "irrationality," however, provides real advantages to a democratic system.[50] If values need not be formally articulated and consistently pursued, legislators can serve many interests at once. They are free to respond to the intensity of constituents' beliefs, so that groups whose values are difficult to formalize or explain, but nevertheless are strongly held, can be accommodated. Even if no one objective is fully achieved, many groups can be partially satisfied and can therefore be expected to retain some sense of loyalty to the governmental process. Because negotiation and trading "across substantive fields" are encouraged, the hard sacrifices that different allocations of resources require are implicitly recognized.[51] In the bartering process, people with widely divergent interests are compelled to deal with each other and to recognize the probable costs that their own preferences will inflict on others; thus new understandings and new values emerge as citizens experience firsthand the processes of self-government. Because compromise is necessary and abstract argument is of limited value, groups are encouraged to find the common ground in their positions, rather than to insist on apparently irreconcilable differences of principle. When legislators are free to act "irrationally," they can act even when full information about the consequences of their decisions is unavailable. Because values need not be abstractly identified before action, and because legislators can attempt partial effectuation of those values that are identified, government can experiment with possible solutions, retaining the capacity for quick reversal in the face of evidence of failure. Because information is received and evaluated by a large number of individuals (with differing sensitivities), a legislative body can respond rapidly to a wide range of perceived imperfections in the initial policy. The risks of taking action in an imperfectly understood world can thereby be minimized.

The legislative process need not be romanticized. It works imperfectly and looks worse. But attempts to evaluate the integrity of the legislative process and its products by the unconstrained standards of constitutional rationalism undermine much of the usefulness of legislatures in a democracy.

Conclusion

Judges find so many parts of the Constitution to mean essentially the same thing because, in interpreting the document, they mistake their own intellectual habits for its content. The pressures on judges to do this are probably inexorable and are unlikely to diminish significantly with changes in the political complexion of the federal bench. Not only is rationalism a powerful influence generally, but the political insulation of the judiciary—often touted as the reason it can contribute usefully to public discourse—ensures excessive, uncritical reliance on one narrow analytic method:

> How appropriate rationalist politics are to the man who, not brought up or educated to their exercise, finds himself in a position to exert political initiative and authority, requires no emphasis. His need of it is so great that he will have no incentive to be skeptical about the possibility of a magic technique of politics which will remove the handicap of his lack of political education. The offer of such a technique will seem to him the offer of salvation itself.[52]

Behind the judge, moreover, stands the whole apparatus of legal education. This enterprise, so often a caricature of the general educational developments that Oakeshott described as ominous, too often stamps out minds that are "finely-tempered, neutral instrument[s] . . . well-trained rather than . . . educated."[53] Neither the judges' position nor education is likely to encourage doubts about the power of one version of intellect to erect a pervasively just society.

CHAPTER 7

The Formulaic Constitution

The preceding chapters have been concerned with certain substantive characteristics of the judiciary's interpretations of the Constitution. The purpose of this final chapter is to examine the form in which the Court expresses its constructions. During roughly the past thirty years, a new style of opinion writing has emerged as the most common method of constitutional exegesis.[1] This style is an impressive display of the rationalist's preference for knowledge that is "susceptible of formulation in rules, principles, directions, maxims—comprehensively, in propositions."[2] It emphasizes carefully framed doctrine expressed in elaborately layered sets of "tests," "prongs," "requirements," "standards," or "hurdles." The judicial opinions in which these "analytical devices" appear tend to be characterized by tireless, detailed debate among the Justices.[3] The apparently definitive formulations, standing amidst a welter of separate opinions and contentious footnotes, seem forlorn testaments to the ideals of clarity and consensus. But, taken together, the formulae and the extensive explanation comprise a consistent pattern of earnest argumentation.

The formulaic style is so familiar and so consonant with the times that judges, academics, and lawyers take it for granted. This inattention, while not entirely surprising, is misguided. In the often variable and fragmented world of constitutional interpretation the formulaic style is one of the few basic fixtures. It has been used to explicate freedom of speech, separation of church and state, state sovereignty, equal protection, due process (both substantive and procedural), the case and controversy requirement, the commerce power, the contract clause, the privileges and immunities clause of article IV, the fifth amendment right against self-incrimination, and the cruel and unusual punishment clause.[4] Its influence can also be seen in cases interpreting the sixth amendment (both the right to effective counsel and the right to conduct one's own defense) and the fourth amendment (including cases defining "reasonable" and "searches").[5] Moreover, although it is now customary, the style is not especially natural; it is obtrusively elaborate rather than economical or elegant. Why has the modern Supreme Court so persistently adopted this cumbersome expository device?

This chapter explores the ways in which the formulaic style is different from other, older forms of constitutional doctrine. It argues that the modern style affects the content that the Court finds in the Constitution and that it illuminates the current interpretive functions of the judiciary. Perhaps most important, the formulaic style establishes an identifiable relationship between the Court and the public and thus constrains the way the Court's version of the Constitution bears upon the larger political culture.

This subject matter might seem to put too much weight on the shape, as opposed to the substance, of opinions. Therefore, before turning to a detailed examination of the formulaic style, I address the relationship between form and substance in constitutional law.

Form and Substance

In some ways it is certainly plausible to believe that only the substance of judicial opinions matters. To take the most significant example, no one doubts the profound importance of the Court's declaration that racial segregation in schools and other public arenas is unconstitutional. The great mass of the public, whose jobs do not require reading or dwelling on judicial opinions, was made to understand this result. But it is doubtful that the Court's reasoning, much less the manner of its presentation, filtered past a few elite groups. The Court's more prosaic efforts at constitutional interpretation are certainly understood even more dimly and basically; they are obscured by inattention and by layers of imprecise reports from newspapers, attorneys, word-of-mouth within bureaucracies, and so on. Thus even to say that the "result" is important—in the sense that police give *Miranda* warnings or school officials provide hearings before suspensions—is to overstate the case, for bottom-line constitutional requirements are frequently distorted in the public perception. In that perception the Court's results are converted into vague intuitions and diffuse values. Prison officials sometimes interpret judicial decisions that provide only limited protection for inmates' constitutional rights as broad attacks on institutional authority.[6] Many journalists apparently understand the "malice" requirement of *New York Times Co. v. Sullivan* as being far more an absolute protection than it is.[7] When even fundamental outcomes and reasoning are so imprecisely communicated, claiming an importance for expository style seems absurdly otherworldly.[8]

Justice Benjamin Cardozo, nevertheless, once dismissed lawyers' generally "amused or cynical indifference" to literary style as an indication of a failure of understanding. In judicial opinions, he asserted somewhat dogmatically, form and substance are inseparable: "The strength that is born of form and the feebleness that is born of lack of form are in truth qualities of the substance. They are tokens of the thing's identity. They make it what it is."[9] Form, perhaps, makes substance "what it is" for those few specialists who view Supreme Court opinions more as intellectual or aesthetic efforts than as coercive acts of the sovereign. For some academics and judges, form is inseparable from substance because they read opinions in order to be persuaded or moved or even inspired.[10] Still, from the perspective of the general citizenry (and its lawyers), Cardozo's emphasis on style seems a precious irrelevancy. Insofar as the issue is identifying behavior that might have to be altered because of judicial decrees, form is important only to the extent that it renders essential information too unclear to be understood.

In at least two other respects, however, form is of real, general importance. First, *because* judicial decisions are coercive, the public has the strongest possible interest in the capacity of the Court to resolve constitutional issues. Both traditional justifications for judicial review (for example, enforcing the framers' intentions under current conditions) and disparate modern justifications (removing impediments to effective democratic accountability, protecting "personhood," giving meaning to "public values," and so on) require the Court to resolve issues of enormous difficulty.[11] One need not believe that form and substance are identical to understand that ways of talking about the Constitution must influence patterns of thought. Because analysis and explanation are not entirely separate processes, the form of the opinion must be expressive of the intellectual habits that shape the Court's conclusions. Therefore, to describe the Court's expository style is to identify the idiom that not only expresses the Court's version of the Constitution but also inclines the

Court toward it. It is important to know, then, whether a formulaic constitution provides intellectual resources and instincts commensurate with the functions that are thought to legitimize the Court's power to coerce.

Second, neither the Court nor its many defenders believe that its authority over the public is exhausted by successful communication of specific behavioral norms.[12] The Court should (it is said) teach a sophisticated theory of free speech to a recalcitrant public. The Court is supposed to lead alienated combatants "toward the pursuit of mutual accommodation." It should provide a forum for the application of moral philosophy to public affairs. It should speak as a prophet, calling the nation back to its animating moral vision. It should be "the voice of the spirit, reminding us of our better selves." The Constitution is said to be "our Mona Lisa, our Eiffel Tower, our Marseillaise," and the Court should have a primary role "in establishing our aesthetic principles."

Oddly, many of those who would assign such weighty, sometimes exotic, communicative functions to the Supreme Court do not dwell on the Court's language. To a surprising extent, they speak as if morally uplifting results (when the Court produces them) are a sufficient mechanism for achieving objectives like cultural or historical identity and moral growth.[13] An exception is James B. White, who writes:

> [The law] . . . provides a place that is at once part of the larger culture and apart from it, a place in which we can think about a problematic story by retelling it in various ways and can ask in a new and self-conscious way what it is to mean. Law works by a process of argument that places one version of events against another and creates a tension between them (and between the endings appropriate to each); in doing so it makes our choice of language conscious rather than habitual and creates a moment at which controlled change of language and culture becomes possible.[14]

White describes the constitutional text as speaking both authoritatively and modestly—forcefully allocating responsibility and yet leaving much to be decided later. The document establishes "the fundamental terms of new kinds of conversations; for it creates a set of speakers [and] defines the occasions for and topics of their speech."[15]

There is nothing magical or obscure about the claim that the Constitution (and decisions applying it) create a rhetorical "community" by which aspects of our culture are defined and redefined. The form of the Constitution is expressive, and the document's power is symbolic as well as behavioral. Think about the almost preternatural force of the Constitution in our political and legal culture. Judges (and others) have long employed religious terms in speaking of the Constitution.[16] Serious scholars refer to constitutional interpretation as moral prophecy and as giving voice to the spirit. A congresswoman stirs, not embarrassment, but deep admiration when she declares that her faith in the Constitution is "whole. It is complete. It is total."[17] A prominent scholar, tight-lipped and angry, responds to skeptics by saying that their nihilism about constitutional interpretation "threatens our social existence and the nature of public life as we know it in America; and it demeans our lives."[18] Even those nihilists try to find in the Constitution a vindication of their morality and of themselves.[19] What is it about the document that arouses such impassioned loyalty and such ceaselessly fervent hopes?

The great wisdom contained in its text notwithstanding, the emotive power of the Constitution does not result merely from the substance of the document. Some of that content is thought to be petty, wrongheaded, outdated, or even reprehensible.[20] Moreover, one of the central problems of constitutional theory is that many of the most admirable values attributed to the Constitution are exceedingly difficult to trace convincingly to its text.[21]

Alternatively, the Constitution's lure might be thought to rest, not on a complete reading of the text itself, but on American experience with interpretations of aspects of the text. The text, that is, might be thought to contain enough parts or hints of grand values that judges have been able to fill it out with inspirational interpretations. It is this potential, revealed in the brilliant adaptations of American institutions throughout the nation's history, that fascinates and attracts.

Although this explanation surely contains seeds of truth, it has much to overcome. As I have indicated in previous chapters, to a degree that is often underestimated, the most basic institutional successes—such as the regular relinquishment of the office of the presidency, the timely assembly of Congress each year, and the continued existence of the states as governments—have occurred without significant assistance from legal interpretation. Some successful adaptations, moreover, have consisted in emptying inconvenient provisions of any meaning.[22] Through much of our history, parts of the document now thought to be especially inspirational were largely ignored by the judiciary.[23] Parts that were not ignored were interpreted so as to help bring on the Civil War, to block the effort to achieve equal rights for blacks during Reconstruction, and to threaten the authority of the central government to deal with the Great Depression. For every truly inspirational interpretation, there are many failures: the chaotic efforts to define "obscenity," the willingness to uphold convictions under the Espionage Act during World War I, and the failure to protect Japanese-Americans from internment during World War II. Moreover, many decisions that for some count as "successes" in fact involve tawdry facts or painfully ambiguous moral dilemmas. If our deep attachment to the Constitution arises from its capacity to be interpreted to prohibit visual barriers around outdoor theaters or to sanction a nearly absolute personal prerogative to destroy fetal life, then our attachments come from strange sources.[24]

Only an exceedingly selective view of the history of constitutional interpretations can explain the fervor of the American fascination with "our Mona Lisa." The document, plainly, is able to represent our highest hopes despite much of its content and despite much of our historical experience. The emotional pull generated by the Constitution no doubt has many explanations. But some part of the document's power must result from the relative simplicity and authority of the language, as well as from its frequently inspirational generality.

In order to appreciate the significance of the Constitution's form, it is only necessary to imagine a radical proposal to amend the present text. The proposal might, for example, begin with two widely different provisions: the first amendment's flat injunction that "Congress shall make no law . . . abridging the freedom of speech" and article I's simple declaration that "Congress shall have power . . . to regulate commerce . . . among the several states." One provision withholds power, the other authorizes it. The unequivocal language in each promises that governmental affairs can be arranged properly and that the correct principles need not be complicated or compromised. These are powerfully attractive promises that still work their effect on those beguiled by the "possibility that there are right answers" and on those who fear for the republic whenever some putative constitutional principle is compromised.[25]

The absolutism of the language in both provisions, of course, is a matter of tone. In fact neither provision is absolute, because each is so general and cryptic—characteristics that allow many divergent groups to see their "truths" as authoritatively enshrined. While appearing to sanction only a single proper mechanism, the language permits many, various arrangements. It is a fundamental law that invites everyone to be right, that creates a culture of inclusive rectitude.

Now, suppose that the free speech clause and the commerce clause were to be replaced by the kinds of formulae that the Court has used to implement them. The first amendment would become a forbiddingly complex set of tests, including:

> When "speech" and "nonspeech" elements are combined in the same course of conduct . . . a government regulation is sufficiently justified if it is within the constitutional power of the Government; if it furthers an important or substantial governmental interest; if the governmental interest is unrelated to the suppression of free expression; and if the incidental restriction on alleged First Amendment freedoms is no greater than is essential to the furtherance of that interest.[26]

The commerce clause would also be a series of elaborate provisions, one of which would require inquiry into

> (1) whether [a state] statute regulates evenhandedly with only "incidental" effects on interstate commerce, or discriminates against interstate commerce either on its face or in practical effect; (2) whether the statute serves a local purpose; and if so, (3) whether alternative means could promote this local purpose as well without discriminating against interstate commerce.[27]

If such judicial constructions were substituted for the present text, the importance of style would be sadly evident. The amended constitution would replace a simple authorization to the central government with a complex set of constraints on the states. It would change an absolute prohibition ("Congress shall make no law") into an equivocal authorization ("a governmental regulation is sufficiently justified if . . ."). It would substitute uncertain modifications and redundancies ("an important or substantial" and "either on its face or in practical effect") for self-confident simplicity ("no law" and "shall have"). The specific and the banal ("When speech and nonspeech elements are combined," and "promote this local purpose as well without discriminating") would replace the general and the cryptic. In short, the new constitution would be complicated, hesitant, specific yet confusing, and demanding yet without natural authority. It would be contrived rather than inspired. It could promise neither certitude nor inclusiveness. It could promote debate and litigation but not loyalty, passion, or faith.

Although much that is conveyed in modern Supreme Court opinions is this formulaic constitution, the Court has not, of course, exactly amended the Constitution. The formulaic opinions supplement rather than replace the original text. Moreover, the form appropriate for the original document is not necessarily appropriate for its application. Nevertheless, the Court's opinions are the most authoritative way in which the original text is explained to the public. There is a yawning gap between the Court's preferred style of communication and its functions. Those functions require that the Court's style of expression, although perhaps different from that of the original text, be capable of great subtlety and force.

The debate over the Court's role, however, proceeds for the most part with a strange disregard for the capacities and limitations suggested by the idiom with which the Court so often intervenes in the culture.

Form and Function

The formulaic style does not inspire, but what functions does it serve? Why does the Court often use language so different from that of the document that it is interpreting? To what audience and with what voice is the Court speaking? Reliance on the formulaic style begins to become understandable if its vaguely familiar outlines are filled in. The style is an amalgam of the bureaucratic and the academic.

Although the Court's formulae are not as long or involved as many administrative rules and guidelines, some of the same characteristics are plainly evident.[28] Both are complex, layered, and equivocal. Both employ words in a puzzlingly artificial way. (What, for instance, is a "nonspeech element"? Why does the Court say that a regulation must further an "important and substantial" governmental interest?) Typically, both attempt to cover all contingencies. (A state law may not discriminate against interstate commerce "either on its face or in practical effect.") In both an air of authority is established by illusory precision. (The abridgment of speech can be no greater than is "essential" to furtherance of a governmental interest. But, if inquiry is directed at *how* "furthered" the governmental interest must be and at what cost, the apparent decisiveness in the word "essential" evaporates.)[29]

Bureaucratic language is characteristically ridiculed as awkward and ineffective when read directly by the general public, but it can be useful when used to achieve cohesion within a profession or control within official hierarchies.[30] Within organizations, the complexity and completeness is aimed at preventing predictable efforts at evasion; the stilted use of words quickly seems normal, as those sharing expertise and a common working milieu are socialized to understand the words as terms of art. Delegation of responsibility through the organization and across time requires systematic delineation and standardization.

The use of bureaucratic style by the Supreme Court is an effort to achieve similar purposes. To the extent that clerks have substantial drafting responsibilities and rotate frequently, it saves time to have established frameworks or recipes for various classes of opinions. Moreover, in a field where *stare decisis* is of limited significance and at a time when there is intense intellectual and ideological diversity at all levels of the judiciary, the elaborateness and detail of the formulae are an obvious effort to achieve control and consistency.[31] The Court, in short, has adopted the formulaic style in part because its primary audience is not the general public. It is addressing itself, its clerks, and the lower courts. The language sounds bureaucratic because the objectives are organizational.

The formulaic style is not, however, fully or only bureaucratic. It is also academic. The opinions look like law review articles. They have the same pattern of laborious footnoting and detailed argumentation. They have the same formalized organization—introductions, major divisions, subdivisions, conclusions. More important, like academic writing, opinions analyze endlessly. Ideas, especially as expressed in the formulae, are treated with deadly seriousness.[32] How, precisely, should a given formula be phrased? Should it be applied more generally, be restricted, or perhaps even be abandoned? Should a single prong (or subprong) be dropped? Should analysis under one "prong" be merged with analysis under another or kept separate? Are apparently different formulations "really" different? Indeed, the Court sometimes debates whether a long-used test actually means anything at all. Only academics, one would have thought, could have such patience for explanation or could so objectify ideas. One reason the formulaic style is little noticed by commentators is that it so resembles the voice of the academy.

It is no wonder that opinions have begun to look like legal scholarship, for legal scholars have removed the available alternatives. Formalistic explanations, whether expressed in a short statement of a rule accompanied by a string of citations or in a mechanical restatement of the relevant text, have long been discredited as aridly conceptualistic and hopelessly literalistic.[33] But realistic explanations, exemplified in daringly moralistic *ipse dixit*s or by bald "balancing" tests that seek to maximize some set of interests, too obviously separate the Court from its sources of legitimacy.[34] In this age of intellectual anxiety, when judicial power is extended but its bases are more problematic than ever, it is only natural that the Court should imitate its most skeptical and demanding audience.[35] And, despite vigorous debate within the academy, the Court has been able to identify among scholars disparate elements of a working consensus on appropriate constitutional explanations. This consensus, which at its best might be thought to contain the beginnings of a sophisticated instrumentalism, is reflected in several aspects of the formulaic style.

First, the formulae are framed as complex explications of the Constitution.[36] In insisting that its "tests" have the Constitution as their ultimate referent, the Court seeks to avoid the threat to its legitimacy inherent in some of the radically subjectivist proposals of the realists and other skeptics. However, by using multifaceted formulations, the Court also attempts to avoid some of the familiar criticisms of naive textualism or historicism. The multiple layers of explanation implicitly acknowledge that the task of interpretation is difficult and must proceed in a way that allows for the simultaneous utilization of various sources.[37]

Second, the complexity and detail of formulaic opinions reflect the Court's felt responsibility to convince. Constitutional answers can no longer be thought certain, and it is thus not enough that they simply be announced. One or more of the prongs is usually openly cast as instrumental—a concession that the meaning of the Constitution will vary according to the vagaries of social and political experimentation.[38] The Court labors under a heavy burden of explanation because it knows it is exercising choice.

Third, the layered "standards" are an effort to create impersonal, formal rules that can constrain the Court itself. Precisely because the difficulty of following the rules laid down is now well known, the Court resorts to multiple, tentative, self-imposed restrictions. The aspiration is that, once established, these rules be sufficiently clear and external to the judges to allow for objectivity.[39]

Fourth, the formulae apparently allow for moderate fact-responsiveness. The opinions are typically divided into two major sections—the first discussing the "prongs" in the abstract and the second applying them to the facts of the case. Moreover, different formulae are established for fairly narrow classes of cases.[40] The more extreme realists' proposals that only facts are relevant to the outcome of cases could never be assimilated to more general notions of lawfulness, but the Court cannot ignore the power of the attack on abstract, general legal principles.[41] The form of modern decisions suggests an effort to moderate (but not abandon) conceptualism by using complex sets of principles that apply to relevant classes of cases.

In short, the formulaic style reflects a view, aspects of which are shared among influential legal scholars, that as a practical matter the advantages of realism can be successfully combined with elements of formalism. The result is more conceptualistic than the "grand style" admired by the realists but more elaborate and sophisticated than the formalism that they discredited. Having seen the judiciary's traditional intellectual habits undercut by decades of legal scholarship, the Justices have turned to scholarship for substitutes. The academics' analytic style—more explanation, finer distinctions, greater clarity—does not inspire but is taken seriously, at least by those whose style is being imitated. As the Court seeks intellectual legitimacy, the voice of the judge and the voice of the legal scholar converge.

The elements of this attempted synthesis of formalism and realism are evaluated serially below, where I argue that the modern style is a superficial and unsatisfactory response to (admittedly) serious problems. It achieves organizational control and intellectual respectability, to the extent it does so, by excluding the general public from the Court's audience and by impoverishing the Court's thought. A successful accommodation of realism and formalism, if it is possible, would require a style of communication far different from the formulaic style. Perversely, the task would sometimes require imperfection—evocation, incompleteness, tentativeness, and even a willingness *not* to explain. Much may be wrong with older forms of constitutional doctrine, but in some important respects they are all superior to the style now so prevalent.

The Effort to Retain the Authority of the Text

Because the modern effort to combine realism and formalism rejects radically subjectivist approaches to interpretation, its constitutional explanations all have a referent outside themselves. Whether the authority of constitutional law is thought to be grounded in specific text, in the document's history, in the relationship among provisions, or somewhere else, judicial decisions are an effort to approximate a standard external to the opinion itself. Although all types of doctrine have the natural effect of substituting themselves for primary constitutional meaning, formulaic explanations are especially incompatible with maintaining the authority of the original text.[42]

In part, this incompatibility arises because of the formulae's characteristic elaborateness, which reflects an intention to make meaning clear and certain, but which quickly becomes an end in itself. Words, for example, are piled on; the repetition, with its own reassuring cadence, is an effort at completion. Thus, the "principal or primary" effect of a statute must "neither advance nor inhibit" religion; a state must show that its "purpose or interest" is constitutionally "permissible and substantial" or "significant and legitimate"; the means must be necessary to the "accomplishment of its purpose or the safe guarding of its interest"; a court must examine "additional or substitute" procedural safeguards. Extra words are so essential to the rhetorical force of the formulae that they are used, as in the case of the prohibition against "advancing *or inhibiting*" reli-

gion, even when plainly irrelevant to the constitutional text being interpreted.[43] Occasionally, an entire clause is added to a formula more for the
satisfactory sense of rounding out that the extra words give than for the
addition of any substantive meaning.[44] Formulae sometimes exist in
order to explicate words in other formulae, doctrine to explain doctrine,
so the reader is removed by formal stages from the animating text.[45]
Strange phrasing, like elaborateness and complexity, fascinates and centers attention narcissistically around itself. The Justice who argued that
the "minimal scrutiny prong of this two-tiered approach has led to an
unfortunate diminution of First Amendment protection" was struggling
against the dead weight of words to get back to the Constitution.[46]

The self-absorption associated with formulae is not an unfortunate by-
product of unnecessary prolixity or complexity. It is a distinctive purpose
of the formula and is implicit in the basic design. Compare, for example,
naive literalism, which in Justice Owen Roberts's notorious formulation
requires that courts "lay the article of the Constitution . . . beside the
statute . . . [and] decide whether the latter squares with the former."[47]
There is no reason here to review the many difficulties that stand in the
way of comparing words as if they were physical objects. Justice Roberts's
prescription for the judicial role may be impossible, but it is nevertheless
helpful. Because a simple examination of the words is sufficient to determine the issue under Roberts's apparent assumptions, his approach requires the Court to rely on its readers' attention to the relevant external
authority. The decision in which the prescription was urged, *United
States v. Butler*, held that a system of expenditures for farm price supports
was a regulation of agriculture rather than an expenditure for the general
welfare under article I, section 8, and therefore exceeded congressional
power.[48] Because the words "regulation" and "expenditure" are not objects with precise contours, the *Butler* opinion could not conclusively—
nor did it even persuasively—demonstrate why the Agricultural Adjust-
ment Act was one rather than the other. But the opinion did ask the
reader to grapple with the meaning of words that appear in the Constitution. If the Court's comparison was necessarily incomplete, it was at least
palpably incomplete; the deficiencies were there to see for anyone with a
common claim to the English language. Indeed, Justice Roberts did not
think that a conclusive demonstration was possible. He wrote, "All the
Court does, or can do, is to announce its considered judgment upon the
question."[49] The simple announcement of a judgment (no matter how
unsatisfactory in other respects) is generous to the reader, for it allows
room for other judgments.

Some such modesty is necessary in any real appeal to external authority. If in the end a court can do no more than announce its judgment about the meaning of the constitutional text (or other external authority), that text remains separate from the court's opinion about it. When a court claims something more ambitious—when it seeks to demonstrate rather than to announce—there is correspondingly less reason to distinguish the external authority from the court's opinion. When the issue is certain and the reader is disallowed an opinion, the judicial construction comes to be interchangeable with the original text. Interpretation can then stand in place of the original text.

The disappearance of the external authority is a matter of degree. To some extent it occurs with any style of explanation. It depends not so much on the number or strength of the reasons given for a judicial construction as on the tenor of the rhetorical claims of certainty and closure made by the court. *McCulloch v. Maryland* illustrates both the varied ways in which these claims can be made and the special quality of the claim made by use of the formulaic style.[50] In *McCulloch* Chief Justice John Marshall made a sophisticated literalistic argument that largely obliterated the original text. The issue was whether the word "necessary" in the necessary and proper clause of article I, section 8 was to mean something closer to "merely convenient" than to "absolutely essential." Marshall's argument advanced like an avalanche.[51] He began by asserting that "nothing is more common than to use words in a figurative sense." Indeed, "almost all compositions contain words, which, taken in the rigorous sense, would convey a meaning different from that which is obviously intended." Having characterized the use of a word in its simplest and plainest sense as exceedingly unlikely, Marshall asserted that the figurative meaning "is essential to just construction."

Marshall then proceeded to draw from a range of sources.[52] In an audacious argument made to seem entirely obvious, he suggested that it is logically impossible for a constitution to constrain power narrowly. "To have prescribed the means by which government should, in all future time, execute its powers, would have been to change, entirely, the character of the instrument." As if this were not enough, Marshall repeatedly described the "baneful influence" of the narrower construction on the operations of government. He invoked "the absolute impracticability of maintaining [the narrower meaning] without rendering the government incompetent to its great objects." Finally, he claimed that to have used the word "necessary" in a sense other than "convenient" would have been "an extraordinary departure from the usual course of the human mind."

The force of Marshall's argument was created in part by the cumulation of different arguments and in part by the dramatic exaggeration in his choice of words. He buried the doubting reader under appeals to common understanding, analogies to the wording of other constitutional provisions, claims about the nature of constitutions, prudential arguments about the capacities of legislatures to avail themselves of experience, and assurances about the drafters' intent. The doubter also had to stand against Marshall's barrage of words: "nothing," "almost all," "obviously," "essential," "impossible," "compelled," "absolute," "conclusively," "extraordinary," and so on. Justice Marshall's opinion is far more forceful than that of Justice Roberts; it is not, however, more true that "necessary" means "convenient" than that a complex system of acreage controls is a "regulation" rather than an "expenditure." Marshall's task was not to announce a judgment. His purpose was to create a fact. To the extent that he was successful—if "necessary" is the same as "convenient"—there is no further reason for the reader's eye to wander back to the words of the necessary and proper clause.

Even powerful arguments about particular words, however, can fail to replace the external text completely. The mere substitution of a single word for another is precarious; the recalcitrant reader is still left room to note that the word "convenient" is different from the word "necessary." Marshall summarized, therefore, not with an argument but with a complex pronouncement: "Let the end be legitimate, let it be within the scope of the constitution, and all means which are appropriate, which are plainly adapted to that end, which are not prohibited, but consist with the letter and spirit of the constitution, are constitutional." [53]

Almost nothing in *McCulloch* presaged the complexity and ambiguity of this passage. The thrust of all the arguments had been that the necessary and proper clause enlarged Congress' power and permitted the use of any means *it* thought useful. The pronouncement, however, suggested that courts should decide whether the means chosen are "appropriate" and whether they are "plainly adapted" to their ends. These words seem to reintroduce the narrower (and emphatically rejected) meaning of "necessary," and the restriction that the means must be consistent with "the letter and spirit of the constitution" is potentially a broad one indeed.

Despite the equivocation, the reader remains untroubled, carried along by the uncompromising power of the preceding arguments. In fact, the passage successfully completed the process of substitution for the original text because it had a substantive, finished quality. One word was not replaced by another. One word was replaced by a systematic inquiry, a series of standards that seem complete and authoritative. In the end the force of *McCulloch* does not lie in its persuasive interpretation of an external authority. It lies in its obliteration of its reader's attention to external authority and in its substitution of promised, announced judicial inquiries for that authority.

Chief Justice Marshall's summarizing passage is an eerie precursor of the modern formulaic style. Today the passage would be written without the magisterial tone but otherwise would be little changed. It might look like this:

> Legislation under the necessary and proper clause is sufficiently justified if: (1) the purpose is legitimate and within the scope of the constitution; (2) the means chosen are appropriate or plainly adapted to that purpose; (3) the means are not specifically or impliedly prohibited.

The changes suggest increased formalization. Each "prong" is numbered and it is both necessary and sufficient to satisfy all three. Each of Marshall's clauses has become more emphatically a hurdle in its own right. Together they are more woodenly, but more plainly, what Marshall intended them to be: a doctrine, a legally effective text rather than an imperfect description of something else.

The rhetorical end point of the *McCulloch* opinion—the replacement of external authority—has in recent years become the customary beginning point of constitutional decisions. The prevalence of the formulaic style makes routine what Marshall's opinion worked so hard toward. Indeed, today the problematic opinion is the one that does not stand in the place of the Constitution. In order to illustrate modern dissatisfaction with incomplete displacement of the text, it is necessary to return to the subject of chapter 4, the sad history of the Court's effort to define state sovereignty as an affirmative limitation on the commerce power.

Recall the much discredited, and now formally overruled, case of *National League of Cities v. Usery,* in which the Court struck down the extension of the Fair Labor Standards Act (FLSA) to most state and local employees.[54] The decision, notable for its tentative and uncompleted quality, was an unusual departure from the formulaic style. It began by identifying its external referents as a general principle ("our federal system of government") and a specific text (the tenth amendment). The rest of the opinion consisted of unstructured, but suggestive, examples, analogies, contrasts, and phrases. This groping discussion began with the sensible, if limited, assertion that Congress may not impair a state's "'ability to function effectively in a federal system.'"[55] The Court proceeded to draw

an analogy between the FLSA and taxes on a state's capitol, without explaining how such taxes might impair this "ability." It then referred to
"the essential role of the States in our federal system," and quickly distinguished federal regulation of private persons from regulation of "States
as States." In the remainder of the opinion, the Court repeated and supple-
mented the illustrations (again distinguishing private behavior and adding
an analogy to the states' power to locate their own capitals). And without
especially building on them, it piled on more phrases: an "undoubted attribute of state sovereignty," functions that are "essential to [the states']
separate and independent existence," "a coordinate element in the system
established by the Framers," "traditional aspects of state sovereignty," interference "with the integral governmental functions," and so on.

While more functional than literal, the argument in *Usery* has much in
common with Justice Roberts's opinion in *United States v. Butler.* Just as
Butler did not attempt a definitive description of a "regulation," *Usery*
began, but did not at all complete, a description of "state sovereignty."
Both decisions are a series of gestures that leave the reader with the ultimate judgment about an authority that remains distinct from the Court's
opinion. Although annoying to scholars, the unclosed and tentative
quality in *Usery* itself attests to the effort in the opinion to get at an external constitutional standard. The phrases and examples indicate—point
to—but do not replace the tenth amendment.

Within a few years, what was unformed and indicative in *Usery* became formulaic and self-referenced:

> In order to succeed, a claim that congressional commerce power legislation is
> invalid . . . must satisfy *each* of three requirements. First, there must be a
> showing that the challenged statute regulates the "States as States." Second,
> the federal regulation must address matters that are indisputably "attribute[s]"
> of state sovereignty." And third, it must be apparent that the States' com-
> pliance with the federal law would directly impair their ability "to structure
> integral operations in areas of traditional governmental functions."[56]

Despite superficial similarities between this formula and the phrases that
appear in *Usery,* systemization utterly changed the nature of the constitutional interpretation. What had been an effort to explain the principle of
federalism became a substitute for it. Under the formula, a statute that
failed to satisfy any *one* of the prongs would be constitutional. Under
Usery, on the other hand, because the phrases are proxies for the external
idea of the states' capacity to function effectively in the federal system, a
devastating blow to any factor relevant to that standard might render the
statute in question unconstitutional. The illustrations used in *Usery* clearly

demonstrate this, for they do not involve violations of all the elements later extracted from the opinion. For example, the Court noted that the national government may not control the placement of a state capital.[57] Controlling this location does involve the state "as a State"; perhaps, but not "indisputably," this decision (like the adoption of legislation) is an attribute of state sovereignty; once the capital is located, the ability of a state to structure integral operations, whether in traditional or nontraditional areas, is not necessarily affected.

It is logically possible, and not inconsistent with *Usery*, that a now unimagined federal statute might violate none of the three requirements of the subsequently developed formula and yet present a serious threat to the capacity of the states to function as governments. For example, suppose a federal statute preempted all state regulatory power over any issue susceptible to regulation under the commerce power except for state activities themselves.[58] This statute would not violate any of the requirements; yet such a broadscale withdrawal of regulatory power from the states might seriously threaten their capacity to govern.[59] The interposition of formal doctrine would block serious consideration of this issue. The analogies, comparisons, and aphorisms of *Usery* on the other hand, while intellectually unfashionable, would permit analysis of the unexpected variation because they do not substitute themselves for the external constitutional issue.

Although cases that use formulae sometimes state that the doctrine is only a starting point for resolving the ultimate issue, the rhetorical force of the formulae—their systematic, finished quality—is inconsistent with such assurances.[60] If unexpected facts in new cases do not seem sensibly resolvable under an established formula, attention does not easily shift back to the external constitutional issue. At the extreme, a wholly different formula (also self-contained and completed) might be established for a class of cases or, as occurred with efforts to define state sovereignty, the ultimate constitutional inquiry might simply be abandoned.[61] When doctrine becomes an end in itself, either some perfected formula must stand in place of external authority or that authority must be nullified.

The Effort to Persuade

Modern judicial opinions aim somewhere between the revealed certainties of formalism and the highly personalized fiats of extreme realism. If in part the Constitution means what judges want it to mean, the Court is obliged to attempt to convince others that its choices are desirable.

Thus the formulaic style seems designed to clarify and convince. Each issue is given wholly separate formulation and discussion. Every shading of understanding is given explicit treatment in separate opinions. Nearly any criticism or doubt is sufficiently important to deserve a reply, if only in a footnote. The modern Court's burden is neither simply to reveal nor even to explain; it is to enlist the volition of others. Persuasion in this sense requires an unconstrained audience and a responsible speaker, for common volition is impossible without both. Unfortunately, the rhetorical force of the formulaic style is consistent with neither.

Persuasion is always an effort to make the listener feel compelled to a certain conclusion. However, most forms of persuasion create a sense of constraint by first addressing an independent audience; such arguments begin in the readers' territory and move from there, always acknowledging the importance of their understanding and assent.[62] Accordingly, most forms of judicial explanation depend for their force on the communicative power of common language. Even highly formalistic opinions depend, in their literalism, upon conventional understanding.[63] That is why such opinions frequently rely heavily on synonyms and antonyms. In *Carter v. Carter Coal Co.*, for instance, the Court tried to explain the difference between "direct" and "indirect" effects on commerce this way: "The word 'direct' implies that the activity or condition . . . shall operate proximately—not mediately, remotely, or collaterally—to produce the effect."[64] The additional words can help persuade if they match some existing understanding. Similarly, analogies are used to make the unintuitive seem familiar. Thus in *Butler* the Court tried to explain how an expenditure could be a regulation by emphasizing the similarity between the binding quality of a contractual "obligation" and the authoritative quality of a regulation.[65] Metaphors like the "throat" of commerce and the "current" of commerce are also efforts to appeal to common experience and perceptions.[66] Despite their reputation for sterility, formalistic opinions appeal to the linguistic community as authority.

In different degrees, the same is true of other forms of explanation. The modern "balancing test," for example, typically involves the specification of a series of factors and the announcement that, after weighing them, the Court has reached a certain conclusion. Whatever its deficiencies and despite its different parentage, this form of explanation appeals to common experience in almost the same way that formalism does. The listing of various considerations, like the use of synonyms or metaphors, calls upon everyday experience. Like the recitation of plain words, the recitation of the factors in the balance can convince a reader whose experiences and understandings are coordinate with the judges'. Both forms stop short of demonstration because both assume that little need be said when much is shared.

To a lesser extent, Chief Justice Marshall's grand pronouncements, described earlier, depend in part on the warrant of common usage.[67] Justice Holmes's famous aphorism allowing restriction of only that speech that involves a "clear and present danger" has had enduring influence largely because it came paired with its famous example from ordinary life.[68] Justice Brandeis's lyrical concurrence in *Whitney v. California* was, despite its reference to the opinions of "those who won our independence," transparently an appeal to his readers' impulses toward courage and tolerance.[69] The most persuasive passage in *Brown v. Board of Education,* a decision notable for its simplicity, called up what was already commonly known and felt: "To separate them from others of similar age and qualifications solely because of their race generates a feeling of inferiority . . . that may affect their hearts and minds in a way unlikely ever to be undone."[70]

The form of explanation that least appeals to the audience as an independent authority is the formulaic style, which does not so much move its readers as disqualify them. The phrasing of the formulae often creates a specious sense of certainty. There are no "indisputable" attributes of state sovereignty nor is any particular method ever "essential" to furthering a state's interest.[71] Similarly, words common in the formulae—"directly," "apparent," "incidental," "sufficiently," "substantial," "excessive," and so on—promise clarity or measurement where only judgment is possible.

The second "prong" of the establishment clause test, for instance, asks whether the statute's "principal or primary" effect is to advance religion. The Court in *Meek v. Pittenger* found that the loan of secular instructional aids to religious schools violated this standard, despite the existence of the secular legislative purpose of developing children's intellectual capacities.[72] Of course, any aid to parochial schools has the effect of advancing religion, but what does it mean to say that the principal effect of providing maps and laboratory equipment is religious? As the Court acknowledged, a school does not cease to be educational because it instills religious values, and a map does not "change in use" to a religious tract. The Court's answer was to emphasize the degree to which parochial schools integrate secular and religious education, so that educational assistance "inescapably" advanced religion. This answer only emphasized the problematic nature of the Court's announced inquiry. If a school were to achieve perfect identity between its religious and educational functions, aid of any kind could not—by definition—be said to advance one aspect more than the other. The use of the words "principal or primary," then, lent the Court's discussion the authority of measurement but not its substance. Indeed, nothing in the opinion explained why the measured effect of the aid was greater on the religious function than on the educational function. Nor would this measurement have been of much relevance, since an aid program could be dangerous to constitutional values whether or not its educative effects were marginally greater than its tendency to advance religion. Words like "principal or primary" must be read as efforts to explain why the religious effects were especially important or threatening. The metaphor of measurement added only deceptive precision, preventing the reader from participating fully in the matter of judgment that was actually at issue.

The prongs themselves are frequently impervious to common understanding—a specialized code directed at the initiated rather than an explanation directed to the governed. The first part of the test for enforcing the establishment clause, for example, assumes the possibility of a unitary legislative intention, which is a possibility that anyone passingly familiar with even one person's motivational structure would think so unlikely as to be unworthy of inquiry.[73] The same test's second prong involves identifying the primary effect of legislation; but the Court, while openly acknowledging that the consequences are the same, has enforced the rule by differentiating between direct subsidies to parents and tax deductions.[74] Whatever the Court means by "primary effect," it is not what most people would expect. Under the third prong, which asks whether there is "excessive government entanglement with religion," the Court puzzlingly inquires about the amount of political debate engendered by a statute.[75] The "mere rationality" test, discussed in chapter 5 above, states that a statute is void if it serves no legitimate purpose at all, a possibility that would only occur to someone in a fever (or to a judge who in fact meant something else). For many years now the Court, apparently using the phrase "potential life" to mean "actual life," has insisted that the state's interest in the potential life of the fetus is somehow less in the second trimester than in the third.[76] The requirement that a state tax "be fairly related to the services provided by the State" does not, as a normal reader would expect, measure the amount of the tax in relation to the value of the services actually provided by the tax; instead it requires merely that the tax be related to the extent of the contact of the taxed party with the state.[77] In each of these instances, the Court's tests are difficult and obscure, not because the language is legalistic or technical, but simply because the Court uses words in an unusual and often wholly unrealistic way.

In other instances, the artificiality is less obvious but still undermines the capacity of the Court's doctrines to serve as vehicles of communication. It is not possible to know, for example, whether "alternative means" might equally well promote a valid local purpose "without discriminating against interstate commerce."[78] The failure in a particular instance to imagine the alternative that satisfies this requirement is no proof that further effort might not yield one. Nor is it possible to know whether a governmental interest is "unrelated to the suppression of free expression."[79] In every case in which expression is restricted, that restriction is the means by which the valid governmental objective is achieved; thus it would always be strange to say that the objective is "unrelated" to the suppression. The use of tests that cannot mean what they say does not necessarily foreclose useful judicial inquiry, but it does involve indirection and artificiality that exclude the reader.

As important as the words is the structure of the formulae. Their design suggests that all the relevant issues have been identified, separated, and answered. The doctrine is comprehensive and definitive. Only one answer can emerge from the machine. The vitriolic exchanges among the Justices that are becoming customary are not merely evidence of ideological cleavages.[80] They result from the same excessive pursuit of certainty that is reflected in the form of modern doctrine. When only one answer is possible, disagreement even among members of the Court is treated as a sign of irresponsibility or obduracy. A fortiori, the formulaic style forecloses independent judgment by the wider publics that are affected by the decisions but that have no special claims to understanding or authority.

To establish common volition, the Court not only must permit the participation of the reader but also must acknowledge the responsibility of the speaker. Because legal traditions generally deny the creative component of the choices made by judges, most forms of explanation obscure the speaker at least as a matter of appearances. Legal authority—whether a case, principle, rule, or the words of a test—always describes the judge's felt sense of constraint. Even the modern balancing test, in which the judge most plainly relies on private assessments and values, is expressed by the metaphor of weighing, as if the judge were a set of scales rather than a person actively deciding. But the judge's own voice can often break through from beneath the surface. It can be heard in Justice Roberts's tired admission that all a court can do is "announce its considered judgment."[81] Most frequently it is heard in the urgency and emotion that a judge allows into the opinion—in the power of the words, in the cadence, in the massing of arguments. Whether the tone is that of prophet, royalty, accountant, or weary soul, judicial opinions traditionally permit glimmers of the judges' view of themselves and of their responsibility.

The tone of the formulaic style, however, is distinctively mechanical.[82] Its operative metaphor is the observer. The opinions describe the performance of contestants, not the judgment of the Court. One side's position does not "pass muster," "fail[s]" a test, "fare[s]" badly, "runs afoul" of a standard, or does not get over a hurdle.[83] The words of the doctrines are so carefully selected because they will "yield" the results in case after case.[84] Everything turns on whether the state's interest must be "legitimate," or "important," or "compelling." Worlds evolve around the difference between a "reasonable relationship" and a "substantial relationship"; between "pure" speech and "mixed" speech; between ordinary legislative classifications, "suspect" classes and (naturally) "semi-suspect" classes. Such words are divided neatly into separate sections, and the relationship among the sections is explicitly established. All this precision is an attempt to achieve one effect: that the words, once in place, will do the work as the judges watch, recording the score. The formulaic style strains hard, too hard, to convince. By disqualifying the reader and by reducing the judge to observer, it achieves a specious definiteness rather than persuasive power.

The Effort to Constrain

It has become increasingly common to justify judicial enforcement of constitutional norms on the surprising ground that judges are at least somewhat constrained by impersonal standards.[85] The argument is surprising because it is so modest. It divorces authoritativeness from legitimacy. A precedent that misconstrues the constitutional text but is nevertheless capable of constraining future judges is impersonal and, therefore, is thought to legitimize judicial power.[86] Moreover, objectivity is compatible with some amount of unconstrained choice; it contemplates only some "boundary" on choice and thus is vague as to the amount of judicial discretion that is acceptable.[87] Since the behavior of most, if not all, government officials is responsive (in some degree) to external constraints, the emphasis on objectivity as a justification for judicial power hardly distinguishes judges from anyone other than the pure tyrant who is able to govern by personal whim.

Despite its weakness as a justification, the idea of objectivity is essential to the modern effort to accommodate realism and formalism. Current practice is too sophisticated to rely on the capacity of the judge to find a single, authoritative interpretation of constitutional text, yet it is too wedded to the ideal of the rule of law to permit judges to operate beyond legal constraint. Therefore, the formulaic style is designed to extract the maximum possible force from objectivity. In modern decisions, judges are bound not merely by simple and undefined maxims nor by the mysterious flux of prior cases, but by rules that are specific and multiple. The doctrines that in fact largely supplant constitutional text must be sufficiently detailed and schematic to bind judges who otherwise might seem beyond the law.

The apparent definiteness of the formulae does help to convey a promise of impersonal constraint. This is so, however, only because precision involves (or seems to involve) the possibility of checking a court's judgment against some identifiable, agreed-upon standard other than the judge's own inclinations. Most forms of constitutional explanation have this capacity not because of their internally systematic character, but because of their persuasiveness as an interpretation of constitutional text. That text provides an appeal against which any later change in construction can be measured. For example, in his famous treatment of the question of whether a state could tax an activity of a federal bank, Chief Justice Marshall wrote that the issue could be resolved by a principle "blended with . . . [the] texture" of the Constitution: "This great principle is, that the constitution and the laws made in pursuance thereof are supreme; that they control the constitution and laws of the respective States, and cannot be controlled by them."[88] This pronouncement purports to be a direct explanation, almost a restatement, of constitutional provisions. The passage speaks with enormous authority, not so much because it states a rule that is itself capable of constraining judges as because it is a forceful statement of what the text requires. It is the persuasiveness of the interpretation that promises constraint in the future.

Even a decision that uses no principles or rules—a decision that depends upon argument from the facts of the case rather than any formal, encapsulated statements—can convey the possibility of some objectivity if it is the external text to which the opinion appeals. *Burton v. Wilmington Parking Authority* is a well-known and extreme illustration.[89] The issue was whether the actions of a privately owned coffee shop located within a public parking garage were actions of the "state" for purposes of applying the strictures of the fourteenth amendment. The decision relied on a detailed recitation of facts: the public purposes of the garage were subsidized by renting to the restaurant; in some respects the conduct of the restaurant was controlled by a lease; the garage had signs and flags indicating its public character; the building's acquisition and maintenance costs were paid out of public funds. Having massed these and other facts, the Court concluded:

> The State has so far insinuated itself into a position of interdependence with [the coffee shop] that it must be recognized as a joint participant in the challenged activity, which, on that account, cannot be considered to have been so "purely private" as to fall without the scope of the Fourteenth Amendment.[90]

By modern standards, the extraordinary aspect of the Court's opinion was its refusal to formalize its reasoning into principles:

> Because readily applicable formulae may not be fashioned, the conclusions drawn from . . . this record are by no means declared as universal truths on the basis of which every state leasing agreement is to be tested. . . . A multitude of relationships might appear to some to fall within the Amendment's embrace, but that . . . can be determined only in the framework of the peculiar facts or circumstances present.[91]

The Court's unwillingness to state explicit formulations was criticized as a failure of objectivity; the absence of rules was seen as a refusal to constrain future decisions.[92] And, indeed, the Court's own summation of what it had decided in *Burton* appeared to promise only that future cases with identical facts would be decided in the same way.[93]

The failure to formalize a rule in *Burton,* however, did not fatally undermine the capacity of the decision to constrain judges in future cases. To the extent that the Court's arguments persuasively related the facts of the case to the "state action" requirement, *Burton* was, as later cases demonstrate, pregnant with possibilities for influencing the Justices in subsequent decisions.[94] After all, the *Burton* Court did not merely list facts; it used facts to argue about constitutional meaning.[95] It argued that the state ought not benefit financially or programmatically from discriminatory policies; it suggested that the purposes of the fourteenth amendment were implicated when private action was perceived by the public as state action; it claimed a practical policy against permitting easy evasion by the state of its constitutional obligations. To the extent that *Burton* was persuasive in these respects, its attention to particularized facts was rich and emphatic, certainly more so than a mechanically stated rule. In short, in *Burton* objectivity (or the capacity to constrain) did not de pend on the precision of verbal formulations but on the continuing persuasive power of the complex marshaling of facts.

In contrast, the formulaic constitution is a series of judicial demands. The Court refers to the subparts of its formulations as "tests," "requirements," and even "hurdles." One side "must satisfy" each of three requirements; a party "must show"; or "it must be apparent that. . . ."[96] The possibility of impersonal constraint is belied by the explicit and reiterated demand that the judge be addressed and satisfied. Occasionally discretionary power is openly acknowledged. The burden on the government in sex discrimination cases is to show "*at least* that the classification serves 'important . . . objectives and that the . . . means employed' are 'substantially related to the achievement of those objectives.'"[97] Fulfilling the announced requirements, the test itself announces, might not always be sufficient. The Court sometimes describes apparently definitive formulae as "helpful" or as mere "guidelines."[98] Although the careful design and elaborate structure of the formulae assign to the words the responsibility for the outcome, in various ways the phrasing emphasizes that the judge has the power to give (or not to give) the words meaning.

Even the structured and finished quality of the formulae works against their capacity to communicate constraint to either judge or reader. Like the language itself, the complex structure of the formulae emphasizes the need to persuade the judge and, therefore, subtly highlights the power inherent in applying or altering the hurdles. For example, because they are designed to be complete and precise, formulae often separate issues that are roughly similar. Thus the formulations are characterized by a redundant or, at least, overlapping quality.[99] The systemizations of state sovereignty that followed *Usery,* for instance, demanded that the state demonstrate both regulation of the states "as States" and impairment of states' "ability to structure integral operations in areas of traditional governmental functions." To the uninitiated, the impairment of integral operations would necessarily involve regulation of the states "as States." The two prongs are not, however, identical: "to regulate" is not necessarily "to impair"; and the state could be regulated "as a State" in a nontraditional area. Nevertheless, the complete separation of two such closely related sets of issues emphasizes their cumulative, hurdlelike quality. The litigant must jump and then jump again.

Formal separation of overlapping rules communicates discretionary power in other ways as well. Systematic formulation of doctrine makes the Court's use of inconsistent propositions stand out, and compartmentalized analysis provides abundant opportunities for the Court to exploit such inconsistencies. In applying the "dormant" commerce clause to state truck-length regulations in *Kassel v. Consolidated Freightways Corp.*, for instance, a plurality of the Court summarized the relevant "general principles" as follows:

> A State's power to regulate commerce is never greater than in matters traditionally of local concern. . . . Regulations that touch upon safety—especially highway safety—are those that "the Court has been most reluctant to invalidate." . . . Indeed, "if safety justifications are not illusory, the Court will not second-guess legislative judgment about their importance in comparison with . . . burdens on interstate commerce." . . .
>
> But [the Court will weigh] ". . . the asserted safety purpose against the degree of interference with interstate commerce" . . . [by means of] "a sensitive consideration of the weight and nature of the state regulatory concern in light of the extent of the burden imposed on the course of interstate commerce."[100]

The reader is thus put on notice that the Court retains the option either to defer to or to second-guess the legislative judgment. The remainder of the plurality opinion insisted on appearing to exercise both these choices. In one section, it found that the state's safety interest was inadequate, despite acknowledging evidence demonstrating at least some safety considerations behind the statute.[101] Dismissing this evidence, of course, could be read as "second-guessing" the legislative judgment. This possibility seems confirmed by a later, separate section, where the plurality argued that "special deference" to the state's safety judgment was inappropriate *because* the local regulation placed disproportionate burdens on out-of-state businesses.[102] However, the language of the section that discussed the safety rationale purported to be the language of deference. The state had "failed to present *any* persuasive evidence," and its safety interest was "illusory."[103] Moreover, the plurality had asserted that it would not second-guess the legislative judgment on whether the burdens on commerce were disproportionate to the safety benefits unless the state's safety interests were essentially nonexistent. So, one might think, an exacting inquiry into safety considerations could not have been triggered by a balancing process that itself was triggered by the finding that safety interests were illusory. The justification for discounting the evidence on safety, then, remains somewhat mysterious despite the later discussion of the inappropriateness of special deference. Perhaps some Talmudic distinction could resolve the confusion, but rhetorically at least the opinion blithely insisted on having it both ways: it did and did not second-guess the legislative judgment.

In offering the Court opportunities to treat related issues repetitively, multiple "prongs" permit the Court to treat closely related issues differently under different headings. Consider again the cases in which the Court has found that state aid to private schools was motivated by the secular legislative purpose of improving education but had the primary effect of advancing religion.[104] While to most people this combination of findings would be surprising, it is not formally inconsistent. The intended purpose of the program need not turn out to be its main consequence. Nevertheless, the issues of institutional motivation and primary effect are closely related, if only because intent is normally inferred from consequences. Compartmentalizing the discussions of motive and effect allowed the Court to characterize the program both benignly and harshly.[105] The effect of simultaneously exculpating the legislators and condemning the program is to drive home to the reader the extent to which the nature of the program can be viewed in different ways, thus emphasizing the range of choices available to the Court.

Despite their superficial precision, neither the content nor the shape of modern formulae communicates clarity and constraint. The formulae are demands—multiple, repetitive, shifting, and sometimes inconsistent. The style reflects intellectual embarrassment about the existence of judicial discretion, but is designed to assure plentiful opportunities for its exercise. In combination with the mechanical tone of formulaic opinions, the palpable range of choice inherent in the formulae communicates, not objectivity, but power without responsibility. Rather than binding, the formulaic style frees the Court, like some lumbering bully, to disrupt social norms and practices at its pleasure.

The Effort to Moderate Conceptualism

The modern style uses intermediate principles in an attempt to combine conceptualism with fact-responsiveness. Despite the arguments of the realists, abstract constitutional principles cannot be reduced to circumstantial factual judgments. But the dangers of conceptualism are now too well understood to permit decisions by reference to a few abstract legal principles. The Court's middle ground is to emphasize analysis of how subclasses of cases should be resolved. Overarching principles like equal protection are broken down into three or more sets of formulae, and the Court expends large parts of its effort and creativity in deciding which formula should govern a moderately specific category of fact situations. More than a decade of opinions has been spent on many of these issues.[106] In particular cases, the contrast between the space and energy devoted to selecting doctrine and that devoted to applying doctrine is frequently striking.[107] Throughout modern constitutional law—from first amendment questions about obscenity to commerce clause issues arising from state regulation of truck lengths—much of the Justices' intellectual energy is not directed at the actual resolution of cases at hand. It is directed at the difficult, complex, but preliminary, issue of determining the proper test to be applied in a defined class of cases. This painstaking and self-conscious attention to preliminary and moderately abstract questions reflects and enhances a perspective that is regulatory, abstract, and adversarial.

The Regulatory Perspective

The first of the consequences arises because the vigor and seriousness of the argumentation about choice of doctrine stands in such distinct contrast to the mechanical tone of judicial application of doctrine. This contrast emphasizes the personal responsibility of judges at the level of policy determination. Although the doctrine determines the outcome (as the judges watch), the Justices do take responsibility for the precise wording and relationships within the formulae.[108] What is communicated, then, is that the important part of the modern Justice's task is deciding how sets of problems should be handled. This acceptance of responsibility *for choosing the words* casts the Court as a regulator rather than as an adjudicator. Thus the shape of the opinions emphasizes a relocation of the judges' moral responsibility and a redefinition of their institutional role.

Paradoxically, more general legal pronouncements—such as Chief Justice Marshall's maxim that the federal rule must never be controlled by the state rule, or Justice Holmes's principle that *all* free speech questions can be resolved by reference to the "clear and present danger" test—are so broad that they necessarily channel judicial effort into an assessment of the particularities of the case.[109] Similarly, the analogical thinking characteristic of case analysis forces comparison and evaluation of relevant facts in cases.[110] Balancing, too, explains so little that its major consequence is judicial discussion of the specifics of the case.[111] Whatever their deficiencies, then, conventional forms of legal explanation are either so general or so free of content that the judge's job is primarily to think about a manageably specific set of circumstances. Thus in the past, inattention to questions of intermediate generality has been consistent with the traditional view that the important part of the Court's role is the resolution of specific controversies. The modern Court's emphasis on doctrine selection expresses and consolidates a radical shift in role from adjudicator to regulator.

This shift affects the quality of judicial opinions in important and dismaying ways. Because the broad issue of how a class of cases ought to be treated is a regulatory matter, general social facts seem naturally relevant. Therefore modern opinions tend to convert moral choices into social or political description. In the plurality opinion in *Frontiero v. Richardson*, for example, four members of the Court argued that "classifications based upon sex, like classifications based upon race, alienage, and national origin, are inherently suspect and must therefore be subjected to close judicial scrutiny."[112] Most of the justification for this determination was an interpretation of American social and political history.[113] The plurality said that the nation's experience with sex discrimination was "long and unfortunate"; women were "put . . . not on a pedestal, but in a cage"; "throughout much of the nineteenth century the position of women in our society was, in many respects, comparable to that of blacks under the pre–Civil War slave codes"; "women still face pervasive . . . discrimination in our . . . institutions"; and, finally, "the sex characteristic frequently bears no relation to ability to perform or contribute to society."

This sweeping discussion is dismaying in part because the level of the rhetoric was inappropriate to the facts of the case. The statute struck down in *Frontiero* required that female members of the armed services prove that their husbands were financially dependent, but permitted the wives of male members of the services to be treated as dependent regardless of their actual financial situations. The complexity here, as in so many sex discrimination cases, is that a discrimination against a female member of the service also (inevitably) is to the disadvantage of her husband, and a discrimination in favor of a male member of the service also (inevitably) is to the advantage of his wife—a complexity with specific relevance to a "dependency benefit" program. General analogies between sex and race ring hollow in the context of a case that clearly illustrates one concrete respect in which the history of sex discrimination is highly and specially ambiguous: the lives of men and women are so closely tied together that harm and benefit cannot be cleanly divided.[114]

There may be good reasons for deciding to view the discrimination involved in *Frontiero* as a disadvantage to women. Such reasons, however, would have to reply to the marginally employed wife who, because she did not have to risk her dependency benefits, was not discouraged from remaining in the work force. Broad historical or social descriptions are of little use here, for the ambiguity of the situation lies in the fact that both the servicewomen and the working women married to servicemen have interests. So severe is the Court's shift from adjudicator to regulator in cases like *Frontiero* that the dispute is merely an occasion for social theorizing. As the plurality's opinion demonstrates, in such instances the force of grand pronouncements can be critically undercut by the (largely ignored) circumstances of the case.

Frontiero illustrates another respect in which reliance on social facts is dismaying. The analogy of women to blacks is a highly controversial one.[115] Some of the same facts pointed to by the plurality can be used to emphasize the ways in which women have been favored, protected, and loved. Arguments about the analogy between sex and race are not simply historical arguments that can be finally resolved by more or better information. They are arguments for a moral vision; they are depictions of ourselves and our history and our future.[116] Such visions change vocabulary and self-perception. The cultural decision to view American history as invidious to women or to view gender as irrelevant to capacity is only partly responsive to facts. It is also responsive to moral goals—to the changes people want to make in each other. The *Frontiero* plurality is strikingly silent about matters of will and vision. The fixation on historical, social, and physical facts that tends to characterize debates about moral choice when cast at the level of social policy impoverishes the plurality's opinion. Words that "make and remake the world" require an "attitude of looking away from . . . principles, 'categories' . . . toward . . . consequences, facts."[117] A people creates its culture in part through constitutional controversies; attention to the specifics of a case is a small guarantee that this process of self-definition will not be debased by the simplifications and false determinism evoked by "scientific" descriptions of social or historical facts.

The Abstract Perspective

The second general consequence of emphasizing the choice of intermediate principles is that doctrine selection is separated from doctrine application. This separation results naturally because the importance attached to doctrine selection calls for separate and self-conscious treatment. The effect of the separation is to permit the decision as to choice of doctrine to be couched in cerebral tones, the intricacy and fullness of the actual dispute having been reserved for a subsequent section of the opinion. It is largely this bifurcation of fact and formula that makes the task of doctrine selection seem a practical endeavor. That task, after all, requires a Court to choose in advance three or four specific questions that will properly resolve myriads of possible cases in areas as broad and unpredictable as "mixed speech and nonspeech." Such endeavors do not seem quixotic at first, because complexity and variety are acknowledged only after the doctrine is selected. As cases continue to arise, however, the variety of possible fact configurations gradually becomes more and more difficult to ignore. In several areas, such as separation of church and state, probable cause, state sovereignty, and abortion regulation, the incessant pressure of this variety eventually has begun to force the Justices to acknowledge what should have been immediately obvious: the formulae are too simple and specific for the range of issues they are designed to resolve.[118]

Because the facts of the case tend not to affect doctrine selection, decisions often contain painful incongruities, direct confrontation of which would reveal the problematic nature of the moral premises underlying the doctrine-selection decision. In *Bakke*, for instance, Justice Brennan's opinion contained (in section III) an almost philosophical comparison of gender discrimination and remedial race discrimination.[119] Pointing to similar potential for stigmatizing "powerless segments of society" and the immutability of both gender and race, the opinion concluded that such classifications must be struck down when a "searching" (but not "'strict' in theory and fatal in fact") judicial inquiry indicates that the program stigmatizes the politically powerless.[120] The need for this extended discussion arose because early in section III the opinion had rejected the possibility that the university's purposes themselves contravened the "cardinal principle that racial classifications that stigmatize—because they are drawn on the presumption that one race is inferior to another or because they put the weight of government behind racial hatred . . .—are invalid without more."[121] Having established the Court's proper "role," the opinion moved in section IV to a more particularized assessment of the preferential admissions program under review. Here Justice Brennan wrote:

> If it was reasonable to conclude—as we hold that it was—that the failure of minorities to qualify for admission at Davis under regular procedures was due principally to the effects of past discrimination, then there is a reasonable

likelihood that, but for pervasive racial discrimination, respondent would have failed to qualify for admission even in the absence of Davis' special admissions program.[122]

This extraordinary passage suggests that a *particular* white applicant would have had worse credentials than unnamed minority applicants if American history had been entirely different. It purports to be a claim about social causality. Its complexity is masked by simpleminded reciprocity: if past discrimination can reasonably be said to have *reduced* the qualifications of minorities, then there is a "reasonable likelihood" that Bakke's qualifications are artificially *inflated*. In fact, of course, it is not clear how racial configurations in general would have been affected by a different social and political history, and it is entirely uncertain how a changed history would have affected Bakke's fortune even had that changed history led to a larger number of qualified minorities.[123]

The passage, then, cannot be read as a serious statement about social causality. It does, nevertheless, communicate the moral judgment that white people have benefited unfairly from racial injustices. Although adorned with unsupportable assumptions about social causality, the force of the argument is not about hypothetical qualifications but about moral entitlements. White people in general and Bakke in particular, having benefited unfairly from racial injustices, are less worthy than competing minority applicants.

A fundamental objection to remedial racial discrimination, of course, is precisely that it inevitably involves the government in conscious decision making about how much various races deserve. This course is feared because it requires judgments about the relative moral worth of the races and, more pragmatically, because it might fuel racial competition and hatred. In Justice Brennan's opinion, these concerns were reflected in the word "stigma," defined in section III as resulting from racial classifications that draw "on the presumption that one race is inferior to another or [that] put the weight of the government behind racial hatred."[124] The crucial step in doctrine selection was the dismissal of the possibility that the purposes of remedial racial discrimination might be inherently stigmatizing. However, the specific justifications for the Davis program in the doctrine application section plainly undercut this dismissal, for these justifications themselves are painful illustrations of racially based moral judgments and competition. A mind attuned to the sounds being made in section IV would have been far less certain of the moral issues decided with such self-confidence in section III. The compartmentalization so characteristic of the formulaic style impoverishes the Court's moral discourse by allowing relatively abstract moral arguments to be uninformed by the richness and difficulty suggested by the case itself.

The Adversarial Perspective

A third consequence of independent emphasis on doctrine selection is that the judiciary's adversarial relationship with the general culture is encouraged yet made to seem more natural and acceptable. Formulae are calibrated judicial demands for justification of classes of decisions made by others. One might expect that self-conscious concern about selection of formulae—about how closely the courts should review decisions made by others—might sometimes lead to a less adversarial relationship with other decision makers. Because of this reassurance, the full and separate discussion of the Court's proper role does tend to legitimize extension of judicial power. However, the bases for reassurance are largely illusory. One reason is that doctrine selection is couched as a preliminary matter and therefore, like such esoteric legal issues as standing or ripeness, is made to seem somehow a technical matter of special concern to the judiciary. In a given category of cases, should judges have to be convinced of a compelling state interest, of an important one, or merely of a legitimate one? Should judges accept post hoc rationalizations for a statute or should they demand to be shown the actual motives of the legislators? The perspective implicit in such questions emphasizes the judiciary's capacities, and thus questions of power allocation tend to revolve narrow-mindedly around the courts. To justify partial insulation from judicial oversight, the advocate must argue against judges' self-respect and institutional self-interest. Moreover, those representing other decision makers are put in the awkward position of arguing to judges that judges ought not be "conscientious," that they ought not examine a set of decisions closely. Cases begin, in short, with the Court's prestige, self-importance, and power set against the diffuse interests of other decision makers.

The interests of these other decision makers are assessed, at least as a formal matter, independently of, and prior to, the resolution of the case itself. Thus the need for judicial oversight is established in an antiseptic setting. No matter what the Court decides about the issue of doctrine selection, the competing decision maker might still prevail in the doctrine application section. The concerns of the myriad unrepresented decision makers seem less immediate and less pressing because the discussion of greatest relevance to them contains no announcement of consequences. On the other hand, the emphasis on highly specific considerations in the doctrine application section distances the eventual announcement of real consequences from those nonparties who may eventually be affected but who do not share all the parties' peculiarities.

During doctrine selection, the Court is not judging the case as a set of identifiable transactions or events. Instead it is demanding that political and social institutions justify their insulation from judicial oversight. This puts the culture itself—its language, its stereotypes, and its institutions—on trial. The issue that opens nearly every major constitutional decision is the extent to which some aspect of the culture can be trusted. The Justices' first duty in constitutional cases is to set themselves apart from the larger culture. The law that emerges from decisions structured in this way cannot appreciate or build from the traditions, understandings, and behaviors commonly shared outside the nation's courtrooms.

Conclusion

This chapter started by asking why the modern Court has adopted the cumbersome formulaic style. The immediate reasons were not hard to locate: the style is a conscientious effort to maintain intellectual respectability while attempting to formulate and implement complex policies through institutional layers and across time. The "constitution" has become an ambitious political and social agenda; the courts have become a kind of elevated bureaucracy, busily crafting formulae that will bend the nation's affairs toward various visions dignified by constitutional status. The difficulty is, as Benjamin Barber said in a larger context, that those who "have been set on securing rights, realizing purposes, protecting interests, and in general getting things done . . . have had a difficult time making sense of conversation as a political art."[125] The less immediate, but more basic, question, then, is why Justices and scholars have not been more dissatisfied with the awkward and degraded way of talking that has developed naturally along with the Court's instrumentalist role. Why are those who want the Court to intervene with wisdom and effectiveness in the culture not dismayed by a communicative style that isolates the Court from the governed and from their ordinary experiences and understandings?

Here I can offer only a speculation that returns to where this book began. The single most significant event for present-day judges and scholars was the federal judiciary's extended and often heroic assault on racial segregation in the South. The profound formative influence of this struggle has shaped as has nothing else law, role, and aspiration. The operative image has been of the courts attacking a pernicious and deeply engrained part of popular culture. By degrees, I believe, this image of the judiciary as antagonist to the popular culture has consolidated and grown, so that the courts' basic function has become that of critic and reformer of the general culture. No more than the arrogant modern painter or composer, whose roles also are to uplift an unappreciative and uncomprehending mass sensibility, need the judiciary employ an idiom that draws on and is understandable to ordinary people.

It was one thing for the Warren Court to attack an aspect of a largely regional culture. In doing so, it could draw on a more broadly shared set of beliefs, attitudes, and perceptions. It is another thing for the current Court to isolate itself from the general culture, retaining ties of language and intellectual approach only to an academic elite. Unlike many, I have no definite prescriptions for what the Court's roles ought to be or even how it should write its opinions. But if its roles require sensitive moral judgments and the capacity to educate and move the people who provide continuing consent to the authority of the Constitution, the Court must learn (and, to some extent, rediscover) other ways of speaking. If the fundamental law is to retain the people's loyalty and support, both the content and form of its announced meaning must be kept somewhere within reach of the public's comprehension. This discipline would require that courts accomplish less, but it might enable them to achieve more. Constitutional law, certainly, helps to shape the culture, but it cannot routinely assault that culture. Law must begin somewhere, and it must shape by participating.

Notes

1. See generally Nagel, *Controlling the Structural Injunction,* 7 Harv. J.L. & Pub. Pol. 395 (1984), and sources cited therein.

2. Legislative veto: *Immigration and Naturalization Serv. v. Chadha,* 462 U.S. 919 (1983); see also *Bowsher v. Synar,* 106 S. Ct. 3181 (1986). Gerrymandering: *Davis v. Bandemer,* 106 S. Ct. 2797 (1986). For a discussion of the ways in which a cautious, "restrained" court can encourage dependence on judicial power, see Nagel, *A Comment on the Burger Court and "Judicial Activism,"* 52 U. Colo. L. Rev. 223 (1981).

3. Contract clause: e.g., Epstein, *Toward a Revitalization of the Contract Clause,* 51 U. Chi. L. Rev. 703 (1984). Guarantee clause: e.g., Note, *The Rule of Law and the States: A New Interpretation of the Guarantee Clause,* 93 Yale L.J. 561 (1984).

4. For some current approaches to the Court's function, see text related to notes 11–13 in chapter 7. Some of the most effective indictments of theories of judicial review have been written to clear the ground for the proposal of a new theory. See, e.g., Ely, *On Discovering Fundamental Values,* 92 Harv. L. Rev. 5 (1978); Perry, *Noninterpretive Review in Human Rights Cases: A Functional Justification,* 56 N.Y.U. L. Rev. 278 (1981). In their turn the new theories have been subjected to severe criticism. On M. Perry, THE CONSTITUTION, THE COURTS, AND HUMAN RIGHTS (New Haven: Yale University Press, 1982), see *Symposium: Judicial Review and the Constitution—The Text and Beyond,* 8 U. Dayton L. Rev. 443 (1983). On J. Ely, DEMOCRACY AND DISTRUST (Cambridge: Harvard University Press, 1980), see, e.g., Tribe, *The Puzzling Persistence*

of Process-Based Constitutional Theories, 89 Yale L.J. 1063 (1980); Tushnet, *Darkness on the Edge of Town: The Contributions of John Hart Ely to Constitutional Theory,* 89 Yale L.J. 1037 (1980). See generally *Symposium: Judicial Review Versus Democracy,* 42 Ohio St. L.J. 1 (1981); *Symposium: Constitutional Adjudication and Democratic Political Theory,* 56 N.Y.U. L. Rev. 259 (1981). Raoul Berger has produced an insistent drumbeat of criticism; see, e.g., R. Berger, GOVERNMENT BY JUDICIARY (Cambridge: Harvard University Press, 1977), which in turn has spawned comment. See Perry, *Interpretivism, Freedom of Expression, and Equal Protection,* 42 Ohio St. L.J. 261, 285 n.100 (1981). Some skeptics now have gone so far as to question whether interpretation of a written constitution can be anything other than an exercise of the reader's imagination. See, e.g., Levinson, *Law as Literature,* 60 Tex. L. Rev. 373 (1982). Accordingly, some proponents of judicial review think it is important to establish that the Constitution's text can provide *some* constraint external to the judge. See, e.g., Fiss, *Objectivity and Interpretation,* 34 Stan. L. Rev. 739 (1982). In short, recent constitutional scholarship has amounted to a virtual torrent of criticism and backpeddling.

5. Family life: see, e.g., *Planned Parenthood v. Danforth,* 428 U.S. 52 (1976). Public schools: *Goss v. Lopez,* 419 U.S. 565 (1975). Congress and executive agencies: *Immigration and Naturalization Serv. v. Chadha,* 462 U.S. 919 (1983).

6. 347 U.S. 483 (1954).

7. See *Plessy v. Ferguson,* 163 U.S. 537 (1896).

CHAPTER 2

1. *Marbury v. Madison,* 5 U.S. (1 Cranch) 137, 176–77 (1803).

2. A. Bickel, THE SUPREME COURT AND THE IDEA OF PROGRESS 87 (New York: Harper & Row, 1970).

3. Hart, *The Time Chart of the Justices,* 73 Harv. L. Rev. 84, 99 (1959).

4. See, e.g., Sandalow, *Constitutional Interpretation,* 79 Mich. L. Rev. 1033 (1981); Brest, *The Misconceived Quest for the Original Understanding,* 60 B.U.L. Rev. 204 (1980); Munzer and Nickel, *Does the Constitution Mean What It Always Meant?* 77 Colum. L. Rev. 1029 (1977). See also L. Tribe, AMERICAN CONSTITUTIONAL LAW 816 passim (Mineola, N.Y.: Foundation Press, 1978); C. Miller, THE SUPREME COURT AND THE USES OF HISTORY 189–201 (Cambridge: Harvard University Press, 1969).

5. *Marbury v. Madison,* 5 U.S. (1 Cranch) 137 (1803).

6. *McCulloch v. Maryland,* 17 U.S. (4 Wheat.) 316 (1819).

7. E.g., *Palko v. Connecticut,* 302 U.S. 319 (1937).

8. *Regents of University of California v. Bakke,* 438 U.S. 265 (1978).

9. *Rostker v. Goldberg,* 453 U.S. 57, 83–86 (1981) (White and Brennan, JJ., dissenting).

10. E.g., L. Tribe, supra note 4.

11. These titles were drawn, as examples, from 20 INDEX TO LEGAL PERIODICALS, SEPTEMBER 1980 TO AUGUST 1981 (New York: H. W. Wilson, 1982).

12. For an extended analysis that reaches much the same conclusion, see Sandalow, supra note 4.

13. *Schechter Poultry Corp. v. United States,* 295 U.S. 495 (1935); *Panama Ref. Co. v. Ryan,* 293 U.S. 388 (1935).

14. J. Nowak, R. Rotunda, J. Young, CONSTITUTIONAL LAW 147 (2d ed.; St. Paul: West, 1978).

15. *National Cable Television Ass'n v. United States,* 415 U.S. 336 (1974); J. Ely, DEMOCRACY AND DISTRUST 133 (Cambridge: Harvard University Press, 1980).

16. E.g., *Carter v. Carter Coal Co.,* 298 U.S. 238 (1936).

17. *United States v. Darby,* 312 U.S. 100, 124 (1941). The Court recently formalized its withdrawal from this area. *Garcia v. San Antonio Metropolitan Transit Authority,* 105 S. Ct. 1005 (1985).

18. *Katzenbach v. Morgan,* 384 U.S. 641 (1966). See also *Jones v. Alfred H. Mayer Co.,* 392 U.S. 409 (1968).

19. The Court insists, instead, that the Congress shares only remedial power. *Oregon v. Mitchell,* 400 U.S. 112 (1970); *Rome v. United States,* 446 U.S. 156 (1980).

20. As to prisons, see, e.g., *Siegel v. Ragen,* 88 F. Supp. 996 (N.D. Ill. 1949), *cert. denied,* 339 U.S. 990 (1950), *reh'g denied,* 340 U.S. 847 (1950). As to reapportionment, see *Colegrove v. Green,* 328 U.S. 549 (1946).

21. Compare *Vlandis v. Kline,* 412 U.S. 441 (1973), with *Weinberger v. Salfi,* 422 U.S. 749 (1975).

22. *Levy v. Louisiana,* 391 U.S. 68 (1968); *Labine v. Vincent,* 401 U.S. 532 (1971); *Weber v. Aetna Casualty & Sur. Co.,* 406 U.S. 164 (1972); *Trimble v. Gordon,* 430 U.S. 762 (1977).

23. Compare, e.g., *Allgeyer v. Louisiana,* 165 U.S. 578 (1897), and *Lochner v. New York,* 198 U.S. 45 (1905), with *Williamson v. Lee Optical Co.,* 348 U.S. 483 (1955), and *New Motor Vehicle Bd. v. Orrin W. Fox,* 439 U.S. 96 (1978).

24. *Griswold v. Connecticut,* 381 U.S. 479 (1965); *Roe v. Wade,* 410 U.S. 113 (1973).

25. The exclusionary rule was first applied to the states in *Mapp v.*

Ohio, 367 U.S. 643 (1961). In *United States v. Calandra,* 414 U.S. 338, 348 (1974), the Court described the right as remedial "rather than a personal constitutional right of the party aggrieved."

26. For a history, see J. Nowak, R. Rotunda, and J. Young, supra note 14, at 411–16.

27. *Engel v. Vitale,* 370 U.S. 421 (1962).

28. *Elrod v. Burns,* 427 U.S. 347 (1976).

29. *New York Times Co. v. Sullivan,* 376 U.S. 254 (1964).

30. *Williams v. Florida,* 399 U.S. 78 (1970).

31. *Willson v. The Black Bird Creek Marsh Co.,* 27 U.S. (2 Pet.) 245 (1829).

32. *Cooley v. Board of Wardens,* 53 U.S. (12 How.) 299 (1851).

33. Compare *Champion v. Ames,* 188 U.S. 321 (1903), *Hipolite Egg Co. v. United States,* 220 U.S. 45 (1911), and *Hoke v. United States,* 227 U.S. 308 (1913), with *Hammer v. Dagenhart,* 247 U.S. 251 (1918).

34. On the original importance of property, see B. Siegan, ECONOMIC LIBERTIES AND THE CONSTITUTION 30–40 (Chicago: University of Chicago Press, 1980). On more recent priorities, consider, e.g., *Schad v. Mount Ephraim,* 452 U.S. 61 (1981) (nude dancing); *Planned Parenthood of Missouri v. Danforth,* 428 U.S. 52 (1976) (right to abortion for unmarried minor without parental consent); *Carey v. Population Services Int'l,* 431 U.S. 678 (1977) (right of unmarried minors to decide whether or not to beget or bear a child); *Stanley v. Georgia,* 394 U.S. 557 (1969) (right to private use of obscene literature). See generally, Posner, *The Uncertain Protection of Privacy by the Supreme Court,* 1979 Sup. Ct. Rev. 173.

35. On the kinds of concerns that led to the adoption of the tenth amendment, see C. Kenyon, ed., THE ANTI-FEDERALISTS (Indianapolis: Bobbs-Merrill, 1966). On the present scope of national power with respect to the states, see, e.g., *Perez v. United States,* 402 U.S. 146 (1971); *United States v. Darby,* 312 U.S. 100 (1941); *Katzenbach v. McClung,* 379 U.S. 294 (1964). The suspicion with which the Court views state authority is especially evident in the expansion of federal judicial power at the expense of powers traditionally or textually reserved to the states. See, e.g., *Baker v. Carr,* 369 U.S. 186 (1962); *Elrod v. Burns,* 427 U.S. 347 (1976); *Griswold v. Connecticut,* 381 U.S. 479 (1965); *Roe v. Wade,* 410 U.S. 113 (1973); *Columbus Bd. of Educ. v. Penick,* 443 U.S. 449 (1979).

36. On the ambiguity of legal categories and their relation to change, see E. Levi, AN INTRODUCTION TO LEGAL REASONING (Chicago: University of Chicago Press, 1949).

37. In his study of the British Constitution, Albert Dicey used the word "convention" rather than "practice." A. Dicey, INTRODUCTION TO

THE STUDY OF THE LAW OF THE CONSTITUTION (7th ed.; London: Macmillan, 1908). Herbert Horwill, applying Dicey's idea to the American Constitution, employed the word "usage." H. Horwill, THE USAGES OF THE AMERICAN CONSTITUTION (London: Oxford University Press, 1925). I have chosen a different word to emphasize, as the British tradition does not, that behavior can define the written words of a constitution. For a different treatment of a similar theme, see C. Miller, supra note 4, at 128–42, 189–220.

38. *Minor v. Happersett*, 88 U.S. (21 Wall.) 162 (1875); *Forsyth v. Hammond*, 166 U.S. 506 (1897); *In re Duncan*, 139 U.S. 449 (1891).

39. As a rough measure, consider that in one year (1977), 13,113 civil rights cases were commenced in U.S. district courts. Between 1971 and 1977 the total was 63,227. JUDICIAL CONFERENCE OF THE UNITED STATES: REPORT OF THE PROCEEDINGS at 189 (1977).

40. Cf. T. Schelling, THE STRATEGY OF CONFLICT 73 (New York: Oxford University Press, 1963).

41. For a more comprehensive discussion, see Munro, *Law and Conventions Distinguished*, 91 L.Q. Rev. 218 (1975).

42. U.S. CONST. art. I, § 9; U.S. CONST. amend. XX, § 2.

43. U.S. CONST. art. II, § 1, para. 6; U.S. CONST. amend. XX, § 3; U.S. CONST. amend. XXV.

44. U.S. CONST. art. I, § 2, para. 5; U.S. CONST. art. I, § 3, para. 6; U.S. CONST. art. II, § 4.

45. L. Henkin, FOREIGN AFFAIRS AND THE CONSTITUTION 173–76 (Mineola, N.Y.: Foundation Press, 1972).

46. See H. Horwill, supra note 37, at 104–5.

47. For an analysis of the meaning of the ninth amendment, see Berger, *The Ninth Amendment*, 66 Cornell L. Rev. 1 (1980).

48. *United States v. Klein*, 80 U.S. (13 Wall.) 128 (1872).

49. *Flint v. Stone*, 220 U.S. 107 (1911).

50. Definition of a quorum: *United States v. Ballin*, 144 U.S. 1 (1892). Veto override: *Missouri Pac. Ry. Co. v. Kansas*, 248 U.S. 276 (1919). Presidential signature: *Gardner v. Collector*, 73 U.S. (6 Wall.) 499 (1868); *Lapeyere v. United States*, 84 U.S. (17 Wall.) 191 (1873); *La Abra Silver Mining Co. v. United States*, 175 U.S. 423 (1899); *Edwards v. United States*, 286 U.S. 482 (1932). Veto power: *The Pocket Veto Cases*, 279 U.S. 655 (1929).

51. Wechsler, *The Political Safeguards of Federalism: The Role of the States in the Composition and Selection of the National Government*, in A. MacMahon, ed., FEDERALISM, MATURE AND EMERGENT 97 (New York: Doubleday, 1955).

52. *National Mut. Ins. Co. v. Tidewater Transfer Co.*, 337 U.S. 582 (1949) (opinion by Frankfurter, J.).

53. R. Berger, GOVERNMENT BY JUDICIARY 193–200 (Cambridge: Harvard University Press, 1977).

54. See supra note 50.

55. Impairment of contracts clause: *Home Bldg. & Loan Assoc. v. Blaisdell,* 290 U.S. 398 (1934). Internment of Japanese-Americans: *Korematsu v. United States,* 323 U.S. 214 (1944).

56. Corwin, *Judicial Review in Action,* 74 U. Pa. L. Rev. 639, 659–60 (1926).

57. See H. Horwill, supra note 37, at 104–5.

58. Id. at 175–82.

59. For a complete description of the varying interpretations of the tenth amendment, see G. Gunther, CONSTITUTIONAL LAW CASES AND MATERIALS 195–211 (10th ed.; Mineola, N.Y.: Foundation Press, 1980). On the meaning of "jury," see *Williams v. Florida,* 399 U.S. 78 (1970); *Apodaca v. Oregon,* 406 U.S. 404 (1972); *Burch v. Louisiana,* 441 U.S. 130 (1979); *Ballew v. Georgia,* 435 U.S. 223 (1978). On "legislative powers," see, e.g., *Immigration and Naturalization Serv. v. Chadha,* 462 U.S. 919 (1983).

60. *Young v. Klutznick,* 497 F. Supp. 1318 (E.D. Mich. 1980).

61. See, e.g., *Boston v. Kentucky,* 106 S. Ct. 1712 (1986).

62. See U.S. CONST. art. I, § 2, para. 5; U.S. CONST. art. I, § 3; U.S. CONST. art. I, § 5.

63. *Powell v. McCormack,* 395 U.S. 486 (1969).

64. Id. at 521.

65. See supra note 1. See generally R. Berger, FEDERALISM: THE FOUNDERS' DESIGN 8–15 (Norman: University of Oklahoma Press, 1987).

66. This is a pervasive and complex theme, for example, in Henry James's THE GOLDEN BOWL (1904).

67. Cf. *Youngstown Sheet & Tube Co. v. Sawyer,* 343 U.S. 579, 593, 610–11 (1952) (Frankfurter, J., concurring). Justice Frankfurter proposed that "a systematic, unbroken, executive practice, long pursued to the knowledge of the Congress and never before questioned" might be treated as a gloss on "executive power" (id.). Frankfurter's position, consistent with the recommendation in this chapter, stops well short of placing undue pressure on every particular congressional decision. But it does suggest how even judicial deference to a practice might undercut the development of stable norms to the extent that the practice is thereby formalized into an explicit legal rule.

68. Compare the Court's treatment of the governmental interest in potential life in *Roe v. Wade,* 410 U.S. 113 (1973), with *Harris v. McRae,* 448 U.S. 297 (1980).

69. S. 158 97th Cong., 1st sess. (1980) ("The Human Life Bill") was introduced by Senator Jesse Helms in 1981.

70. *Gannett Co. v. DePasquale,* 443 U.S. 368 (1979).

71. *Richmond Newspapers, Inc. v. Virginia,* 448 U.S. 555, 565 (1980).

72. See *Richmond Newspapers, Inc. v. Virginia,* 448 U.S. 555, 602 n.2 (Blackmun, J., concurring).

73. See supra note 71.

74. For a general discussion of the characteristics of adjudicatory decision making, see D. Horowitz, THE COURTS AND SOCIAL POLICY 1–67 (Washington, D.C.: Brookings Institution, 1977).

75. E.g., *Carter v. Carter Coal Co.,* 298 U.S. 238 (1936).

76. E.g., Corwin, *National-State Cooperation—The Present Possibilities,* 46 Yale L.J. 599 (1937); Koenig, *Federal and State Cooperation Under the Constitution,* 36 Mich. L. Rev. 752 (1938).

77. E.g., M. Frankel, PARTISAN JUSTICE (New York: Hill & Wang, 1980). See also Langbein, *Land Without Plea Bargaining: How the Germans Do It,* 78 Mich. L. Rev. 204 (1979); Damaska, *Evidentiary Barriers to Conviction and Two Models of Criminal Procedure: A Comparative Study,* 121 U. Pa. L. Rev. 506 (1973).

78. E.g., Kaus, *Abolish the 5th Amendment,* Washington Monthly, December 1980, 12–19 (1980).

79. On the trend in judicial decisions, see *Immigration and Naturalization Serv. v. Chadha,* 462 U.S. 919 (1983); *Bowsher v. Synar,* 106 S. Ct. 3181 (1986). On the history of disfavor, see, e.g., W. Wilson, CONGRESSIONAL GOVERNMENT: A STUDY IN AMERICAN POLITICS (Boston: Houghton Mifflin, 1885); K. Lowenstein, POLITICAL POWER AND THE GOVERNMENTAL PROCESS (2d ed.; Chicago: University of Chicago Press, 1965).

80. For a description, see Chayes, *The Role of the Judge in Public Law Litigation,* 89 Harv. L. Rev. 1281 (1976).

81. *Elrod v. Burns,* 427 U.S. 347 (1976); *Branti v. Finkel,* 445 U.S. 507 (1980).

82. R. Dworkin, TAKING RIGHTS SERIOUSLY 143 (Cambridge: Harvard University Press, 1977).

83. For similar views, see Fiss, *The Forms of Justice,* 93 Harv. L. Rev. 1, 10–13 (1979); M. Shapiro, FREEDOM OF SPEECH: THE SUPREME COURT AND JUDICIAL REVIEW 30 (Englewood Cliffs, N.J.: Prentice-Hall, 1966); A. Bickel, THE SUPREME COURT AND THE IDEA OF PROGRESS 86 (New York: Harper & Row, 1970).

84. *Miranda v. Arizona,* 384 U.S. 436, 483–86 (1966).

85. See supra note 82.

86. The phrase is taken from Linde, *Judges, Critics, and the Realist Tradition,* 82 Yale L.J. 227, 230 (1972).

87. See Dahl, *Decision-Making in a Democracy: The Supreme Court as a National Policy-Maker,* 6 J. Pub. L. (1957).

88. J. Wilkinson, FROM BROWN TO BAKKE: THE SUPREME COURT

AND SCHOOL INTEGRATION, 1954–1978 (New York: Oxford University Press, 1979). See also Kurland, *"Brown v. Board of Education was the beginning": The School Desegregation Cases in the United States Supreme Court, 1954–79,* 1979 Wash. U.L.Q. 309.

89. Bickel's proposals were made in A. Bickel, THE LEAST DANGEROUS BRANCH (Indianapolis: Bobbs-Merrill, 1962). They were attacked in Gunther, *The Subtle Vices of the "Passive Virtues": A Comment on Principle and Expediency in Judicial Review,* 64 Colum. L. Rev. 1 (1964).

90. A. Bickel, supra note 83, at 99, 173–81; A. Bickel, supra note 89, at 68–72.

CHAPTER 3

1. 250 U.S. 616, 624 (1919) (Holmes & Brandeis, JJ., dissenting).

2. See Rabban, *The First Amendment in Its Forgotten Years,* 90 Yale L.J. 514 (1981).

3. See, e.g., *Fox v. Washington,* 236 U.S. 273 (1915); *Patterson v. Colorado,* 205 U.S. 454 (1907).

4. Rabban, supra note 2, at 559.

5. Patronage dismissals: see *Branti v. Finkel,* 445 U.S. 507 (1980); *Elrod v. Burns,* 427 U.S. 347 (1976). Campaign finances: see *Buckley v. Valeo,* 424 U.S. 1 (1976). Obscenity: see *Miller v. California,* 413 U.S. 15 (1973). Defamation: see *New York Times Co. v. Sullivan,* 376 U.S. 254 (1964); but see *Gertz v. Robert Welch, Inc.,* 418 U.S. 323 (1974). Billboards: see *Metromedia, Inc. v. City of San Diego,* 453 U.S. 490 (1981). Nude dancing: see *Schad v. Mount Ephraim,* 452 U.S. 61 (1981); *Doran v. Salem Inn, Inc.,* 422 U.S. 922 (1975); but cf. *New York State Liquor Auth. v. Bellanca,* 452 U.S. 714 (1981) (upholding New York state law prohibiting nude dancing in establishments licensed by state to sell liquor). Jacket patches: see *Cohen v. California,* 403 U.S. 15 (1971). License plates: see *Wooley v. Maynard,* 430 U.S. 705 (1977). Schoolchildren: see *Board of Educ. v. Pico,* 457 U.S. 853 (1982); *Tinker v. Des Moines Indep. Community School Dist.,* 393 U.S. 503 (1969). Prisoners: see *Procunier v. Martinez,* 416 U.S. 396 (1974). Corporations: see *First Nat'l Bank v. Bellotti,* 435 U.S. 765 (1978).

6. Probably the most influential article was Chafee, *Freedom of Speech in War Time,* 32 Harv. L. Rev. 932 (1919), which is discussed infra in the text related to notes 18–28. For an account of the influence of other scholars, see Rabban, supra note 2, at 559–79.

7. 250 U.S. 616, 630 (1919).

8. See id.: "The best test of truth is the power of the thought to get itself accepted in the competition of the market."

9. *New York Times Co. v. Sullivan,* 376 U.S. 254, 270 (1964).

10. *Richmond Newspapers, Inc. v. Virginia,* 448 U.S. 555, 576 (1980), quoting *First Nat'l Bank v. Bellotti,* 435 U.S. 765, 783 (1978) and *Branzburg v. Hayes,* 408 U.S. 665, 681 (1972).

11. *Elrod v. Burns,* 427 U.S. 347, 357 (1976); *Richmond Newspapers,* 448 U.S. at 576, quoting *Williams v. Rhodes,* 393 U.S. 23, 32 (1968).

12. *Branzburg v. Hayes,* 408 U.S. 665, 693 (1972).

13. *Miller v. California,* 413 U.S. 15, 35 (1973).

14. *Terminiello v. Chicago,* 337 U.S. 1, 4–5 (1949).

15. See, e.g., J. Higham, STRANGERS IN THE LAND: PATTERNS OF AMERICAN NATIVISM, 1860–1925 (New York: Atheneum, 1963). Higham, for example, traced anti-Catholic repression in part to a public perception that the Roman Catholic Church was authoritarian and thus a threat to "the concept of individual freedom imbedded in the national culture" (id. at 6). The resulting distrust of the church, when combined with economic and international uncertainties (see id. at 77–96, 194–233), often led to full-blown moods of repression against the church. Thus, devotion to liberty can itself be one of the ingredients of intolerance. On the other hand, enforced outward conformity can sometimes reduce the fears that might otherwise have led to serious repression. See infra note 168.

16. For a study that is unusually explicit in detailing how speculative most explanations for repressive periods are, see Hyman, *England and America: Climates of Tolerance and Intolerance—1962,* in D. Bell, ed., THE RADICAL RIGHT 227, 246–50 (Garden City, N.Y.: Doubleday, 1963). Educational levels: see S. Stouffer, COMMUNISM, CONFORMITY, AND CIVIL LIBERTIES: A CROSS-SECTION OF THE NATION SPEAKS ITS MIND 91 (Garden City, N.Y.: Doubleday, 1955). Methods of child-rearing: see id. at 97–99 (maintaining that parental attitudes toward child-rearing reflect parents' level of tolerance of nonconformists); see also T. Adorno, E. Frenkel-Brunswik, D. Levinson, and R. Sanford, THE AUTHORITARIAN PERSONALITY 337–89 (New York: Harper, 1950). Economic conditions: see J. Higham, supra note 15, at 77–96. International politics: see id. at 8, 194–263; E. Latham, THE COMMUNIST CONTROVERSY IN WASHINGTON: FROM THE NEW DEAL TO McCARTHY 393–94 (Cambridge: Harvard University Press, 1966); R. Murray, RED SCARE: A STUDY IN NATIONAL HYSTERIA, 1919–1920, at 12–15 (Minneapolis: University of Minnesota Press, 1955). Institutional rivalries: see E. Latham, supra, at 373–99, 416–23. National character: one prominent American trait is disinclination to defer to elites—see Hyman, supra, at 250. Social status: see D. Bell, THE END OF IDEOLOGY 101–2 (Glencoe, Ill.: Free Press, 1960); cf. D. Potter, FREEDOM AND ITS LIMITATIONS IN AMERICAN LIFE 46–48 (Stanford: Stanford University Press, 1976) (describing pressures for conformity as a function of social

status and desire for advancement). Weather: cf. R. Murray, supra, at 122 (describing how weather in the fall of 1919 exacerbated tensions between employers and labor).

17. See L. Hand, THE SPIRIT OF LIBERTY 189–90 (3d ed.; New York: Knopf, 1960):

> I often wonder whether we do not rest our hopes too much upon constitutions, upon laws and upon courts. These are false hopes; believe me, these are false hopes. Liberty lies in the hearts of men and women; when it dies there, no constitution, no law, no court can save it; no constitution, no law, no court can even do much to help it. While it lies there it needs no constitution, no law, no court to save it.

Although the passage is often dismissed as unnecessarily dismal and foreboding, it actually appears as part of an impassioned and lyrical patriotic speech that concludes: "In the spirit of liberty and of America I ask you to rise and with me pledge our faith in the glorious destiny of our beloved country" (id. at 191).

18. Chafee, supra note 6, at 960. *Schenck v. United States,* 249 U.S. 47 (1919).

19. See Chafee, supra note 6, at 946, 956, 958, 960.

20. Chafee elaborated on this suggested broad test of certain danger:

> Every reasonable attempt should be made to maintain [the] interests [in public safety and the search for truth] unimpaired, and the great interest in free speech should be sacrificed only when the interest in public safety is really imperiled, and not, as most men believe, when it is barely conceivable that it may be slightly affected. (id. at 960)

21. See, e.g., L. Levy, FREEDOM OF SPEECH AND PRESS IN EARLY AMERICAN HISTORY: LEGACY OF SUPPRESSION (New York: Harper & Row, 1963).

22. See, e.g., Rabban, supra note 2, at 586–94.

23. Chafee, supra note 6, at 933.

24. Id. at 934.

25. See id. at 935.

26. Id. at 944: "'The gradual process of judicial inclusion and exclusion,' which has served so well to define other clauses in the federal Constitution by blocking out concrete situations on each side of the line until the line itself becomes increasingly plain, has as yet been of very little use for the First Amendment."

27. See id. at 943–44.

28. Thus Chafee asserted:

> The problem of locating the boundary line of free speech is solved. It is fixed close to the point where words will give rise to unlawful acts. We cannot define the right of free speech with the precision of the Rule against Perpetuities

or the Rule in Shelley's Case, because it involves national policies which are much more flexible than private property, but we can establish a workable principle of classification in this method of balancing and this broad test of certain danger. (id. at 960)

29. T. Emerson, THE SYSTEM OF FREEDOM OF EXPRESSION 4–5 (New York: Random House, 1970).

30. Id. at 16.

31. Id. at 4.

32. "Those who warn us not to rely too much on legal forms are entirely correct that excessive emphasis can easily be placed upon the role of law" (id. at 5).

33. Id. See also id. at 11: "Because of certain characteristics of a system of free expression, the role of law is of particular significance in any social effort to maintain such a system."

34. See id. at 13.

35. Id. at 17. Although Emerson emphasized that these distinctions were to be drawn functionally, his discussion of the difference between "action" and "expression" illustrates his conceptual approach:

The line in many situations is clear. But at some points it becomes obscure. All expression has some physical element. Moreover, a communication may take place in a context of action, as in the familiar example of the false cry of "fire" in a crowded theater. Or, a communication may be closely linked to action, as in the gang leader's command to his triggerman. Or, the communication may have the same immediate impact as action, as in instances of publicly uttered obscenities. . . . In these cases it is necessary to decide, however artificial the distinction may appear to be, whether the conduct is to be classified as one or the other. (id. at 18)

36. A. Meiklejohn, POLITICAL FREEDOM 33 (New York: Harper, 1960).

37. Id. at 101 (responding to Justice Frankfurter's concurring opinion in *Dennis v. United States,* 341 U.S. 494, 517 [1951]).

38. A. Meiklejohn, supra note 36, at 51.

39. W. Berns, THE FIRST AMENDMENT AND THE FUTURE OF AMERICAN DEMOCRACY 232 (New York: Basic Books, 1976).

40. See id. at 200 (noting that the argument that law cannot distinguish between vulgarity and important speech is "almost jejune").

41. Id.

42. See id. at 195–96, 201, 204–5 passim. Berns argued that the framers intended to protect only decent and orderly speech. Once the Court returned to and accepted this view as to the kinds of speech that the first amendment should protect, Berns urged the Court to adhere more closely to precedent to preserve those values (id. at 233–34, 236).

43. See H. Commager, MAJORITY RULE AND MINORITY RIGHTS 46, 82 (New York: Oxford University Press, 1943). Commager at this stage in his career placed his faith in majority rule as the chief protector of civil liberties, arguing that "men need no masters—not even judges" (id. at 82).

44. See id. at 47–53. Id. at 55: "[The Court's record] discloses not a single case, in a century and a half, where the Supreme Court has protected freedom of speech . . . against congressional attack."

45. See H. Commager, FREEDOM AND ORDER 25–29 (New York: G. Braziller, 1966); quoted passage at 48.

46. Indeed, Commager maintained that "it is as an educational institution that the Court may have its greatest contribution to make to the understanding and preservation of liberty" (id. at 49).

47. See S. Krislov, THE SUPREME COURT AND POLITICAL FREEDOM 91, 220 (New York: Free Press, 1968).

48. See M. Shapiro, FREEDOM OF SPEECH: THE SUPREME COURT AND JUDICIAL REVIEW 103–4 (Englewood Cliffs, N.J.: Prentice-Hall, 1966).

49. See Bork, *Neutral Principles and Some First Amendment Problems*, 47 Ind. L.J. 1, 23 (1971). Bork argued that the "Smith Act cases of the 1950's" represent the ideas expounded in prior dissents and concurrences by Justices Holmes and Brandeis, opinions that suffer from "the considerable handicap of being deficient in logic and analysis as well as in history." He asserted that he was "looking for a theory [of freedom of speech] fit for enforcement by judges" (id.).

50. R. Jackson, THE SUPREME COURT IN THE AMERICAN SYSTEM OF GOVERNMENT 80 (Cambridge: Harvard University Press, 1955). He did qualify that suggestion, however, stating that "it is my belief that the attitude of a society and of its organized political forces, rather than its legal machinery, is the controlling force in the character of free institutions" (id. at 81).

51. L. Hand, THE BILL OF RIGHTS 69 (Cambridge: Harvard University Press, 1958).

52. Different theorists, of course, think that maintaining the amount and variety of information in the system is relevant to different objectives. Emerson, for example, believes that a system of free expression serves four separate but interrelated values: individual self-fulfillment, discovering truth, allowing for participation in decision making, and achieving a more adaptable and therefore stable community. See T. Emerson, supra note 29, at 6, 7. A number of theorists emphasize the protection of the democratic decision-making process. See, e.g., W. Berns, supra note 39, at 233; J. Ely, DEMOCRACY AND DISTRUST, ch. 5 (Cambridge: Harvard University Press, 1980); A. Meiklejohn, supra note 36, at 33;

M. Shapiro, supra note 48; Bork, supra note 49. See also Blasi, *The Checking Value in First Amendment Theory*, 1977 Am. B. Found. Research J. 521. Martin Redish centers the justification on the value of "individual self-realization." Redish, *The Value of Free Speech*, 130 U. Pa. L. Rev. 591, 593 (1982).

53. J. Ely, supra note 52, at 105. Similarly, Michael Perry stated that modern freedom of expression cases have "served, on balance, as . . . instrument[s] of moral growth." Asserting that these cases have not been the "focus of significant controversy," Perry stated that "only a few persons . . . upon surveying the broad features of the Court's work product . . . would today take issue with much of what the Court has done." Perry, *Noninterpretive Review in Human Rights Cases: A Functional Justification*, 56 N.Y.U. L. Rev. 278, 314–15 (1981). Perhaps by "persons" Perry intended to exclude anyone not a law professor.

54. See, e.g., T. Emerson, supra note 29, at 13: "[The courts'] competence to . . . [maintain our system of freedom of expression] rests upon their . . . relative immunity to immediate political and popular pressures." But see Richardson, *Freedom of Expression and the Function of Courts*, 65 Harv. L. Rev. 1, 54 (1951): "The great battles for free expression will be won . . . not in the courts but in committee rooms and protest-meetings, by editorials and letters to Congress. . . . The proper function of courts is narrow."

55. T. Emerson, supra note 29, at 9.

56. Id. at 10–11.

57. See id. at 11.

58. Id. at 14.

59. This seems likely, although Emerson did purport to base his fears on "the lesson of experience." See id. at 11.

60. See id. at 10. Emerson further observed that "such exceptions must be clear-cut, precise and readily controlled. Otherwise the forces that press toward restriction will break through the openings, and freedom of expression will become the exception and suppression the rule."

61. See infra text related to notes 77–78. It is, of course, easy to dismiss those who are willing to recognize the occasionally heavy costs of protecting speech on the grounds that they have not fully analyzed the problem or have neglected to consider some long-term policy considerations. Thus Emerson wrote:

> The longer-run logic of the traditional [free speech] theory may not be immediately apparent to untutored participants in the conflict. Suppression of opinion may thus seem an entirely plausible course of action; tolerance a weakness or a foolish risk.
> Thus it is clear that the problem of maintaining a system of freedom of expression . . . is one of the most complex any society has to face. Self-

restraint, self-discipline, and maturity are required. The theory is essentially a highly sophisticated one. (id. at 9–10)

62. J. Randall commented:

The exercise of this form of newspaper control [the arrest of editors], how-ever, was usually unfortunate. The more prominent the editor, the greater was the newspaper's gain in prestige in the eyes of its readers and sympathizers because of the martyr's pose which the editor invariably assumed. When, for example, F. Key Howard, editor of the *Baltimore Exchange,* was arrested and confined in Fort Lafayette and elsewhere, he sent a vigorous letter to the Sec-retary of War demanding instant and unconditional release. He stood his ground heroically and demanded, not pardon, but vindication. He refused to appear before an "irresponsible tribunal," and would not seal his lips to obtain discharge. The paper continued publication for a time while its editor and proprietor were in prison, and the net result was simply to afford this journal a more conspicuous rostrum from which to hurl its anathemas against the Gov-ernment. On the morrow of Howard's arrest the *Exchange* declared in an in-dignant editorial that the unrestricted right of the press to discuss and con-demn the war policy of the Government is identical with the freedom of the people to do the same thing, and thus the trumpet blasts for journalistic free-dom were added to the general chorus of anti-war sentiment. (CONSTITU-TIONAL PROBLEMS UNDER LINCOLN 503–4 [Gloucester: P. Smith, 1963])

63. R. Murray, supra note 16, at 26.

64. See, e.g., R. Brown, LOYALTY AND SECURITY: EMPLOYMENT TESTS IN THE UNITED STATES 475–76 (New Haven: Yale University Press, 1958): "Our current experience with loyalty oaths shows once again that those who refuse to subscribe to them are more often than not people of stout conscience whom we should cherish rather than punish." See also id. at 95, detailing lack of evidence that any of the University of California faculty members dismissed for refusing to submit to loyalty oaths were communists.

65. For other examples, see infra note 70.

66. Act of June 25, 1798, ch. 58, 1 Stat. 570.

The severity of the Sedition Law failed to prevent the "overthrow" of the Adams administration by the Jeffersonian "disorganizers." Indeed, the law furnished a ready text which the Democratic-Republicans used to incite the American people to legal "insurgency" at the polls; the election resulted in the repudiation of the party which tried to protect itself behind the Sedition Law. It elevated to power a party whose leaders stressed the concept that freedom of opinion is an essential part of an all-encompassing freedom of the mind. (J. Smith, FREEDOM'S FETTERS: THE ALIEN AND SEDITION LAWS AND AMERICAN CIVIL LIBERTIES 431 [Ithaca: Cornell University Press, 1956])

67. Efforts at news suppression during the war included government control and censorship over the telegraph lines from Washington, D.C.,

which, in turn, led to the excision of comments representing the opinions of writers and news reports addressing diplomatic issues and criticizing cabinet officers (see J. Randall, supra note 62, at 482–83); prosecutions under the military code against anyone "holding correspondence with, or giving intelligence to, the enemy, either directly or indirectly" (id. at 490); numerous instances of the military suspending publication of specific newspapers (id. at 492–93); seizure of particular editions and blanket prohibitions against circulating particular papers (id. at 499–500); and arrest of editors (id. at 502).

Despite these efforts at suppression, the press continued to relay effective news and opinions to the public. Randall describes the period as one "of remarkable activity in journalistic enterprise" (id. at 484). Not only criticism but also specific military plans were widely publicized (id. at 484–85, 489, 508, 521).

68. See J. Higham, supra note 15, at 232–33; R. Murray, supra note 16, at 239, 242–44.

69. Here again, the mood of suppression proved self-limiting because its excesses engendered effective opposition. See E. Latham, supra note 16, at 358–59; A. Theoharis, SEEDS OF REPRESSIONS: HARRY S. TRUMAN AND THE ORIGINS OF MCCARTHYISM 182–92 (Chicago: Quadrangle Books, 1971).

70. Another period of serious repression was the prolonged effort to suppress antislavery sentiment in the South before the Civil War. Beginning in earnest after Nat Turner's insurrection in 1831, these efforts consisted of a variety of censorship devices, often buttressed by mob action. See generally H. Hyman and W. Wiecek, EQUAL JUSTICE UNDER LAW: CONSTITUTIONAL DEVELOPMENT, 1835–1875, at 91–92 (New York: Harper & Row, 1982); R. Nye, FETTERED FREEDOM: CIVIL LIBERTIES AND THE SLAVERY CONTROVERSY, 1830–1880, at 153 passim (East Lansing: Michigan State University Press, 1963). See also Nye at 176:

> Though these statutes served to hamper free expression of antislavery opinion in the South, they did not fully suppress it. Most of the laws dealt out punishment for "incendiary" talk, or "opinions tending to incite insurrection,"—terms vaguely defined and charges difficult to establish—a fact recognized by Southern courts, whose verdicts were usually lenient. Legal processes were often slow, loopholes could be found.

In the North the effect was to bolster the abolitionists' position by allying their cause with the "firm moral ground" of free speech (R. Nye, supra at 215).

> The abolitionists . . . were the martyrs, the oppressed and persecuted, the defenders of free speech and free criticism. When the abolitionists emerged as guardians of white liberties . . . their cause gained immeasurably in moral

> strength. The influence of the era of mob violence . . . was a significant factor
> in cementing support in the North for the antislavery movement. (id. at 218)

Efforts to "gag" debate in Congress over slavery as well as efforts in the
South to block the distribution of antislavery mail had similar perverse
results, legitimizing and strengthening the antislavery movement. See id.
at 41–85. See also H. Hyman and W. Wiecek, supra, at 118–19; infra
note 169.

71. See generally Wellington, *On Freedom of Expression,* 88 Yale L.J.
1105 (1979) (absence of empirical evidence makes it difficult to determine whether increased protection of defamatory speech has contributed
to a more efficient political process); supra text related to notes 9–11;
infra note 79. The lack of empirical substantiation is evident in the opinions. See, e.g., *Elrod v. Burns,* 427 U.S. 347, 359 (1976); *New York Times
Co. v. Sullivan,* 376 U.S. 254, 279 (1964).

72. This problem was given sensitive treatment in H. Kalven, THE
NEGRO AND THE FIRST AMENDMENT 132–35 (Columbus: Ohio State
University Press, 1965). See also id. at 135 (making analogous comparison between protecting civil rights protestors but not labor union
members).

73. See, e.g., Kurland, *The Irrelevance of the Constitution: The First
Amendment's Freedom of Speech and Freedom of Press Clauses,* 29 Drake L.
Rev. 1 (1979).

74. Cf. H. Kalven, supra note 72, at 133 (permitting civil rights protest gives black community powerful communicative resource it might not
otherwise have).

75. See id. at 165–66.

76. Cf. M. Shapiro, supra note 48, at 111–15 (concept of preferred
position for speech is a statement about interests court should represent
and should not be understood as a ranking of values); Black, *Mr. Justice
Black, the Supreme Court, and the Bill of Rights,* Harper's, February 1961,
at 63, 66–68 (emphasizing increase in personal freedom that would result from absolutist view of first amendment).

77. T. Emerson, supra note 29, at 17.

78. Id. at 12.

79. In *New York Times Co. v. Sullivan,* for example, the Court's entire
support for enunciating the new defamation doctrine was contained in
one paragraph:

> Allowance of the defense of truth, with the burden of proving it on the defen-
> dant, does not mean that only false speech will be deterred. Even courts ac-
> cepting this defense as an adequate safeguard have recognized the difficulties
> of adducing legal proofs that the alleged libel was true. . . . Under such a rule,
> would-be critics of official conduct *may be deterred* from voicing their criti-
> cism . . . because of doubt whether it can be proved in court or fear of the

expense of having to do so. . . . The rule *thus dampens* the vigor and limits the variety of public debate. (376 U.S. 254, 279 [1964] [footnotes and citations omitted; emphasis added])

In short, the Court moved from a plausible hypothesis to a firm certainty without reference to any evidence other than previous judicial pronouncements.

80. See *Village of Skokie v. National Socialist Party of Am.*, 69 Ill. 2d 605, 373 N.E. 2d 21 (1978). This decision was made in a timely fashion after the Supreme Court ordered the village to grant an expedited review or face dissolution of the injunction prohibiting the march. See *National Socialist Party of Am. v. Village of Skokie*, 432 U.S. 43 (1977) (per curiam).

81. See *Schad v. Borough of Mt. Ephraim*, 452 U.S. 61, 73–76 (1981) (because first amendment protects nonobscene, live nude dancing, municipality must justify as reasonable any restriction).

82. See supra note 61; infra note 110. Indeed, one prominent scholar dismissed as a "bizarre proposition" the idea that the public's understanding of rights like the freedom of speech might be relevant to the proper legal definition of those rights. See R. Dworkin, TAKING RIGHTS SERIOUSLY 146 (Cambridge: Harvard University Press, 1978).

83. See *New York v. Ferber*, 456 U.S. 962 (1982) (dictum) (New York statute did not prohibit enough nonobscene material to merit striking it down on overbreadth grounds).

84. See *Richmond Newspapers, Inc. v. Virginia*, 448 U.S. 555, 581 (1980) (dictum).

85. See infra note 111.

86. See J. Randall, supra note 62, at 518–19.

87. See id. at 515–22. The pattern of suppression during the Civil War was in sharp contrast with that which accompanied World War I and the beginnings of active judicial protections of freedom of speech. The suppression accompanying World War I resulted from statutes and judicial enforcement rather than from executive decrees and military actions. See id. at 524–28.

88. 372 U.S. 539 (1963). The Court's explanations, however, have been remarkably general. See, e.g., *NAACP v. Alabama*, 357 U.S. 449, 460 (1958). For efforts to provide a fuller rationale for the judicial doctrines, see Emerson, *Freedom of Association and Freedom of Expression*, 74 Yale L.J. 1 (1964); Raggi, *An Independent Right to Freedom of Association*, 12 Harv. C.R.–C.L.L. Rev. 1, 2–11 (1977).

89. 372 U.S. at 544, quoting *NAACP v. Alabama*, 357 U.S. 449, 462 (1958).

90. The Court did, however, strain to show "the utter failure [of the state] to demonstrate the existence of any substantial relationship between the N.A.A.C.P. and subversive or Communist activities" (372

U.S. at 554–55). The Court could not find sufficient justification for burdening associational rights in the absence of "any indication of present subversive infiltration" (id. at 555). Thus, the Court implied that the government's interest would have sufficed if a substantial basis for suspecting communist infiltration had existed.

91. See id. at 584–85 (White, J., dissenting), discussing *Graham v. Florida Legislative Investigation Comm.*, 126 So. 2d 133, 134–35 (Fla. 1960).

92. See 372 U.S. at 548 n.3. See also *NAACP v. Alabama*, 357 U.S. 449, 462–63 (1958).

93. Justice Harlan argued in dissent that the Court, in effect, required "an investigating agency to prove in advance the very things it is trying to find out" (372 U.S. at 580). To the extent that parts of the majority's opinion reflected the Court's judgment that communists had not actually infiltrated the NAACP (see id. at 554), the Court was simply prejudging an issue made complicated not only by some evidence of infiltration but also by the nature of clandestine infiltration itself (see id. at 583 [White, J., dissenting]). The Court's holding ultimately was based on its judgment that the legislative committee had not laid an adequate foundation demonstrating that communists had infiltrated the NAACP (see id. at 557).

94. See id.

95. Justice Douglas, for example, expressed concern about forcing information "upon an audience incapable of declining to receive it" (*Lehman v. City of Shaker Heights*, 418 U.S. 298, 307 [1974] [Douglas, J., concurring]).

96. See Wellington, supra note 71, at 1119.

97. See *Lehman v. City of Shaker Heights*, 418 U.S. 298, 304 (1974).

98. See *Red Lion Broadcasting Co. v. FCC*, 395 U.S. 367, 390 (1969).

99. See *Gertz v. Robert Welch, Inc.*, 418 U.S. 323, 369 (1974) (White, J., dissenting).

100. Martin Shapiro commented that "Justice Black's opinions get anthologized and Justice Frankfurter's get explained" (M. Shapiro, supra note 48, at 109).

101. 403 U.S. 15 (1971).

102. See id. at 18.

103. See id. at 18–19.

104. See id. at 19–24 (citation omitted).

105. See id. at 24–25.

106. T. Emerson, supra note 29, at 10.

107. 403 U.S. at 27 (Blackmun, J., dissenting).

108. Nudity on outdoor movie screen: see *Erznoznik v. City of Jacksonville*, 422 U.S. 205 (1975). Noncommercial billboards: see *Metromedia, Inc. v. City of San Diego*, 453 U.S. 490 (1981). Obscene dancing:

Miller v. California, 413 U.S. 15, 24–25 (1973). Nude dancing apparently is a protected activity (see supra note 5), but only if it does not violate the obscenity standard set forth in *Miller.*

109. See S. Stouffer, supra note 16, at 39–47, 78–79.

110. See supra note 61. Thus, Stouffer took a benign view of American attitudes toward civil liberties:

> Many of them . . . are simply drawing quite normal and logical inferences from premises which are false because the information on which the premises are based is false. They have not been as yet sufficiently motivated by responsible leaders . . . to give "sober second thought" to the broader and long-range consequences of specific limitations of freedom. (S. Stouffer, supra note 16, at 223)

The idea that the public is unable to understand or appreciate the principle of free speech is often reflected in a denigration of the purposes underlying short-term suppressions. When, for example, the Court justified the FCC sanctions imposed on stations airing George Carlin's "Filthy Words" monologue as an effort to protect unwilling listeners and their children from offensive intrusions (see *FCC v. Pacifica Found.,* 438 U.S. 726, 748–50 [1978]), Justice Brennan dissented, asserting that the majority's professed reliance on these objectives did not reflect the actual reasons for approving the rule: "In this context, the Court's decision may be seen for what . . . it really is: another of the dominant culture's inevitable efforts to force those groups who do not share its mores to conform to its way of thinking, acting, and speaking" (438 U.S. at 777 [Brennan, J., dissenting] [citation omitted]).

111. See H. Kalven, supra note 72, at 15–16. The Sedition Act of 1798, Act of June 25, 1798, ch. 58, 1 Stat. 570, led to some prosecutions but to no Supreme Court decisions. It expired two years after enactment—§ 6 of the Act provided that it would expire at the end of two years—and President Jefferson pardoned those who had been convicted. See H. Kalven, supra, at 17–18. The next opportunity to deal with seditious libel did not occur until the Sedition Act of 1918, and Kalven asserted that the Court did not directly confront the issue until 1964 (see id. at 17).

112. *New York Times Co. v. Sullivan,* 376 U.S. 254 (1964). See H. Kalven, supra note 72, at 17. Although Kalven did not state expressly that he believed this case was the proper occasion, it is clear that that was his belief given his reference to March 1964—the date of the decision in the case—as the proper occasion. Even if *Sullivan* was the proper occasion, the Court certainly failed to avail itself fully of the opportunity; its opinion in some respects went far beyond what was necessary to deal with seditious libel and in other respects did not altogether prohibit that form of repression. See H. Kalven, supra note 72, at 53–64.

113. *New York Times Co. v. United States,* 403 U.S. 713 (1971) (per curiam).

114. See, for example, Justice Stewart's concurring opinion in the *Pentagon Papers* case, in which he stated that the Court should have considered the need for secrecy in foreign affairs (*New York Times Co. v. United States,* 403 U.S. 713, 728 [1971] [Stewart, J., concurring]). Even so, Justice Stewart voted against allowing the government to suppress publication of the papers on the facts of the case stating that "I cannot say that disclosure of any of [the Pentagon Papers] will surely result in direct, immediate, and irreparable damage to our Nation or its people" (id. at 730). Absence of authorizing legislation: see id. at 732 (White, J., concurring). Failure of the president to act without the aid of the judiciary: see id. at 730 (Stewart, J., concurring). Although Stewart observed that the judiciary should act in conjunction with the executive branch in certain situations, he did not find this to be one of them.

115. 403 U.S. at 762 (Blackmun, J., dissenting), quoting with approval the dissenting opinion of Judge Wilkey in *United States v. The Washington Post Co.,* 446 F. 2d 1327, 1329 (D.C. Cir. 1971) (Wilkey, J., dissenting in part, concurring in part).

116. Even the argument made by the *New York Times* before the Court was notably short of a ringing endorsement for freedom of the press:

JUSTICE STEWART:

Q. Mr. Bickel, it is understandably and inevitably true that in a case like this, particularly when so many of the facts are under seal, it is necessary to speak in abstract terms, but let me give you a hypothetical case. Let us assume that when the members of the Court go back and open up this sealed record we find something that absolutely convinces us that its disclosure would result in the sentencing to death of 100 young men whose only offense had been that they were 19 years old and had low draft numbers. What should we do?

A. Mr. Justice, I wish there were a statute that covered it.

Q. Well there is not. We agree, or you submit, and I am asking in this case what should we do. . . .

A. No, sir, but I meant it is a case in which the chain of causation between the act of publication and the feared event, the death of these 100 young men, is obvious, direct, immediate.

Q. That is what I am assuming in my hypothetical case.

A. I would only say as to that that it is a case in which in the absence of a statute, I suppose most of us would say—

Q. You would say the Constitution requires that it be published, and that these men die, is that it?

A. No, I am afraid that my inclinations to humanity overcome the somewhat more abstract devotion to the First Amendment in a case of that sort. . . .

Q. I get a feeling from what you have said, although you have not addressed yourself directly to it, that you do not weigh heavily or think that the courts should weigh heavily the impairment of sources of information, either diplomatic or military intelligence sources. I get the impression that you would not consider that enough to warrant an injunction.

A. In the circumstances of this case, Mr. Justice, I think, or I am perfectly clear in my mind, that the President, without statutory authority, no statutory basis, goes into court, asks an injunction on that basis, that if Youngstown Sheet and Tube Co. v. Sawyer means anything, he does not get it. Under a statute, we don't face it in this case, and I don't really know. I would have to face that if I saw it. If I saw the statute, if I saw how definite it was—

JUSTICE DOUGLAS:

Q. Why would the statute make a difference, because the First Amendment provides that Congress shall make no law abridging freedom of the press. Do you read that to mean that Congress could make some laws abridging freedom of the press?

A. No, sir. Only in that I have conceded, for purposes of this argument, that some limitations, some impairment of the absoluteness of that prohibition is possible, and I argue that, whatever that may be, it is surely at its very least when the President acts without statutory authority because that inserts into it, as well—

Q. That is a very strange argument for The Times to be making.

> (*Transcript of Oral Argument in Times and Post Cases Before the Supreme Court,* New York Times, June 27, 1971, § 1, at 25, col. 4 [transcript of oral argument by Alexander M. Bickel], reprinted in J. Goodale, ed., 2 THE NEW YORK TIMES V. UNITED STATES: A DOCUMENTARY HISTORY 1226 [New York: Arno Press, 1971])

117. The dissenters were particularly concerned about the hurried procedures through which the case came before the Court. See 403 U.S. at 748 (Burger, C.J., dissenting); id. at 752 (Harlan, J., dissenting); id. at 759 (Blackmun, J., dissenting).

118. See *Richmond Newspapers, Inc. v. Virginia,* 448 U.S. 555 (1980). Although the Court specifically stated that "overriding considerations" might justify some exceptions, it did not specify the situations in which an exception would be appropriate (id. at 581 n.18).

119. 403 U.S. at 25.

120. T. Emerson, supra note 29, at 10 (emphasis added).

121. The Court's decisions in *Gitlow v. New York,* 268 U.S. 652 (1925) and *Dennis v. United States,* 341 U.S. 494 (1951) are representative of the Court's attempt to avoid the potentially dangerous result of absolutely principled application of the doctrine.

122. This concern underlies much of the dissatisfaction with cases

like *Gitlow* and *Dennis*. For a delineation of the complex judgments underlying the apparently "hard" test, see P. Freund, ON UNDERSTANDING THE SUPREME COURT 27 (Boston: Little, Brown, 1951).

123. The Court apparently took this position in *Valentine v. Chrestensen*, 316 U.S. 52 (1942).

124. The Court has observed that a consumer's interest in the free flow of commercial information "may be as keen, if not keener by far, than his interest in the day's most urgent political debate" (*Virginia State Bd. of Pharmacy v. Virginia Citizens Consumer Council*, 425 U.S. 748, 763 [1976]).

125. See *Metromedia, Inc. v. City of San Diego*, 453 U.S. 490 (1981) (invalidating as unconstitutional under first amendment San Diego's ban on billboards).

126. See *Miller v. California*, 413 U.S. 15 (1973).

127. See Van Alstyne, *A Graphic Review of the Free Speech Clause*, 70 Calif. L. Rev. 107 (1981).

128. See *Erznoznik v. City of Jacksonville*, 422 U.S. 205 (1975).

129. Libraries: see *Board of Educ. v. Pico*, 457 U.S. 853, 871–72 (1982). Theaters: see *Southeastern Promotions, Ltd. v. Conrad*, 420 U.S. 546 (1975).

130. *New York Times Co. v. Sullivan*, 376 U.S. 254, 271–72 (1964): "Authoritative interpretations of the First Amendment . . . have consistently refused to recognize an exception for any test of truth. . . . Erroneous statement is inevitable in free debate, and . . . it must be protected if the freedoms of expression are to have the 'breathing space' that they 'need . . . to survive'" (quoting *NAACP v. Button*, 371 U.S. 415, 433 [1963]). More recently, the Court has said: "There is no constitutional value in false statements in fact. . . . [Nevertheless,] the First Amendment requires that we protect some falsehood in order to protect speech that matters" (*Gertz v. Robert Welch, Inc.*, 418 U.S. 323, 340–41 [1974]).

When the Court approved a zoning ordinance designed to disperse motion picture theaters that showed sexually explicit "adult" movies, the plurality's efforts to take note of the kind of movies subject to the regulation elicited portentious reminders of the standard judicial wisdom:

> The fact that the "offensive" speech here may not address "important" topics . . . does not mean that it is less worthy of constitutional protection. . . .
> . . . Much speech that seems to be of little or no value will enter the marketplace of ideas, threatening the quality of our social discourse and, more generally, the serenity of our lives. But that is the price to be paid for constitutional freedom. (*Young v. American Mini Theatres, Inc.*, 427 U.S. 50, 87–88 [1976] [Stewart, J., dissenting])

At times, some Justices have become so entranced with the idea that it is dangerous for a court to try to distinguish the useful from the useless that they appear to believe that it is an impossible task. Thus, Justice Brennan defended a radio broadcast of George Carlin's long monologue of "filthy words" on the ground that "some parents may actually find Mr. Carlin's unabashed attitude toward the seven 'dirty words' healthy. . . . It is only an acute ethnocentric myopia that enables the Court to approve the censorship" (*FCC v. Pacifica Found.*, 438 U.S. 726, 770, 775 [1978] [Brennan, J., dissenting]). The monologue is funny and for some it may be useful; nevertheless, it is possible to evaluate its overall worth negatively without being ethnocentric.

131. For an argument that "the law should teach civility," see W. Berns, supra note 39, at 201.

132. See id.

133. Libraries: see *Board of Educ. v. Pico*, 457 U.S. 853, 871–72 (1982). Theaters: see *Southeastern Promotions v. Conrad*, 420 U.S. 546, 561 (1975).

134. The current standard permits governments to regulate or prohibit any works that "taken as a whole, appeal to the prurient interest in sex, which portray sexual conduct in a patently offensive way, and which, taken as a whole, do not have serious literary, artistic, political, or scientific value" (*Miller v. California*, 413 U.S. 15, 24 [1973]). For an account of the different obscenity standards applied by individual Justices, see B. Woodward and S. Armstrong, THE BRETHREN: INSIDE THE SUPREME COURT 192–204 (New York: Simon & Schuster, 1979).

135. See *New York v. Ferber*, 102 S. Ct. 3348 (1982).

136. Examples of this category include "adult movies" (see *Young v. American Mini Theatres, Inc.*, 427 U.S. 50 [1976]) and an extended radio monologue entitled "Filthy Words" (see *FCC v. Pacifica Found.*, 438 U.S. 726 [1978]).

137. L. Bollinger, THE TOLERANT SOCIETY (New York: Oxford University Press, 1986).

138. For example, Bollinger argues that there is symbolic clarity in extraordinary efforts in a discrete and concrete area (id. at 123–25) and communicative potential in the literary abilities of at least some of the great jurists (id. at 213). Moreover, he notes that judges can speak in relative unison and that some of their professional norms involve appreciation for tolerance (id. at 134–35). He also observes, "In this society the terminology of 'rights' sometimes seems to perform . . . [the] psychological function of providing an automatic, and socially accepted, way of separating oneself from the acts of others, which is usually an important predicate for tolerance" (id. at 168; see also id. at 135, 200).

139. Id. at 233.

140. At my university, for example, protests have been mounted against CIA recruiting. In one instance, negotiations between the police and protest leaders resulted in a system for facilitating orderly arrests: "As

police stood at the door of a bus, protesters filed toward them, crossed a line to be arrested, [and] were hauled off" (Boulder Daily Camera, November 19, 1985, at 1A). This method was decided upon because, although the "demonstrators wanted to make their point by getting arrested in large numbers with news reporters and photographers on hand," for several hours the police would make no arrests. A year later, a planner of a protest on the same issue commented, "The little game the protesters played with the police [last year] minimized the significance of our stance" (Boulder Daily Camera, November 13, 1986, at 1C).

141. To take two prominent examples: The Court said in 1964 that "vehement, caustic" and "erroneous" statements must be protected from the danger of self-censorship in order to ensure adequate democratic accountability (*New York Times Co. v. Sullivan,* 376 U.S. 254, 270–72 [1964]). Some years later, it suggested that in principle suppression of "one particular scurrilous epithet" threatened the creation of "a more capable citizenry and more perfect polity" (*Cohen v. California,* 403 U.S. 15, 22–24 [1971]). Bollinger discusses both cases. L. Bollinger, supra note 137, at 34, 48–50, 170–72.

142. L. Bollinger, supra note 137, at 222–23, 245.

143. Id. at 191.

144. Id. at 192–93, 247.

145. See Gibson, *Literary Minds and Judicial Style,* 36 N.Y.U. L. Rev. 915 (1961).

146. L. Bollinger, supra note 137, at 235.

147. Id. at 195.

148. Bollinger provides some evidence. See id. at 29, 235. Other evidence, if any is needed, can be found in Gibson, supra note 145, at 916.

149. L. Bollinger, supra note 137, at 222.

150. Id. at 235.

151. See, e.g., T. Emerson, supra note 29, at 13–14. For a recent variation on the theme, see Perry, supra note 53, at 295–96, 314–15. For a similar but more cautious view, see J. Ely, supra note 52, at 107, 112.

152. *Newberg Area Council, Inc. v. Board of Educ.,* nos. 7045, 7291 (W.D. Ky., September 6, 1975) (interim order). Similarly, in Boston, Judge Arthur Garrity issued an order that, in addition to prohibiting racial slurs and epithets, also prohibited

all gatherings of three or more people and all violent conduct, noise audible within the school, picketing, signs or other conduct likely to disturb classes, within 100 yards of any public school building in South Boston and within 50 yards of any other public high school or middle school building elsewhere in the City of Boston at any time between 7:00 A.M. and 4:00 P.M. on a school day; and . . . all gatherings of three or more people engaged in or threatening to engage in violent conduct on or along any route used to transport students into or out of South Boston between 7:00 and 9:30 A.M. and between 1:00 and 4:00 P.M. on a school day and at any other time when such routes are used. (*Morgan v. Kerrigan*, no. 72-911-G [D. Mass., December 17, 1974] [order on motion for relief concerning security])

Although most orders are more general, they are potentially no less chilling on the exercise of freedom of speech. See, e.g., *Kasper v. Brittian*, 245 F. 2d 92, 94 (6th Cir. 1957) (prohibiting all persons from in any way interfering with carrying out of court's orders); *Mims v. Duval County School Bd.*, 338 F. Supp. 1208 (M.D. Fla. 1971) (prohibiting anyone from disrupting operations of schools); *Stell v. Board of Educ.*, no. 1316 (S.D. Ga., March 16, 1972) (order prohibiting interference with plan of desegregation). See generally Comment, *Community Resistance to School Desegregation: Enjoining the Undefinable Class*, 44 U. Chi. L. Rev. 111 (1976).

153. See Landau, *Fair Trial and Free Press: A Due Process Proposal*, 62 A.B.A. J. 55, 57 (1976); and *Court Watch Summary*, 5 News Media and the Law, June–July 1981, at 53.

154. See J. Randall, supra note 62, at 506–7.

155. See, e.g., *Dennis v. United States*, 341 U.S. 494 (1951); *Whitney v. California*, 274 U.S. 357 (1927); *Gitlow v. New York*, 268 U.S. 652 (1925); *Abrams v. United States*, 250 U.S. 616 (1919); *Debs v. United States*, 249 U.S. 211 (1919); *Schenck v. United States*, 249 U.S. 47 (1919).

156. See supra text related to notes 66–69.

157. See, e.g., Rabban, supra note 2.

158. The dissents of Justices Holmes and Black are of particular note. See, e.g., *Communist Party v. Subversive Activities Control Bd.*, 367 U.S. 1, 137 (1961) (Black, J., dissenting); *Dennis v. United States*, 341 U.S. 494, 579 (1951) (Black, J., dissenting); *American Communications Ass'n v. Douds*, 339 U.S. 382, 445 (1950) (Black, J., dissenting); *Gitlow v. New York*, 268 U.S. 652, 672 (1925) (Holmes, J., dissenting); *Abrams v. United States*, 250 U.S. 616, 624 (1919) (Holmes, J., dissenting).

159. See, e.g., *New York v. Ferber*, 102 S. Ct. 3348 (1982); *Gannett Co. v. DePasquale*, 443 U.S. 368 (1979); *FCC v. Pacifica Found.*, 438 U.S. 726 (1978); *Zurcher v. Stanford Daily*, 436 U.S. 547 (1978); *Ohralik v. Ohio State Bar Ass'n*, 436 U.S. 447 (1978); *Jones v. North Carolina Prisoners' Labor Union, Inc.*, 433 U.S. 119 (1977); *Hudgens v. NLRB*, 424 U.S. 507 (1976); *Young v. American Mini Theatres, Inc.*, 427 U.S. 50 (1976); *Buckley v. Valeo*, 424 U.S. 1 (1976); *Pell v. Procunier*, 417 U.S. 817 (1974); *Lehman v. City of Shaker Heights*, 418 U.S. 298 (1974); *Pittsburgh Press Co. v. Pittsburgh Comm'n on Human Relations*, 413 U.S. 376 (1973); *Paris Adult Theatre I v. Slaton*, 413 U.S. 49 (1973); *Miller v. California*, 413 U.S. 15 (1973); *Branzburg v. Hayes*, 408 U.S. 665 (1972); *Laird v. Tatum*, 408 U.S. 1 (1972); *Law Student Civil Rights*

Research Council, Inc. v. Wadmond, 401 U.S. 154 (1971); *Red Lion Broadcasting Co. v. FCC*, 395 U.S. 367 (1969); *United States v. O'Brien*, 391 U.S. 367 (1968); *Walker v. Birmingham*, 388 U.S. 307 (1967); *Adderly v. Florida*, 385 U.S. 39 (1966); *Scales v. United States*, 367 U.S. 203 (1961); *Communist Party v. Subversive Activities Control Bd.*, 367 U.S. 1 (1961); *Barenblatt v. United States*, 360 U.S. 109 (1959); *Roth v. United States*, 354 U.S. 476 (1957); *Dennis v. United States*, 341 U.S. 494 (1951); *American Communications Ass'n v. Douds*, 339 U.S. 382 (1950); *Chaplinsky v. New Hampshire*, 315 U.S. 568 (1942); *Valentine v. Chrestensen*, 316 U.S. 52 (1942); *Cox v. New Hampshire*, 312 U.S. 569 (1941); *Whitney v. California*, 274 U.S. 357 (1927); *Gitlow v. New York*, 268 U.S. 652 (1925); *Abrams v. United States*, 250 U.S. 616 (1919); *Debs v. United States*, 249 U.S. 211 (1919); *Schenck v. United States*, 249 U.S. 47 (1919).

160. See, e.g., *Southeastern Promotions, Ltd. v. Conrad*, 420 U.S. 546 (1975) (prior restraint permissible only after proper procedural safeguards); *Miller v. California*, 413 U.S. 15 (1973) (states may regulate or forbid obscenity by specific statutory definitions); *United States v. Robel*, 389 U.S. 258 (1967) (states may exclude individuals from public employment based on their associational ties if statute is narrowly drawn).

161. See, e.g., *Richmond Newspapers, Inc. v. Virginia*, 448 U.S. 555 (1980) (courts may justifiably close criminal trials to public upon finding of "overriding interest"); *Nebraska Press Ass'n v. Stuart*, 427 U.S. 539 (1976) (prior restraints on reporting about criminal trial can be justified by sufficient showing of threat to fair trial and lack of alternative precautions); *New York Times Co. v. United States*, 403 U.S. 713 (1971) (per curiam) (government may justify prior restraint on publication of material allegedly related to national security if "heavy presumption" is overcome); *New York Times Co. v. Sullivan*, 376 U.S. 254 (1964) (defamation against public official actionable if showing of reckless disregard for truth is made).

162. First amendment rights of corporations: see *First Nat'l Bank v. Bellotti*, 435 U.S. 765 (1978). Patronage jobs: see *Elrod v. Burns*, 427 U.S. 347 (1976).

163. See supra notes 15–16.

164. The early Supreme Court decision involving dissent over the war was *United States v. O'Brien*, 391 U.S. 367 (1968), which upheld a statute rather plainly aimed at preventing one of the major forms of protest against the war, the burning of draft cards. By that year there had already been four years of active protests and demonstrations against the war. Some of the most vocal and massive protests occurred in 1969, the year immediately following *O'Brien*.

165. It was *after* five years of vigorous public protest that the Court

protected students' right to wear armbands (*Tinker v. Des Moines School Dist.*, 393 U.S. 503 [1969]), and it was after fully seven years of caustic public criticism of the war that the Court protected the publication of the Pentagon Papers (*New York Times Co. v. United States*, 403 U.S. 713 [1971]). Cf. Dahl, *Decision-Making in a Democracy: The Supreme Court as a National Policy-Maker*, 6 J. Pub. L. 279 (1957) (suggesting that Court follows and lends legitimacy to, only occasionally leading, national policies).

166. See supra note 67.

167. See chapter 2.

168. Higham, for example, described how demands for outward conformity by recent immigrants during World War I resolved insecurities and greatly reduced nativistic intolerance:

> Yet, despite the indiscriminate anti-foreign suspicions omnipresent in the war mood, incidents of this kind [lynchings] were unusual. . . . The average non-German alien passed through 1917 and 1918 unscathed by hatred, and often touched by sympathy. The logic of 100 per cent Americanism was against him, but the war also created powerful forces which held that logic in check. . . . This was the paradox of American nationalism during the First World War. On the one hand it created an unappeasable and unprecedented demand for unity and conformity. On the other, it saved the foreigner from the persecutory or exclusionist consequences of this demand as long as he was non-German and showed an outward compliance with the national purpose. To a remarkable degree the psychic climate of the war gave the average alien not only protection but also a sense of participation and belonging. (J. Higham, supra note 15, at 215)

169. Efforts to suppress abolitionist journalism in the North prior to the Civil War provide an example. Despite these widespread attempts, "abolitionist journalism expanded and flourished, and after 1840 it encountered little significant difficulty" (R. Nye, supra note 70, at 124). One of the major reasons for the cessation of efforts at suppression was that the censorship had gone so far as to "take on dangerous implications" even to those who did not share the abolitionists' cause (see id. at 125–37). For other examples, see supra notes 62, 66, 70.

170. For an insightful analysis that comes to a somewhat similar conclusion, see Blasi, *The Pathological Perspective and the First Amendment*, 85 Colum. L. Rev. 449 (1985).

171. See, e.g., Scanlon, *A Theory of Free Expression*, 1 Phil. & Pub. Aff. 204 (1972). Cf. Wellington, supra note 71, at 1105. T. M. Scanlon analyzes freedom of expression in the context of the proper limitations of governmental power and the requirements of individual autonomy but not as a purely constitutional right. He suggests that, except in extreme situations like wartime, government should not place legal restrictions on expression even where such expression: (1) advances false beliefs; or

(2) incites others to independent harmful acts. Harry Wellington, unlike Scanlon, uses a constitutional analysis in which he discusses the importance of freedom of expression to individual autonomy and the political process. Although Wellington too would bar government from restricting expression that advances false beliefs, he would permit government to restrict advocacy that creates a clear and present danger of unlawful action. For an interesting claim that the relevant value is the individual's freedom to choose belief, see Smith, *Skepticism, Truth and Tolerance in the Theory of Free Expressions,* 60 S. Cal. L. Rev. 649 (1987).

CHAPTER 4

1. For a history, see J. Nowak, R. Rotunda, and J. Young, CONSTITUTIONAL LAW 150–56 (2d ed.; St. Paul: West, 1978).

2. 426 U.S. 833 (1976).

3. The basic constitutional "test" (whether the regulation "affected" commerce) was immediately understood to provide no limitation on national power. "Almost anything—marriage, birth, death—may in some fashion affect commerce" (*National Labor Relations Bd. v. Jones & Laughlin Steel Corp.,* 301 U.S. 1, 99 [1937] [McReynolds, J., dissenting]). By 1959 Herbert Wechsler could refer to "the virtual abandonment of limits" to the federal commerce power (Wechsler, *Toward Neutral Principles of Constitutional Law,* 73 Harv. L. Rev. 1, 23–24 [1959]).

4. 426 U.S. at 858, 860 (Brennan, J., dissenting).

5. Tribe, *Unraveling National League of Cities: The New Federalism and Affirmative Rights to Essential Government Services,* 90 Harv. L. Rev. 1065, 1066 (1977): "I make no claims about what the Justices intended. . . . I haven't a clue what that might have been, but I doubt that the conclusion of this article was it." Michelman, *States' Rights and States' Roles: Permutations of "Sovereignty" in National League of Cities v. Usery,* 86 Yale L.J. 1165, 1166 (1977): "The only interpretation that is compatible with the decision taken as a whole, I shall argue, is a surprising one that leads in directions the Justices do not seem to have intended or anticipated."

6. Choper, *The Scope of National Power Vis-à-Vis the States: The Dispensability of Judicial Review,* 86 Yale L.J. 1552 (1977).

7. E.g., J. Ely, DEMOCRACY AND DISTRUST 224 n.44 (Cambridge: Harvard University Press, 1980); Barber, *National League of Cities v. Usery: New Meaning for the Tenth Amendment?* 1976 Sup. Ct. Rev. 161; Cox, *Federalism and Individual Rights Under the Burger Court,* 73 Nw. U.L. Rev. 1 (1978); Tushnet, *The Dilemmas of Liberal Constitutionalism,* 42 Ohio St. L.J. 411, 420–21 (1981).

8. E.g., Stewart, *Pyramids of Sacrifice? Problems of Federalism in Man-*

dating State Implementation of National Environmental Policy, 86 Yale L.J. 1196, 1224–25, 1271 (1977); Kaden, *Politics, Money, and State Sovereignty: The Judicial Role,* 79 Colum. L. Rev. 847 (1979). For a view much closer to the one proposed here, see P. Bobbitt, CONSTITUTIONAL FATE: THEORY OF THE CONSTITUTION, 191–95 (New York: Oxford University Press, 1982).

9. See cases in infra note 19.

10. 105 S. Ct. 1005 (1985).

11. For an account of some of these cases, see Nagel, *The Legislative Veto, the Constitution, and the Courts,* 3 Const. Comm. 61 (1986).

12. No doubt this is in part justifiable because of the special capabilities and responsibilities of the other branches of government in resolving such disputes. See Choper, supra note 6, at 1560–77 (as to federalism); Frohnmayer, *The Separation of Powers: An Essay on the Vitality of the Constitutional Idea,* 52 Or. L. Rev. 211 (1973) (as to separation of powers). Whatever the reasons, the reluctance of the Supreme Court to rule on cases involving structural values is often dramatic. See, e.g., *McArthur v. Clifford,* 393 U.S. 1002 (1968); *Holmes v. United States,* 391 U.S. 936 (1968); *Velvel v. Nixon,* 396 U.S. 1042 (1970); *Massachusetts v. Laird,* 400 U.S. 886 (1970); *DaCosta v. Laird,* 405 U.S. 979 (1972). See also *Goldwater v. Carter,* 444 U.S. 996 (1979). But it is not invariable. See supra note 11.

13. E.g., *United States v. Five Gambling Devices,* 346 U.S. 441 (1953); *Scarborough v. United States,* 431 U.S. 563 (1977); *National Cable Television Assoc. v. United States,* 415 U.S. 336 (1974).

14. As to equitable discretion, compare *Milliken v. Bradley,* 418 U.S. 717 (1974) with *Columbus Bd. of Educ. v. Penick,* 443 U.S. 449 (1979). As to standing, compare *Warth v. Seldin,* 422 U.S. 490 (1975) with *Duke Power Co. v. Carolina Env'tl. Study Group,* 438 U.S. 59 (1978). As to comity, compare *Younger v. Harris,* 401 U.S. 37 (1971) with *Steffel v. Thompson,* 415 U.S. 452 (1974).

15. E.g., *Milliken v. Bradley,* 418 U.S. 717 (1974); *San Antonio Indep. School Dist. v. Rodriguez,* 411 U.S. 1 (1973); *Labine v. Vincent,* 401 U.S. 532 (1971).

16. As to analyses of motive and legislative purpose, compare, e.g., *Eisenstadt v. Baird,* 405 U.S. 438 (1972); *Trimble v. Gordon,* 430 U.S. 762 (1977); *Craig v. Boren,* 429 U.S. 190 (1976) with *Hoke v. United States,* 227 U.S. 308 (1913); *United States v. Sullivan,* 332 U.S. 689 (1948); *Perez v. United States,* 402 U.S. 146 (1971); *United States v. Kahriger,* 345 U.S. 22 (1953); *Katzenbach v. McClung,* 379 U.S. 294 (1964). With respect to the less drastic means requirement, see *Katzenbach v. McClung.* Also, compare, e.g., *Roe v. Wade,* 410 U.S. 113 (1973) (states' method of protecting potential life sweeps unnecessarily broadly

when protecting fetuses prior to viability) with *Nixon v. Administrator of Gen. Serv.*, 433 U.S. 425 (1977) (statute that provides for the storage and screening of 42 million pages of presidential documents and 880 presidential tape recordings does not unnecessarily subordinate presidential requirements of confidentiality).

17. Balancing: see *South Carolina State Highway Dep't v. Barnwell Bros., Inc.*, 303 U.S. 177 (1938); *Southern Pac. Co. v. Arizona*, 325 U.S. 761 (1945); *Bibb v. Navajo Freight Lines, Inc.*, 359 U.S. 520 (1959); *Raymond Motor Transp., Inc. v. Rice*, 434 U.S. 429 (1978); *Kassel v. Consolidated Freightways Corp.*, 450 U.S. 662 (1981); *Minnesota v. Clover Leaf Creamery Co.*, 449 U.S. 456 (1981); *National League of Cities v. Usery*, 426 U.S. at 856 (Blackmun, J., concurring); see also *Nixon v. Administrator of Gen. Serv.*, supra note 16, at 425.

"Undue impairment": *New York v. United States*, 326 U.S. 572 (1946) (Stone, J., concurring); similarly, the Court has said that "Congress may not exercise power in a fashion that impairs the States' integrity" (*Fry v. United States*, 421 U.S. 542, 547 n.7 [1975]); "neither government *may destroy* the other nor curtail *in any substantial manner* the exercise of its powers" (*Metcalf and Eddy v. Mitchell*, 269 U.S., 514, 523 [1926] [emphasis added]).

Nature of "legislative" acts: *Immigration and Naturalization Serv. v. Chadha*, 462 U.S. 919, 952–57 (1983). A criticism of the Court's conceptualization of "lawmaking" can be found in Nagel, supra note 11, at 67–69.

18. E.g., compare *Brown v. Board of Educ.*, 347 U.S. 483 (1954) with *Keyes v. School Dist. No. 1*, 413 U.S. 189 (1973); *Swann v. Charlotte-Mecklenburg Bd. of Educ.*, 402 U.S. 1 (1971); *Green v. County School Bd.*, 391 U.S. 430 (1968). Also, compare *Roe v. Wade*, supra note 16, with *Planned Parenthood of Cent. Mo. v. Danforth*, 428 U.S. 52 (1976); *Bellotti v. Baird*, 443 U.S. 622 (1979); *Colautti v. Franklin*, 439 U.S. 379 (1979); *Thornburgh v. American College of Obstetricians and Gynecologists*, 106 S. Ct. 1060 (1986).

19. Compare *United States v. Nixon*, 418 U.S. 683 (1974) with *Nixon v. Administrator of Gen. Serv.*, supra note 16. Compare *National League of Cities v. Usery*, 426 U.S. at 833 with *City of Lafayette v. Louisiana Power & Light Co.*, 435 U.S. 389 (1978); *City of Los Angeles v. Manhart*, 435 U.S. 702 (1978); *Massachusetts v. United States*, 435 U.S. 444 (1978); *North Carolina v. Califano*, 435 U.S. 962 (1978); *Hodel v. Virginia Surface Mining & Reclamation Assoc.*, 452 U.S. 264, 276–77, 286–90 (1981); *United Transp. Union v. Long Island R.R. Co.*, 455 U.S. 678 (1982); *FERC v. Mississippi*, 456 U.S. 742 (1982); *EEOC v. Wyoming*, 460 U.S. 226 (1983); *Garcia v. San Antonio Metropolitan Transit Auth.*, supra note 10. Compare *Buckley v. Valeo*, 424 U.S. 1 (1976); *Bowsher v. Synar*, 106

S. Ct. 3181 (1986) with *Morrison v. Olson*, 108 S. Ct. 2597 (1988).

20. C. Black, STRUCTURE AND RELATIONSHIP IN CONSTITUTIONAL LAW (Baton Rouge: Louisiana State University Press, 1969).

21. J. Ely, DEMOCRACY AND DISTRUST (Cambridge: Harvard University Press, 1980).

22. Tribe, *The Puzzling Persistence of Process-Based Constitutional Theories*, 89 Yale L.J. 1063 (1980). See also Benedict, *To Secure These Rights: Rights, Democracy, and Judicial Review in the Anglo-American Constitutional Heritage*, 42 Ohio St. L.J. 69 (1981); Grano, *Ely's Theory of Judicial Review: Preserving the Significance of the Political Process*, id. at 167; Richards, *Moral Philosophy and the Search for Fundamental Values in Constitutional Law*, id. at 319. But see Maltz, *Federalism and the Fourteenth Amendment: A Comment on Democracy and Distrust*, id. at 209.

23. E.g., Chayes, *The Roles of the Judge in Public Law Litigation*, 89 Harv. L. Rev. 1281 (1976); Fiss, *The Forms of Justice*, 93 Harv. L. Rev. 1 (1979); Eisenberg and Yeazell, *The Ordinary and the Extraordinary in Institutional Litigation*, 93 Harv. L. Rev. 465 (1980).

24. E.g., Chayes, supra note 23. Diver, *The Judge as Political Power Broker: Superintending Structural Change in Public Institutions*, 65 Va. L. Rev. 43 (1979).

25. Eisenberg and Yeazell, supra note 23, at 467. Cf. Ely, *On Discovering Fundamental Values*, 92 Harv. L. Rev. 5, 18 n.62 (1978); Fiss, supra note 23, at 53.

26. E.g., Brest, *The Misconceived Quest for the Original Understanding*, 60 B.U.L. Rev. 204 (1980); Cover, book review, New Republic, January 14, 1978, at 26, 27; Munzer and Nickel, *Does the Constitution Mean What It Always Meant?* 77 Colum. L. Rev. 1029 (1977). See also L. Tribe, AMERICAN CONSTITUTIONAL LAW 816 (Mineola, N.Y.: Foundation Press, 1978).

27. E.g., Bickel, *The Original Understanding and the Segregation Decision*, 69 Harv. L. Rev. 1 (1955).

28. For a general discussion, see Ely, supra note 25, at 16–22.

29. "Goodness": Wright, *Professor Bickel, the Scholarly Tradition, and the Supreme Court*, 84 Harv. L. Rev. 769, 797 (1971). "Minimal standards of human dignity": Eisenberg and Yeazell, supra note 23, at 517. "Personhood": L. Tribe, supra note 26, at 914.

30. "Just wants": Michelman, *On Protecting the Poor Through the Fourteenth Amendment*, 83 Harv. L. Rev. 7 (1969). "Mediation of liberal conversation": B. Ackerman, SOCIAL JUSTICE IN THE LIBERAL STATE 311 (New Haven: Yale University Press, 1980). "Equal respect and concern": R. Dworkin, TAKING RIGHTS SERIOUSLY 149, 227 (Cambridge: Harvard University Press, 1977). For other elaborate efforts to conceptualize equal protection, see Alexander, *Modern Equal Protection Theories:*

A Metatheoretical Taxonomy and Critique, 42 Ohio St. L.J. 3 (1981); Simson, *A Method for Analyzing Discriminatory Effects Under the Equal Protection Clause,* 29 Stan. L. Rev. 663 (1977). Roberto Unger: Tushnet, *Darkness at the Edge of Town: The Contributions of John Hart Ely to Constitutional Theory,* 89 Yale L.J. 1037, 1057–62 (1980).

31. Eisenberg and Yeazell, supra note 23, at 497: "Nor do the records of the constitutional convention or the debate surrounding consideration of the Constitution counsel specifically against judicial decisions affecting institutions traditionally regulated by executive officials."

32. See Choper, supra note 6, at 1588–90.

33. Separation of powers: Diver, supra note 24, at 91–92; Chayes, supra note 23, at 1307. See generally the discussion in Nagel, *Separation of Powers and the Scope of Federal Equitable Remedies,* 30 Stan. L. Rev. 661, 686–88 (1978). Democratic accountability: Tribe, supra note 22, at 1063, 1069–79; Tushnet, supra note 30, at 1037, 1045–57. "Meaningful opportunity": Tribe, supra, at 1077.

34. Apparently the idea of a bill of rights "never entered the mind of many of [the framers]" until three days before adjournment of the Constitutional Convention. B. Schwartz, A Documentary History of the Bill of Rights 627 (New York: McGraw-Hill, 1971). A common argument for the exclusion of a bill of rights was that specific protections were unnecessary, since the federal government had been granted only enumerated powers (id. at 634). When Madison proposed the Bill of Rights to Congress, its importance for preserving freedom was not emphasized. He argued that it would be "neither improper nor altogether useless" (id. at 1028). See generally Rumble, *James Madison on the Value of the Bill of Rights,* in J. Pennock and J. Chapman, eds., NOMOS XX, Constitutionalism 122 (New York: New York University Press, 1979). The general defense of the proposed Constitution offered in The Federalist continually emphasizes governmental structure as the basic source of protection against tyranny: "In the compound republic of America, the power surrendered by the people is first divided between two distinct governments, and then the portion allotted to each subdivided among distinct and separate departments. Hence a double security arises to the rights of the people" (The Federalist no. 51, at 323 [A. Hamilton or J. Madison] [Mentor ed.; New York: New American Library, 1961]). See generally Diamond, *The Federalist's View of Federalism,* in Essays in Federalism 21, 53, 61 (Claremont, Calif.: Institute for Studies in Federalism, 1961). It is true, of course, that the Bill of Rights was eventually adopted, and its importance in the constitutional scheme may have been magnified both by the adoption of the fourteenth amendment and by modern experience with judicial enforcement of

rights. But neither consideration justifies losing sight of the framers' original scheme.

35. On the importance of size and heterogeneity, see Diamond, supra note 34, at 55–59. See also Choper, supra note 6, at 1617.

36. Herbert Wechsler, for example, was careful not to exclude altogether a role for judicial review in enforcing limitations on Congress. See Wechsler, *The Political Safeguards of Federalism: The Role of the States in the Composition and Selection of the National Government,* in A. MacMahon, ed., FEDERALISM, MATURE AND EMERGENT 97, 108–9 (New York: Doubleday, 1955). See also Freund, *Umpiring the Federal System,* id. at 159. See also supra text related to notes 12–33.

37. Both arguments are contained in J. Choper, JUDICIAL REVIEW AND THE NATIONAL POLITICAL PROCESS: A FUNCTIONAL RECONSIDERATION OF THE ROLE OF THE SUPREME COURT (Chicago: University of Chicago Press, 1980). The argument with respect to separation of powers is discussed in Monaghan, book review, 94 Harv. L. Rev. 296 (1980). Here I shall deal only with Choper's argument with respect to federalism, and references will be to the article on which this aspect of the book was based. Choper, supra note 6, at 1552.

38. Choper, supra note 6, at 1556, 1581, 1583.

39. Id. at 1556.

40. Id. at 1560, et seq.

41. Choper contrasts federalism to matters of principle by suggesting that principles are enforced without regard to immediate social costs because enforcement protects "the dignity of the individual" (supra note 6, at 1555). But it seems unlikely that he means by this that the definition of rights or their protection is never compromised because of practical trade-offs. Nor is it clear why federalism, as a constitutional requirement, might not have content independent of "practical" considerations and sometimes be enforced despite immediate costs. He denies that principles exclude policy considerations requiring complex factual determinations (id.). Much of his discussion implies that principles have independent intellectual content that involves "technical considerations" and judicial expertise (id. at 1574). In contrast, federalism is often treated as meaning little more than that states must exist (see infra note 56). However, in places Choper acknowledges that federalism might involve content independent of the practical accommodations made in the political process (id. at 1599–1600). E.g., he concedes that Congress might make constitutional errors with regard to what federalism requires (id. at 1574). On special competence of courts, see id. at 1554; cf. id. at 1556.

42. Choper, supra note 6, at 1555–56.

43. Id. at 1611.

44. Id. at 1614.

45. Id. at 1616.

46. Id. at 1555.

47. His acknowledgment is somewhat ambivalent (id. at 1620). It is a further sign of the widespread preoccupation with rights that Choper was criticized for not analogizing states' rights sufficiently to individuals' rights and for underestimating how far the latter depends on the former (Benedict, supra note 22, at 75–76). Compare supra note 22 and related text.

48. Choper, supra note 6, at 1620–21. The discussion of this issue in Choper's book is fuller but not significantly different. There Choper adds, but does not rely on, the argument that "the federalism principle has simply outlived its usefulness" (supra note 37, at 255–56). He also drops the adjective "critical," thus emphasizing the quantitative aspect of his argument that judicial protection of federalism threatens the capacity to protect a wide array of individual rights. But the protection of any single principle or right will naturally seem to be less weighty than the protection of all others, so in this respect the argument proves nothing that is specific to federalism. In short, Choper's book, like his article, does not successfully escape the need to show why self-determination (while difficult to protect) is not worth protecting. See infra text related to notes 49–50.

49. Choper, supra note 6, at 1604.

50. E.g., id. at 1555, 1560, 1616, 1617.

51. See generally G. Wood, THE CREATION OF THE AMERICAN REPUBLIC 608–9 (Chapel Hill: University of North Carolina Press, 1969).

52. On Choper's concern about outcomes, see supra note 6, at 1555, 1617–18.

53. Id. at 1555.

54. See supra note 41.

55. Choper, supra note 6, at 1560–67, 1571, 1576, 1620.

56. Or "trampled," as Choper puts it (id. at 1560). Or "swallow the states whole" (id. at 1594). See also id. at 1563–68, 1570. See also infra text related to note 134. The Court seemed to adopt this view in *Garcia* when it asserted that "to say that the Constitution assumes the continual role of the States is to say little about the nature of that role" (*Garcia v. San Antonio Metropolitan Transit Auth.*, 105 S. Ct. 1005, 1017 [1985]; but see id. at 1020).

57. Choper does briefly recognize that judicial review serves such nonspecific purposes as "nourishment of constitutional understanding" (supra note 6, at 1605). In suggesting that his federalism proposal would not damage public understanding and the Court's role in sustaining that

understanding, Choper is at his least convincing. See Monaghan, supra note 37, at 306–7.

58. The term "instrumentalism" has various meanings. Here I use it to denote those intellectual habits and inclinations described in Summers, *Naive Instrumentalism and the Law*, in P. Hacker and J. Raz, eds., LAW, MORALITY AND SOCIETY: ESSAYS IN HONOUR OF H. L. A. HART (Oxford: Clarendon Press, 1977).

59. A different sort of attack was also made: that *Usery* violated *stare decisis*. For example, Archibald Cox summarizes his criticism this way: "The short of the matter, therefore, is that although the decision in *National League of Cities* is almost surely consistent with the original conception of the federal union and might not have surprised any constitutional scholar prior to the 1930s, it is thoroughly inconsistent with the constitutional trends and decisions of the past forty years" (Cox, *Federalism and Individual Rights Under the Burger Court*, 73 Nw. U.L. Rev. 1, 22 [1978]). In this chapter I do not dispute the accuracy of Cox's revealingly complacent assessment, but I do inquire into how the modern decisional law (as well as the concerns of scholars) could have come to depart so significantly from the constitutional design.

60. Michelman, supra note 5, at 1190; Tribe, supra note 5, at 1088–90.

61. Both Tribe and Michelman deal briefly with the issue of local self-determination. Michelman, supra note 5, at 1191 n.86: "Further investigation of this sensitivity to community self-determination, its role in the cited decisions, its theoretical significance, and its relationship to the issues in NLC, must await another article." Tribe, supra note 5, at 1093 n.109: "Political accountability . . . poses a problem not only for state and local governments, but also for Congress."

62. Tribe, supra note 5, at 1072.

63. Michelman, supra note 5, at 1168; Tribe, supra note 5, at 1074.

64. Michelman, supra note 5, at 1168; Tribe, supra note 5, at 1074–75.

65. Tribe, supra note 5, at 1074; Michelman, supra note 5, at 1172.

66. 426 U.S. at 860.

67. Michelman, supra note 5, at 1166.

68. *Garcia v. San Antonio Metropolitan Transit Auth.*, 105 S. Ct. 1005, 1017, 1019, 1021 (1985).

69. Id. at 1011.

70. Id. at 1018.

71. See Summers, *Professor Fuller's Jurisprudence and America's Dominant Philosophy of Law*, 92 Harv. L. Rev. 433 (1978).

72. A matter that is acknowledged by both Tribe and Michelman. See supra note 60.

73. Tribe, supra note 22, at 1077: "The crux of any determination that a law unjustly discriminates against a group . . . [is] that the law is part of a pattern that denies those subject to it a meaningful opportunity to realize their humanity."

74. *National Labor Relations Bd. v. Jones & Laughlin Steel Corp.*, 301 U.S. at 37. See also supra note 56.

75. Cf. *Stanley v. Georgia*, 394 U.S. 557 (1969).

76. Cf. *New York Times Co. v. United States*, 403 U.S. 713 (1971).

77. Linde, *Judges, Critics, and the Realist Tradition*, 82 Yale L.J. 227, 238 (1972).

78. Id. at 232, 237, 238, 239.

79. See Summers, supra note 58; Linde, supra note 77, at 229–30.

80. See Fiss, supra note 23.

81. E.g., *Carter v. Carter Coal Co.*, 298 U.S. 238 (1936).

82. 426 U.S. at 849, 851.

83. Id. at 851.

84. See Wechsler, supra note 36, passim. See also Freund, supra note 36, at 159–61; C. Friedrich, TRENDS OF FEDERALISM IN THEORY AND PRACTICE 3–11 (New York: Praeger, 1968).

85. 426 U.S. at 845.

86. Id. at 845–51.

87. Id. at 847, 848, 850–51.

88. I am using the modern nomenclature, which nearly reverses the framers' usage. See Diamond, supra note 34.

89. Apparently there was at least some basis for the anti-Federalist fear that some Federalists wished literally to abolish the states. See J. Main, THE ANTI-FEDERALISTS: CRITICS OF THE CONSTITUTION 121 (Chicago: Quadrangle Books, 1964); B. Schwartz, supra note 34, at 597. More generally, however, the anti-Federalists feared that the proposed Constitution provided inadequate safeguards against the enlargement of federal power beyond the enumerated powers. See, e.g., B. Schwartz, supra note 34, at 526, 572, 592–93, 653.

90. See J. Main, supra note 89, at 129; C. Kenyon, ed., THE ANTI-FEDERALISTS xl, xli, li, liii (Indianapolis: Bobbs-Merrill, 1966).

91. C. Kenyon, supra note 90, at 210, xl.

92. Id. at 388. Subsequent writings attest to the importance of such arguments. See, e.g., R. Dahl and E. Tufte, SIZE AND DEMOCRACY (Stanford: Stanford University Press, 1973); G. McConnell, PRIVATE POWER AND AMERICAN DEMOCRACY 190 (New York: Knopf, 1966); A. de Tocqueville, 2 DEMOCRACY IN AMERICA 79, 148, 307–11 (New Rochelle, N.Y.: Arlington House, 1970).

93. See, e.g., J. Lewis, ed., ANTI-FEDERALIST V. FEDERALIST 28 (San Francisco: Chandler, 1967).

94. THE FEDERALIST, supra note 34, no. 10 (J. Madison); THE FEDERALIST, supra note 34, no. 51 (A. Hamilton or J. Madison).

95. See infra text related to notes 100, 107–12, 119.

96. THE FEDERALIST, supra note 34, no. 17, at 9, 20 (A. Hamilton).

97. See J. Main, supra note 89, at 130; R. Dahl and E. Tufte, supra note 92, at 4–11; THE FEDERALIST, supra note 34, no. 9 (A. Hamilton); THE FEDERALIST, supra note 34, no. 10 (J. Madison).

98. THE FEDERALIST, supra note 34, no. 45 (J. Madison). See Wechsler, supra note 36; Choper, supra note 6, at 1560–65. The Court emphatically adopted this view in *Garcia v. San Antonio Metropolitan Transit Auth.*, 105 S. Ct. 1005, 1018–21 (1985).

99. See infra text related to notes 107–12. See generally Diamond, supra note 34, at 46.

100. THE FEDERALIST, supra note 34, no. 46, at 299 (J. Madison). Emphasis added.

101. "Legitimacy" has alternatively been defined as the capacity to engender and maintain the belief that the existing political institutions are "appropriate" (see S. Lipset, POLITICAL MAN 64 [Anchor ed.; Garden City, N.Y.: Doubleday, 1963]) and as "rightful," or "entitled to rule" (see C. Friedrich, TRADITION AND AUTHORITY 89 [New York: Praeger, 1972]). I treat the effectiveness of a government in meeting the needs of its citizens as one source of legitimacy. Compare S. Lipset, supra, ch. 3, with C. Friedrich, supra, at 89.

102. THE FEDERALIST, supra note 34, no. 49, at 314 (A. Hamilton or J. Madison).

103. THE FEDERALIST, supra note 34, no. 17, at 120 (A. Hamilton).

104. Location of state capital: *Coyle v. Oklahoma*, 221 U.S. 559 (1911). Exemption of statehouse from federal tax: *New York v. United States*, supra note 17, at 582. Protection of state court proceedings: *Younger v. Harris*, supra note 14.

105. See supra note 64.

106. Cf. *New York v. United States*, supra note 17. In many other cases, the Supreme Court has shown an inclination to protect "traditional" areas of state governmental activity from federal encroachment. See, e.g., *Rizzo v. Goode*, 423 U.S. 362 (1976); *Milliken v. Bradley*, 418 U.S. 717 (1974); *San Antonio Independent School Dist. v. Rodriguez*, supra note 15; *Labine v. Vincent*, supra note 15.

107. THE FEDERALIST, supra note 34, no. 16, at 116 (A. Hamilton).

108. THE FEDERALIST, supra note 34, no. 17, at 119 (A. Hamilton).

109. Id. at 119–20.

110. "The powers delegated by the proposed Constitution to the federal government are few and defined. Those which are to remain in the State governments are numerous and indefinite. The former will be exer-

cised principally on external objects, as war, peace, negotiation, and foreign commerce; with which last the power of taxation will, for the most part, be connected. The powers reserved to the several States will extend to all the objects which, in the ordinary course of affairs, concern the lives, liberties, and properties of the people, and the internal order, improvement, and prosperity of the State" (THE FEDERALIST, supra note 34, no. 45, at 292–93 [J. Madison]). "It is only within a certain sphere that the federal power can, in the nature of things, be advantageously administered" (THE FEDERALIST, supra note 34, no. 46, at 295 [J. Madison]).

111. THE FEDERALIST, supra note 34, no. 45, at 292 (J. Madison).

112. THE FEDERALIST, supra note 34, no. 17, at 120 (A. Hamilton). See also THE FEDERALIST, supra note 34, no. 45, at 292 (J. Madison); THE FEDERALIST, supra note 34, no. 46, at 295 (J. Madison).

113. See Diamond, supra note 34.

114. Education: e.g., *San Antonio Independent School Dist. v. Rodriguez*, supra note 15; *Brown v. Bd. of Educ. (II)*, 349 U.S. 294 (1955). Family law: e.g., *Labine v. Vincent*, supra note 15. I do not mean to imply, of course, that the Court consistently honors the tradition of state control over such matters. See, e.g., *Carey v. Population Serv.*, 431 U.S. 678 (1977); *Zablocki v. Redhail*, 434 U.S. 374 (1978). But such intrusions are made against a backdrop of the acknowledged propriety of general state authority over such matters. See, e.g., *Griswold v. Connecticut*, 381 U.S. 479, 499 (1965) (Harlan, J., concurring).

115. E.g., 426 U.S. at 833, 875 (Brennan, J., dissenting).

116. See supra note 110. See also Wechsler, supra note 36, at 98: "National action has thus always been regarded as exceptional in our polity, an intrusion to be justified by some necessity, the special rather than the ordinary case."

117. Federal control over state employees who perform general functions, then, is analogous to general federal common law in that both, almost by definition, are at odds with the concept of enumerated powers. Cf. *Erie R.R. Co. v. Tompkins*, 304 U.S. 64 (1938).

118. 426 U.S. at 851.

119. THE FEDERALIST, supra note 34, no. 46, at 300 (J. Madison).

120. Id. at 296–99.

121. For example, typically courts threaten to raise funds themselves but do not directly order state legislatures to raise taxes. E.g., *Wyatt v. Stickney*, 344 F. Supp. 373 (M.D. Ala. 1972), aff'd in part sub. nom. *Wyatt v. Aderholt*, 503 F.2d 1305 (5th Cir. 1974). On the state appointment process, see *Mayor of Philadelphia v. Educ. Equality League*, 415 U.S. 605 (1974); *Carter v. Jury Comm'n*, 396 U.S. 320 (1970); *Lance v. Plummer*, 384 U.S. 929 (1966) (Black, J., dissenting from denial of certiorari).

122. 426 U.S. at 845, 851.

123. *EPA v. Brown,* 431 U.S. 99 (1977).

124. THE FEDERALIST, supra note 34, no. 17, at 119 (A. Hamilton).

125. THE FEDERALIST, supra note 34, no. 46, at 294–95 (J. Madison).

126. Evidence suggests that the sense of identification and participation is possible to a far greater extent in very small units of government. See R. Dahl and E. Tufte, supra note 92, at 60, 63, 84. On the relationship between state authority and local authority, see 1 A. de Tocqueville, supra note 92, at 45, 51, 52, 79, 148; 2 A. de Tocqueville, supra note 92, at 109. For a detailed account of the advantages of localism and of the legal status of cities, see Frug, *The City as a Legal Concept,* 93 Harv. L. Rev. 1057 (1980).

127. E.g., *San Antonio Independent School Dist. v. Rodriguez,* supra note 15; *Milliken v. Bradley,* 418 U.S. 717 (1974).

128. 426 U.S. at 850–51.

129. Id. at 855–56.

130. Michelman, supra note 5, at 1169.

131. 426 U.S. at 845, quoting from *Lane County v. Oregon,* 74 U.S. (7 Wall.) 71 (1869).

132. 1 A. de Tocqueville, supra note 92, at 152.

133. See *Immigration and Naturalization Serv. v. Chadha,* 462 U.S. 99 (1983) (invalidation of the legislative veto).

134. E.g., Tribe, supra note 5, at 1072 ("empty vessels"), 1071 ("gutted shell"); Choper, supra note 6.

135. THE FEDERALIST, supra note 34, no. 45, at 289 (J. Madison). See also supra text related to notes 88–97.

CHAPTER 5

1. E.g., *City of Cleburne v. Cleburne Living Center,* 105 S. Ct. 3249 (1985); *U.S. Railroad Retirement Bd. v. Fritz,* 449 U.S. 166 (1980); *N.Y. Transit Auth. v. Beazer,* 440 U.S. 568 (1979); *U.S. Dept. of Agriculture v. Moreno,* 413 U.S. 528 (1973); *Eisenstadt v. Baird,* 405 U.S. 438 (1972); *Reed v. Reed,* 404 U.S. 71 (1971); *Dandridge v. Williams,* 397 U.S. 471 (1970); *McDonald v. Bd. of Election Comm'rs,* 394 U.S. 802 (1969); *Williamson v. Lee Optical Co.,* 348 U.S. 483 (1955); *Tigner v. Texas,* 310 U.S. 141 (1940); *Smith v. Cahoon,* 283 U.S. 553 (1931); *F.S. Royster Guano Co. v. Virginia,* 253 U.S. 412 (1920); *Miller v. Wilson,* 236 U.S. 373 (1915); *Lindsley v. Natural Carbonic Gas Co.,* 220 U.S. 61 (1911); *Gulf, Colo. & Santa Fe Ry. v. Ellis,* 165 U.S. 150 (1897). Cf. *Levy v. Louisiana,* 391 U.S. 68 (1968); *Carrington v. Rash,* 380 U.S. 89 (1965); *Skinner v. Oklahoma,* 316 U.S. 535 (1942); *Yick Wo v. Hopkins,* 118 U.S. 356 (1886).

2. *Rinaldi v. Yeager,* 384 U.S. 305, 308 (1966) (citations omitted).

3. The principal characteristic of a "fundamental interest" appears to be that the Court calls the interest fundamental. The right to procreate was termed "one of the basic civil rights of man" in *Skinner v. Oklahoma*, 316 U.S. 535, 541 (1942). But, while conceding that the right to a minimal income involved the "most basic economic needs of impoverished human beings," the Court has not treated that right as fundamental. See *Dandridge v. Williams*, 397 U.S. 471, 484–85 (1970). For examples of interests held to be fundamental, see *Shapiro v. Thompson*, 394 U.S. 618 (1969) (right to travel); *Harper v. Virginia Bd. of Elections*, 383 U.S. 663 (1966) (right to vote); *Carrington v. Rash*, 380 U.S. 89 (1965) (right to vote); *Reynolds v. Sims*, 377 U.S. 533 (1964) (right to vote). See generally Note, *Developments in the Law: Equal Protection*, 82 Harv. L. Rev. 1065 (1969). "Suspect classifications" have been described as groups that are in special need of protection because they are "discrete and insular" minorities (*United States v. Carolene Products Co.*, 304 U.S. 144, 152–53 n.4 [1938]). See, e.g., *Graham v. Richardson*, 403 U.S. 365 (1971) (nationality); *Williams v. Rhodes*, 393 U.S. 23 (1968) (political allegiance); *Harper v. Virginia Bd. of Elections*, 383 U.S. 663 (1966) (wealth); *Korematsu v. United States*, 323 U.S. 214 (1944) (race). Cf. *Levy v. Louisiana*, 391 U.S. 68 (1968) (illegitimacy). See Tussman and tenBroek, *The Equal Protection of the Laws*, 37 Calif. L. Rev. 341, 356–64 (1949). See, e.g., *Shapiro v. Thompson*, 394 U.S. 618, 634 (1969): "But in moving from State to State . . . appellees were exercising a constitutional right, and any classification which serves to penalize the exercise of that right, unless shown to be necessary to promote a compelling governmental interest, is unconstitutional." The fact that the classification used must be "necessary to promote a *compelling* governmental interest" means that the Court will examine the statute's classificatory accuracy with more care. See id. at 631–38; infra note 61.

4. But see Ely, *Legislative and Administrative Motivation in Constitutional Law*, 79 Yale L.J. 1205 (1970).

5. Welfare grant rule: *Dandridge v. Williams*, 397 U.S. 471, 485 (1970). Administrators of estates: *Reed v. Reed*, 404 U.S. 71, 76 (1971). Contraceptives: *Eisenstadt v. Baird*, 405 U.S. 438, 446–47 (1972).

6. Both doctrines apparently require not only a compelling governmental interest but also a higher degree of classificatory accuracy to justify a statute that burdens a fundamental interest or suspect category. See supra note 3. The requirement that such a statute's classifications be accurate with respect to the purpose of the statute is simply an alternative formulation of the rationality requirement. See infra text related to notes 60–74.

7. See Westen, *The Empty Idea of Equality*, 95 Harv. L. Rev. 537 (1982).

8. There seems to be an axiom to fit any degree of accuracy the courts might wish to require. See *Skinner v. Oklahoma*, 316 U.S. 535, 540–41 (1942).

9. See, e.g., Tussman and tenBroek, supra note 3, at 343–53.

10. See Ely, supra note 4, at 1224–28, 1237–49.

11. Cf. Tussman and tenBroek, supra note 3, at 344–45.

12. John Ely has previously posited the same concept:

A decision to aid artists rather than oilmen is defensible in terms of promoting the arts; punishing battery more harshly than burglary is defensible in terms of the safeguarding of physical security. And so is any such choice thus defensible, because courts are prepared to credit as acceptable any goal the political branches view as contributing to the general welfare. Thus each choice will import its own goal . . . and the requirement of a "rational" choice-goal relation will be satisfied by the very making of the choice. (Ely, supra note 4, at 1247)

The same idea is also noted in passing in Note, *Developments in the Law: Equal Protection*, supra note 3, at 1082. See also Tussman and tenBroek, supra note 3, at 351. For an excellent, recent illustration, see *United States R.R. Retirement Bd. v. Fritz*, 449 U.S. 166 (1980).

13. See infra text related to note 2. There are, of course, other possible sources for ascertaining legislative purpose. It is possible to look to the legislative history to see what the legislators said they intended to accomplish; one can look at political circumstances, etc., to see what they actually intended or at the actual impact of a statute. Finally, one can look at a combination of these factors along with the statutory terms themselves. Leaving aside the question of whether any of these alternative sources of legislative purpose are empirically determinable (see infra text related to notes 55–56 for the analogous problem with ascertaining motivation), which of these possible purposes is the "real" purpose that must be utilized in the equal protection rationality test? The question has never been answered, perhaps because of the empirical problem.

If it were argued, however, that some other source (as yet undefined) of legislative purpose must be employed in the rationality test, an entirely new doctrine would be invoked. Since the "tautological" purpose of a statute, suggested by its terms, always exists, requiring the use of some other legislative purpose can only be justified on the basis that its importance (for whatever reason) outweighs that of the purpose suggested by a statute's terms. But such explicit balancing of legislative purposes has never been required by the Court as a precondition to the rationality test; nor would it be the traditional rationality requirement itself. See infra text related to notes 57–81.

The terms of a statute, then, while not the only source for determining legislative purpose, are *a* source and the purpose they suggest is *a* purpose to which the statutory classifications may be compared to implement the rationality requirement of the equal protection clause.

14. *Eisenstadt v. Baird,* 405 U.S. 438 (1972). Only Chief Justice Warren Burger dissented from the Court's action. The plurality opinion by Justice William Brennan, voiding the statute on equal protection grounds, drew the support of Justices Thurgood Marshall and Potter Stewart. Justice William Douglas concurred on a first amendment rationale. Justice Byron White, joined by Justice Harry Blackmun, concurred on the ground that the statute was overly broad because it required a medical prescription to obtain vaginal foam. Justices Lewis Powell and William Rehnquist did not participate. MASS. GEN. LAWS ANN. ch. 272 (West 1968) provided in relevant part:

> § 21 Except as provided in section twenty-one A, whoever sells, lends, gives away, exhibits . . . any drug, medicine, instrument or article whatever for the prevention of conception or for causing unlawful abortion, or manufactures or makes any such article shall be punished. . . .
>
> § 21 (A) A registered physician may administer to or prescribe for any married person drugs or articles intended for the prevention of pregnancy or conception. A registered pharmacist actually engaged in the business of pharmacy may furnish such drugs or articles to any married person presenting a prescription from a registered physician.

15. See *Commonwealth v. Corbett,* 307 Mass. 7, 8–14, 29 N.E. 2d 151, 152–55 (1940).

16. 405 U.S. at 447, quoting *Reed v. Reed,* 404 U.S. 71, 75–76 (1971).

17. 405 U.S. at 447.

18. The plurality apparently determined which legislative objectives to consider by examining the terms of the statute and by noting what objectives Massachusetts courts had previously attributed to the statute (id.).

19. Id. at 448–50.

20. Id. at 450.

21. Id. In his dissent Justice Burger properly questioned the plurality's reasoning on this point. "Assuming the legislature too broadly restricted the class of persons who could obtain contraceptives, it hardly follows that it saw no need to protect the health of all persons to whom they are made available" (id. at 468; but see id. at 451, n.8). The plurality opinion also relied on the argument made in a concurrence that the statute was over-broad with regard to this public health objective because too many types of contraceptives were included (id. at 451, n.9).

22. Id. at 454.

23. Id.

24. The statute was contained in a chapter relating to "Crimes Against Chastity, Morality, Decency, and Good Order" (id. at 450).

25. Id. at 454.

26. A legislator might, for example, believe that the use of contraceptives is an evil, although a necessary evil in the case of married couples, since even in Massachusetts people who are married are expected to engage in some sexual activity. The same legislator might also believe that restricting the availability of contraceptives to unmarried persons would discourage the evil of premarital sexual activity and somewhat abate the evil of general use of contraceptives.

27. *Levy v. Louisiana,* 391 U.S. 68 (1968). The statute provided that

the right to recover . . . if the injured person dies, shall survive for a period of one year from the death of the deceased in favor of: (1) the surviving spouse and child or children of the deceased . . . ; (2) the surviving father and mother of the deceased . . . if he left no spouse or child surviving; and (3) the surviving brothers and sisters of the deceased . . . if he left no spouse, child, or parent surviving. . . . As used in this article, the words "child," "brother," "sister," "father," and "mother" include a child, brother, sister, father, and mother by adoption, respectively. (LA. CIV. CODE ANN. art. 2315 [West Supp. 1967])

"Child" had been construed to mean "legitimate child" (*Levy v. State,* 193 So. 2d 193, 195 [La. Ct. App. 1967]).

28. 391 U.S. at 72.

29. See supra note 27.

30. 391 U.S. at 80 (Harlan, J., dissenting).

31. See, e.g., cases cited supra note 3.

32. Cf. Ely, supra note 4, at 1246; A. Bickel, THE LEAST DANGEROUS BRANCH 225 (Indianapolis: Bobbs-Merrill, 1962). The possibility that the "tautological" purpose itself might be determined to be impermissible by some independent standard is discussed infra text related to notes 48–54.

33. Ely, supra note 4, at 1224–28. For example, Ely argues that a court might restrict its attention to the goal of promoting public safety in evaluating a safety regulation also designed to aid farmers economically; with the statute's purposes thus restricted the rationality test could be meaningfully applied (id. at 1226–27, 1237–39).

34. There may in fact be some valid reason for a court to so frame the statutory purpose in any particular case. The point throughout this discussion is not to debate which goal is the "real" goal but to argue that at a minimum the goal suggested by the statutory terms should also be examined and accounted for. If it is, the rationality requirement will be met and the court need go no further with respect to *that* requirement.

35. 105 S. Ct. 3249.

36. 105 S. Ct. at 3259.

37. 283 U.S. 553 (1931).

38. Ely, supra note 4, at 1225–26.

39. For example, should it be *unconstitutional* for the legislature to attempt to aid farmers by excluding them from the requirements of a safety bond merely because such statutes normally are not used as subsidies?

40. Ely, supra note 4, at 1225. Of course, such a purpose might be thought impermissible. See infra text related to notes 48–54.

41. 427 U.S. 307 (1976).

42. See supra text related to notes 27–31. Cf. *Glona v. American Guarantee & Liab. Co.*, 391 U.S. 73, 75 (1968).

43. See supra text related to notes 26–27.

44. See supra notes 19–20.

45. The plurality did acknowledge that "discourage" was the appropriate word, but sometimes switched to "deter." See 405 U.S. at 448 (1972) and supra notes 14–15.

46. *New York Transit Auth. v. Beazer*, 440 U.S. 568 (1979).

47. The dissenters' reason was that they were convinced that patients on long-term methadone maintenance were no more risk-prone for certain jobs than was the general population (440 U.S. at 604–8). Thus, if the purpose had been to decrease risk, including this subgroup would have been irrational. However, the classification itself suggests risk reduction was not the only purpose. The public, out of either fear or disapproval, might desire that transit work be done by those whose deficiencies do not arise out of a history of heroin use, and the transit authority's policy might be a rational response to patrons' preferences. The dissent's rejection of this purpose allowed it to define the employment policy more narrowly than the policy's terms warranted, but this rejection raises the question why the transit authority's concern for public reaction was impermissible. See infra note 48 and related text.

48. 413 U.S. 528 (1973). Another example is *City of Cleburne v. Cleburne Living Center*, in which the Court said that property owners' fears or "negative attitudes" toward the retarded are not permissible bases for public policy (105 S. Ct. at 3259). Similarly, the dissent in *New York Transit Auth. v. Beazer* noted and dismissed the claim that methadone users had been denied employment because of anticipated "adverse public reaction" (440 U.S. at 609, n.15). In each case, it is unexplained why fear or hostility may not be a legitimate basis for public policy.

49. 413 U.S. at 534.

50. Id. (Emphasis in original.)

51. The Court said merely that equal protection must mean this if it is to mean anything (id.). Presumably, however, at least sometimes unpopularity is deserved. Is a "bare" desire to punish a criminal impermissible?

52. 413 U.S. 528, 545, 546 (Rehnquist, J., dissenting).

53. Supra text related to notes 37–40.

54. See generally Ely, supra note 4, at 1235 et seq.

55. See Ely, supra note 4, at 1212–14, 1217–21, 1267.

56. See, e.g., Ely, supra note 4. See also Dworkin, *The Forum of Principle*, 56 N.Y.U. L. Rev. 469 (1981).

57. See A. Bickel, supra note 32, at 225.

58. *Graham v. Richardson*, 403 U.S. 365, 376 (1971).

59. *Shapiro v. Thompson*, 394 U.S. 618, 638 (1969).

60. See supra note 3.

61. "Strict scrutiny *of the classification* . . . is essential . . ." (*Skinner v. Oklahoma*, 316 U.S. 535, 541 [1942] [emphasis added]).

62. See supra text related to notes 11–27.

63. 394 U.S. 618 (1969).

64. Id. at 631.

65. Id. at 630–31.

66. Id. at 634.

67. Id. at 638. That is, the Court held in effect that the importance of the right to travel outweighed the administrative advantages of the residency requirement to the government.

68. Id. at 635–38.

69. Id. at 629, 637–38.

70. Id. at 637–38.

71. But see supra text related to notes 44–47.

72. CONN. GEN. STAT. ANN. § 17–2c (West 1975) provided:

When any person comes into this state without visible means of support for the immediate future and applies for aid to dependent children . . . or general assistance . . . within one year from his arrival, such person shall be eligible only for temporary aid or care until arrangements are made for his return.

An exception was made for those who had a bona fide job offer (i CONN. WELFARE MANUAL, C II, § 219.1–219.2, cited in 394 U.S. at 622 n.2).

73. See supra text related to notes 58–59.

74. See supra text related to note 57.

75. *Reed v. Reed*, 404 U.S. 71 (1971). IDAHO CODE § 15–312 (1947) provided that "of several persons claiming and equally entitled to administer, males must be preferred to females."

76. 404 U.S. at 75–76.

77. Id. at 76. (Emphasis added.)

78. Id.

79. The Court held: "To give a mandatory preference to members of either sex . . . is to make the very kind of arbitrary legislative choice forbidden by the Equal Protection Clause" (404 U.S. at 76). But earlier the Court had stated:

The Court has consistently recognized that the Fourteenth Amendment does not deny to State the power to treat different classes of persons in different ways. . . . [But] a classification "must be reasonable, not arbitrary, and must rest upon some ground of difference having a fair and substantial relation to the object of the legislation." (id. at 75–76; citations omitted)

80. 404 U.S. at 76.

81. See supra text related to notes 2, 26–27.

82. *Reynolds v. Sims,* 377 U.S. 533, 566 (1964).

83. Id. at 565–66.

84. See *Whitcomb v. Chavis,* 403 U.S. 124, 141 (1971); *Lucas v. Forty-fourth Gen. Assembly of Colorado,* 377 U.S. 703, 736 (1964). The general goal of fair representation is most often expressed in the form of a subgoal: requiring legislative districts to be apportioned according to population (one person, one vote). See *Davis v. Mann,* 377 U.S. 678, 690 (1964); *Maryland Comm. for Fair Representation v. James,* 377 U.S. 656, 674 (1964); *Gray v. Sanders,* 372 U.S. 368, 381 (1963).

85. *Reynolds v. Sims,* 377 U.S. 533, 562 (1964).

86. Id. at 567. (Emphasis added.)

87. "The obligation of every school district is to terminate dual [segregated] school systems at once and to operate now and hereafter only unitary schools" (*Alexander v. Holmes County Bd. of Educ.,* 396 U.S. 19, 20 [1969]). Accord *Swann v. Charlotte-Mecklenburg Bd. of Educ.,* 402 U.S. 1, 15 (1971); *Green v. County School Bd.,* 391 U.S. 430, 438–39, 442 (1968). See *Griffin v. County School Bd.,* 377 U.S. 218, 234 (1964).

88. See *Brown v. Board of Educ.,* 347 U.S. 493–95 (1954).

Today, education is perhaps the most important function of State and local governments. Compulsory school attendance laws and the great expenditures for education both demonstrate our recognition of the importance of education to our democratic society. . . . It is the very foundation of good citizenship. (id. at 483, 493)

For an argument that sophisticated theorizing is unnecessary to find state-segregated schools in violation of fourteenth amendment equal protection standards, see Black, Jr., *The Lawfulness of the Segregation Decisions,* 69 Yale L.J. 421 (1960).

CHAPTER 6

1. For the full text of the formulae from which these examples are extracted, see infra notes 4–5, chapter 7. For other examples, see Sunstein, *Naked Preferences and the Constitution,* 84 Colum. L. Rev. 1689 (1984).

2. E.g., Leedes, *The Rationality Requirement of the Equal Protection Clause,* 42 Ohio St. L.J. 640 (1981); Bice, *Rationality Analysis in Consti-*

tutional Law, 65 Minn. L. Rev. 1 (1980); Bennett, *"Mere" Rationality in Constitutional Law: Judicial Review and Democratic Theory,* 67 Calif. L. Rev. 1049 (1979); Perry, *Modern Equal Protection: A Conceptualization and Appraisal,* 79 Colum. L. Rev. 1023 (1979); Perry, *Constitutional "Fairness": Notes on Equal Protection and Due Process,* 63 Va. L. Rev. 383 (1977).

3. Sunstein, supra note 1, at 1732.

4. Commentators have suggested, for example, that the demand be dropped when the decisions under review are "expressive" (see Bice, supra note 2, at 9) or "aesthetic" (see Leedes, supra note 2, at 665).

5. Here is a different comparison: The equal protection clause, of course, generally requires that a distinction be reasonably related to a legitimate public purpose. The eminent domain clause (adopted some eighty years earlier) requires that property be taken only if the taking is "rationally related to a conceivable public purpose" (*Hawaii Hous. Auth. v. Midkiff,* 467 U.S. 229, 241 [1984]).

6. The Court's conclusions were as follows: The 65-foot "doubles" were not more dangerous than shorter trucks (*Kassel v. Consolidated Freightways Corp.,* 450 U.S. 662, 671–74 [1981] [plurality opinion]). The abortion disclosure requirement would achieve "the antithesis of informed consent" because it would increase patients' anxiety (*Thornburgh v. American College of Obstetricians,* 106 S. Ct. 2169, 2180 [1986]). The rule against posters was sufficiently related to preventing a "visual assault" on citizens (*Los Angeles v. Taxpayers for Vincent,* 466 U.S. 789, 807 [1984]). The civil service exclusion was not related to the important purpose of "having an employee of undivided loyalty" (*Sugarman v. Dougall,* 413 U.S. 634, 641–42 [1973]). Punishing only men for statutory rape deterred teenage pregnancy (*Michael M. v. Superior Court,* 450 U.S. 464, 472–73 [1981]). Military uniforms encouraged "the subordination of personal . . . identities in favor of the general group mission" (*Goldman v. Weinberger,* 106 S. Ct. 1310, 1313 [1986]). The prohibitions against distributing child pornography were related to "the protection of children from exploitation through sexual performances" (*New York v. Ferber,* 458 U.S. 747, 757 [1982]). Automatic hearings would serve no purpose if "a foster parent . . . does not care enough about the child to contest the removal" (*Smith v. Organization of Foster Children,* 431 U.S. 816, 850 [1977]). Confining the location for solicitations would serve the state's interest in the "orderly movement of the crowd" (*Heffron v. International Soc'y for Krishna Consciousness,* 452 U.S. 640, 649–50 [1981]).

7. M. Oakeshott, RATIONALISM IN POLITICS 83 (New York: Basic Books, 1962) (emphasis in original).

8. Id. at 32.

9. Id. at 5, 7.

10. Id. at 5.

11. Id. at 4.

12. C. Kenyon, ed., THE ANTI-FEDERALISTS xl, li, liii, 388 (Indianapolis: Bobbs-Merrill, 1966).

13. THE FEDERALIST no. 10 (J. Madison); no. 51 (J. Madison) (Mentor ed.; New York: New American Library, 1961).

14. THE FEDERALIST, supra note 13, no. 16, at 116 (A. Hamilton).

15. *Eisenstadt v. Baird,* 405 U.S. 438, 453 (1972).

16. *Mississippi Univ. for Women v. Hogan,* 458 U.S. 718, 729 (1982).

17. *New York Times Co. v. Sullivan,* 376 U.S. 254, 270 (1964); *Cohen v. California,* 403 U.S. 15, 24 (1971).

18. Redish, *The Value of Free Speech,* 130 U. Pa. L. Rev. 591, 593 (1982); Perry, *Noninterpretive Review in Human Rights Cases: A Functional Justification,* 56 N.Y.U. L. Rev. 278, 314–15 (1981).

19. Epstein, *Toward a Revitalization of the Contract Clause,* 51 U. Chi. L. Rev. 703, 713, 717, 751 (1984).

20. L. Tribe, AMERICAN CONSTITUTIONAL LAW 560 (Mineola, N.Y.: Foundation Press, 1978).

21. Id. at 988.

22. M. Oakeshott, supra note 7, at 6.

23. Id. at 7.

24. E.g., P. Bobbitt, CONSTITUTIONAL FATE: THEORY OF THE CONSTITUTION 182–89 (New York: Oxford University Press, 1982). Perry, *The Authority of the Text, Tradition, and Reason: A Theory of Constitutional Interpretation,* 58 S. Cal. L. Rev. 551, 577 (1985); Burt, *Constitutional Law and the Teaching of the Parables,* 93 Yale L.J. 455 (1984); Cover, *Nomos and Narrative,* 97 Harv. L. Rev. 4 (1983).

25. The case was *Erznoznik v. City of Jacksonville,* 422 U.S. 205 (1975).

26. Aspects of *Roe v. Wade* suggest that the Court may have treated the state's interest as an "outdated worry about the health of women" (L. Tribe, supra note 20, at 931). In some quarters there is a tendency to see restrictions on abortion as efforts to control sexual behavior. An asserted interest in protecting potential human life, however, need not be justified by reference to any external value or result.

27. M. Oakeshott, supra note 7, at 84.

28. Here are two examples from widely different areas: In evaluating a state's rule against 65-foot-long "double" trucks, the Court never mentioned the possibility that the residents were afraid of—and therefore hostile to—those imposing creatures (*Kassel v. Consolidated Freightways Corp.,* 450 U.S. 662 [1981]). The Court's discussion of a child pornography law emphasized the state's purpose of preventing harm to the models, but passed over the purpose of preventing harm to a community in which such material is distributed (*New York v. Ferber,* 458 U.S. 747 [1982]).

29. *Michael M. v. Superior Court*, 450 U.S. 464 (1981).

30. Id. at 470, 472 n.7.

31. See Bryden, *Between Two Constitutions: Feminism and Pornography*, 2 Const. Comm. 147 (1985).

32. *Craig v. Boren*, 429 U.S. 190, 199 (1976). In *Craig* this position was impervious to evidence that gender was correlated to the legislative objective of traffic safety (429 U.S. at 223 [Rehnquist, J., dissenting]). For illustration of sweeping speculation about the relevance of gender differences, see *Frontiero v. Richardson*, 411 U.S. 677 (1973).

33. For example, in *Shapiro v. Thompson*, the Court opined that states can prevent welfare fraud by "investigation" and "cooperation among state welfare departments" (394 U.S. 618, 637 [1969]).

34. The courts may become uninvolved simply because the "case" has been terminated. Even when new cases are initiated, many characteristics of the judicial process discourage receptivity to new information. The original decision may have been rationalized as a matter of principle. In addition, the need for decisional consistency discourages acknowledgment of new information even when the original decision was overtly based on empirical information. For example, school desegregation orders are still entered on the premise that separate schooling instills a feeling of inferiority in minority students that affects educational performance (see *Brown v. Board of Educ.*, 347 U.S. 483, 494 n.11 [1954]), despite the discrediting of the original data upon which that premise was based. See material cited in P. Brest, PROCESSES OF CONSTITUTIONAL DECISIONMAKING 461 n.20 (Boston: Little, Brown, 1975). Moreover, a single judge or panel of judges provides only limited points of access for new information and a limited number of perspectives (and, therefore, less sensitivity to the importance of new information). For a general discussion of the tendencies of central, unitary decisionmakers to be rigid in their use of new information, see C. Lindblom, THE INTELLIGENCE OF DEMOCRACY 196–98, 230–31 (New York: Free Press, 1965).

35. The Court's only hint as to why this might be was a cryptic allusion to the "normative philosophy that underlies the Equal Protection Clause" (*Craig v. Boren*, 429 U.S. 190, 204 [1976]).

36. *Mississippi Univ. for Women v. Hogan*, 458 U.S. 718, 730 (1982); *Kassel v. Consolidated Freightways Corp.*, 450 U.S. 662, 680 (1981) (Brennan, J., concurring). For academic support for this approach, see Leedes, supra note 2, at 665; Bennett, supra note 2, at 1057–60; L. Tribe, supra note 20, at 1085.

37. C. Lindblom, supra note 34, at 142, 137–39, 146–47.

38. For a provocative argument on the need to disregard the known costs of an activity in order to discover unknowable potential benefits, see Gilder, *Prometheus Bound*, Harper's, September 1978, at 35.

39. M. Oakeshott, supra note 7, at 105.

40. *Mississippi Univ. for Women v. Hogan,* 458 U.S. 718, 725 (1982).

41. The pre-1937 commerce clause cases, discussed in chapter 4, might be viewed as examples.

42. M. Oakeshott, supra note 7, at 31.

43. E.g., L. Tribe, supra note 20, at 1091–92.

44. See text related to notes 48–52, chapter 5. Subsequently, the Court upheld a food stamp provision that disfavored families of closely related individuals (*Lyng v. Castillo,* 106 S. Ct. 2727 [1986]).

45. *Planned Parenthood of Cent. Mo. v. Danforth,* 428 U.S. 52, 67–75 (1976).

46. The Court invoked history, for instance, when it announced the right to use contraceptives in *Griswold v. Connecticut,* 381 U.S. 479, 486 (1965). It did the same when holding that states may not condition the right to marry on proof of financial support for noncustodial children (*Zablocki v. Redhail,* 434 U.S. 374, 384 [1978]). Justice Harry Blackmun, dissenting in *Bowers v. Hardwick,* 106 S. Ct. 2841, 2848 (1986), even appealed to values "deeply rooted in our Nation's history" in arguing for a right to engage in private homosexual sodomy. 106 S. Ct. at 2856.

47. The highly ambiguous mingling of humiliation, self-indulgence, and prudery that characterized attitudes toward pregnancy during much of the nineteenth century and well into the twentieth is worth thoughtful consideration:

> "Confinement" never meant simply punishment or bland custody . . . even when applied to criminals or the insane; rather, it betokened society's hope to regenerate a self in institutions modeled upon the regularity, duty, and piety of the home. Thus confinement for childbirth was withdrawal to the supreme source of a woman's identity and purpose, the home. . . .
>
> Prudery . . . concealed a complex mix of public reticence and private concern, a hesitation about revealing one's self to social judgment, but also a desire for better knowledge and advice about a healthy and morally meaningful physicality. (R. Wertz and D. Wertz, LYING-IN: A HISTORY OF CHILDBIRTH IN AMERICA 79–81 [New York: Free Press, 1977])

48. *Cleveland Bd. of Educ. v. La Fleur,* 414 U.S. 632 (1974). Only in an entirely dismissive footnote did the Court mention "the possible role of outmoded taboos" (id. at 632 n.9).

49. See M. Oakeshott, supra note 7, at 168–96.

50. The discussion in this paragraph is based heavily on the work of C. Lindblom, especially chapters 13–15 of THE INTELLIGENCE OF DEMOCRACY, supra note 34, at 192–246.

51. This point is elaborated with regard to environmental decisions in E. Haefele, REPRESENTATIVE GOVERNMENT AND ENVIRONMENTAL

MANAGEMENT 131 (Baltimore: Johns Hopkins University Press, 1973). It is also developed in C. Lindblom, supra note 34, at 87–101, 151–61, 293–310.

52. M. Oakeshott, supra note 7, at 23.

53. Id. at 2. Oakeshott wrote that rationalism, as a technique of knowledge, "can be taught best to those whose minds are empty; and if it is to be taught to one who already believes something, the first step of the teacher must be to administer a purge, to make certain that all prejudices and preconceptions are removed, to lay his foundation upon the unshakable rock of absolute ignorance" (id. at 12).

CHAPTER 7

1. The style is evident in several nonconstitutional areas as well. See, e.g., *Lugar v. Edmondson Oil Co.*, 457 U.S. 922, 930–31 (1982) (meaning of "under color of law" in 42 U.S.C. § 1983); *United States v. Frady*, 456 U.S. 152, 167–69 (1982) (availability of habeas corpus review under 28 U.S.C. § 2254); *Cort v. Ash*, 422 U.S. 66, 78 (1975) (availability of private causes of action).

2. M. Oakeshott, RATIONALISM IN POLITICS 10 (New York: Basic Books, 1962).

3. The phrase was used in *Lynch v. Donnelly*, 465 U.S. 668, 689 (1984) (O'Connor, J., concurring).

4. Modern free speech cases are especially prone to formulae. A clear example is the "*O'Brien* test" for mixed speech and nonspeech. See note 26 infra and related text. Other examples abound.

The "test" for defining obscenity is:

(a) whether "the average person, applying contemporary community standards" would find that the work, taken as a whole, appeals to the prurient interest; (b) whether the work depicts or describes, in a patently offensive way, sexual conduct specifically defined by the applicable state law; and (c) whether the work, taken as a whole, lacks serious literary, artistic, political, or scientific value. (*Miller v. California*, 413 U.S. 15, 24 [1973] [citations omitted])

The standards for evaluating restrictions on "child pornography" are:

The conduct to be prohibited must be adequately defined by the applicable state law, as written or authoritatively construed. . . . The state offense [must] be limited to words that *visually* depict sexual conduct by children below a specified age. The category of "sexual conduct" proscribed must also be suitably limited and described. (*New York v. Ferber*, 458 U.S. 747, 764 [1982] [footnote omitted, emphasis in original])

The "four-part" analysis for commercial speech cases is:

[first] whether the expression is protected by the First Amendment. For commercial speech to come within that provision, it at least must concern lawful activity and not be misleading. Next, we ask whether the asserted governmental interest is substantial. If both inquiries yield positive answers, we must determine whether the regulation directly advances the governmental interest asserted, and whether it is not more extensive than is necessary to serve that interest. (*Central Hudson Gas & Elec. v. Public Serv. Comm'n*, 447 U.S. 557, 566 [1980])

"Time, place and manner" restrictions on speech are approved "provided that they are justified without reference to the content of the regulated speech, that they serve a significant governmental interest, and that in doing so they leave open ample alternative channels for communication of the information" (*Virginia State Bd. of Pharmacy v. Virginia Citizens Consumer Council*, 425 U.S. 748, 771 [1976]).

Programs that aid religious institutions must satisfy this test: "First, the statute must have a secular legislative purpose; second, its principal or primary effect must be one that neither advances nor inhibits religion; finally, the statute must not foster 'an excessive government entanglement with religion'" (*Lemon v. Kurtzman*, 403 U.S. 602, 612–13 [1971] [citation omitted]). For an insightful analysis, see Johnson, *Concepts and Compromise in First Amendment Religious Doctrine*, 72 Calif. L. Rev. 817 (1984).

The test for state sovereignty under the tenth amendment is now at least temporarily abandoned, but was employed by the Court in a series of cases beginning in 1981 with *Hodel v. Virginia Surface Mining & Reclamation Ass'n*, 452 U.S. 264. See note 56 infra and related text.

There are various equal protection standards. One version of the so-called "strict scrutiny" standard is: "In order to justify the use of a suspect classification, a State must show that its purpose or interest is both constitutionally permissible and substantial, and that its use of the classification is 'necessary . . . to the accomplishment' of its purpose or the safeguarding of its interest" (*In re Griffiths*, 413 U.S. 717, 721–22 [1973] [footnotes omitted]). The subtleties of phrasing are clearly presented in the variations on the "middle-level" of scrutiny used in sex discrimination cases. One formulation states: "To withstand constitutional challenge . . . classifications by gender must serve important governmental objectives and must be substantially related to achievement of those objectives" (*Craig v. Boren*, 429 U.S. 190, 197 [1976]). A more recent version is:

> The party seeking to uphold a statute that classifies individuals on the basis of their gender must carry the burden of showing an "exceedingly persuasive justification" for the classification. The burden is met only by showing at least that the classification serves "important governmental objectives and that the

discriminatory means employed" are "substantially related to the achievement of those objectives."

[This test] must be applied free of fixed notions concerning the roles and abilities of males and females. Care must be taken in ascertaining whether the statutory objective itself reflects archaic and stereotypic notions. (*Mississippi Univ. for Women v. Hogan*, 458 U.S. 718, 724–25 [1982] [citations and footnote omitted])

The best-known due process formulation is the trimester-based test for restrictions on the right to abortion:

(a) For the stage prior to approximately the end of the first trimester, the abortion decision and its effectuation must be left to the medical judgment of the pregnant woman's attending physician.

(b) For the stage subsequent to approximately the end of the first trimester, the State, in promoting its interest in the health of the mother, may, if it chooses, regulate the abortion procedure in ways that are reasonably related to maternal health.

(c) For the stage subsequent to viability, the State in promoting its interest in the potentiality of human life may, if it chooses, regulate, and even proscribe, abortion except where it is necessary, in appropriate medical judgment, for the preservation of the life or health of the mother. (*Roe v. Wade*, 410 U.S. 113, 164–65 [1973])

As for procedural due process:

Resolution of the issue whether the administrative procedures . . . are constitutionally sufficient requires analysis of the governmental and private interests that are affected. More precisely, . . . identification of the specific dictates of due process generally requires consideration of three distinct factors: First, the private interest that will be affected by the official action; second, the risk of an erroneous deprivation of such interest through the procedures used, and the probable value, if any, of additional or substitute procedural safeguards; and finally, the Government's interest, including the function involved and the fiscal and administrative burdens that the additional or substitute procedural requirement would entail. (*Mathews v. Eldridge*, 424 U.S. 319, 334–35 [1976] [citations omitted])

The case and controversy standard is as follows:

At an irreducible minimum, Art. III requires the party who invokes the court's authority to "show that he personally has suffered some actual or threatened injury as a result of the putatively illegal conduct of the defendant . . ." and that the injury "fairly can be traced to the challenged action" and "is likely to be redressed by a favorable decision." (*Valley Forge Christian College v. Americans United for Separation of Church & State, Inc.*, 454 U.S. 464, 472 [1982] [citations and footnote omitted])

On the commerce power, see, e.g., notes 27, 100 infra and related text. Another version of the correct "principles" in "dormant" commerce clause cases is:

> (1) The courts are not empowered to second-guess the empirical judgments of lawmakers concerning the utility of legislation.
>
> (2) The burdens imposed on commerce must be balanced against the local benefits actually sought to be achieved by the State's lawmakers, and not against those suggested after the fact by counsel.
>
> (3) Protectionist legislation is unconstitutional under the Commerce Clause, even if the burdens and benefits are related to safety rather than economics. (*Kassel v. Consolidated Freightways Corp.*, 450 U.S. 662, 679–80 [1981] [Brennan, J., concurring])

The test for state taxes on interstate activities sustains the taxes when evaluated according to "practical effect" rather than "formal language": "[The Court has] sustained a tax against Commerce Clause challenge when the tax is applied to an activity with a substantial nexus with the taxing State, is fairly apportioned, does not discriminate against interstate commerce, and is fairly related to the services provided by the State" (*Complete Auto Transit, Inc. v. Brady*, 430 U.S. 274, 279 [1977]).

The formula for the contract clause is:

> The threshold inquiry is "whether the state law has, in fact, operated as a substantial impairment of a contractual relationship." . . .
>
> If the state regulation constitutes a substantial impairment, the State, in justification, must have a significant and legitimate public purpose behind the regulation. . . .
>
> Once a legitimate public purpose has been identified, the next inquiry is whether the adjustment of "the rights and responsibilities of contracting parties [is based] upon reasonable conditions and [is] of a character appropriate to the public purpose justifying [the legislation's] adoption." (*Energy Reserves Group v. Kansas Power & Light Co.*, 459 U.S. 400, 411–12 [1983])

On privileges and immunities of Article IV:

> Application of the Privileges and Immunities Clause to a particular instance of discrimination against out-of-state residents entails a two-step inquiry. As an initial matter, the Court must decide whether the ordinance burdens one of those privileges and immunities protected by the Clause. . . . As a threshold matter, then, we must determine whether an out-of-state resident's interest in employment on public works contracts in another State is sufficiently "fundamental" to the promotion of interstate harmony so as to "fall within the purview of the Privileges and Immunities Clause."
>
> . . . The conclusion that [an] ordinance discriminates against a protected privilege does not, of course, end the inquiry . . . where there is a "substantial reason" for the difference in treatment. "[T]he inquiry in each case must be concerned with whether such reasons do exist and whether the degree

of discrimination bears a close relation to them." (*United Bldg. & Constr. Trades Council v. Mayor of Camden*, 465 U.S. 208, 218–22 [1984] [citations omitted])

The "two-step analysis" for waiver of the fifth amendment right to counsel is:

Before a suspect in custody can be subjected to further interrogation after he requests an attorney there must be a showing that the "suspect himself initiates dialogue with the authorities."

. . . Where reinterrogation follows, the burden remains upon the prosecution to show that subsequent events indicated a waiver of the Fifth Amendment right to have counsel present during the interrogation. (*Oregon v. Bradshaw*, 462 U.S. 1039, 1044 [1983])

A test for identifying cruel and unusual punishment is:

A court's proportionality analysis under the Eighth Amendment should be guided by objective criteria, including (i) the gravity of the offense and the harshness of the penalty; (ii) the sentences imposed on other criminals in the same jurisdiction; and (iii) the sentences imposed for commission of the same crime in other jurisdictions. (*Solem v. Helm*, 463 U.S. 277, 292 [1983])

5. Effective counsel:

A convicted defendant's claim that counsel's assistance was so defective as to require reversal of a conviction or death sentence has two components. First, the defendant must show that counsel's performance was deficient. This requires showing that counsel made errors so serious that counsel was not functioning as the "counsel" guaranteed the defendant by the Sixth Amendment. Second, the defendant must show that the deficient performance prejudiced the defense. This requires showing that counsel's errors were so serious as to deprive the defendant of a fair trial, a trial whose result is reliable. (*Strickland v. Washington*, 466 U.S. 668, 687 [1984])

Right to conduct defense:

First, the *pro se* defendant is entitled to preserve actual control over the case he chooses to present to the jury. . . .

Second, participation by standby counsel without the defendant's consent should not be allowed to destroy the jury's perception that the defendant is representing himself. (*McKaskle v. Wiggins*, 465 U.S. 168, 178 [1984])

On reasonable searches:

[In] determining whether the seizure and search were "unreasonable" our inquiry is a dual one—whether the officer's action was justified at its inception, and whether it was reasonably related in scope to the circumstances which justified the interference in the first place. (*Terry v. Ohio*, 392 U.S. 1, 19–20 [1968])

My understanding of the rule . . . is that there is a twofold requirement, first that a person have exhibited an actual (subjective) expectation of privacy and, second, that the expectation be one that society is prepared to recognize as "reasonable." (*Katz v. United States*, 389 U.S. 347, 361 [1967] [Harlan, J., concurring])

6. An insightful account of the reactions to judicial decisions of both prison officials and inmates is J. Jacobs, STATEVILLE: THE PENITENTIARY IN MASS SOCIETY 107–13, 117–19 (Chicago: University of Chicago Press, 1977).

7. The requirement of "knowing or reckless" disregard for the truth always contained the seeds of intrusive inquiries into the journalists' motivations, but, despite its precise content, *New York Times Co. v. Sullivan*, 376 U.S. 254 (1964) quickly became a symbol of general immunization. These high hopes, perhaps, explain the outraged cries of betrayal that followed, for example, a rather predictable decision holding that political motivations (and "muckraking" styles) are relevant to "recklessness": see Nagel, *How to Stop Libel Suits and Still Protect Individual Reputation*, Washington Monthly, November 1985, at 12.

8. Indeed, scholars sometimes describe the "meaning" of a decision in terms that have almost nothing to do with either holding or reasoning. See, e.g., P. Bobbitt, CONSTITUTIONAL FATE: THEORY OF THE CONSTITUTION 213–19 (New York: Oxford University Press, 1982): "The holding in the Tapes Case [*United States v. Nixon*, 418 U.S. 683 (1974)] is not the preposterous one stated by the Court. . . . The real holding is that a President . . . may not manipulate the instrumentalities of law enforcement both to prevent the law's enforcement and to acquit himself."

9. Cardozo, *Law and Literature*, 14 Yale Rev. 699, 700 (1925). This essay was reprinted in 39 Colum. L. Rev. 119, 120; 52 Harv. L. Rev. 471, 472; and 48 Yale L.J. 489, 490, all in 1939 in special issues upon the occasion of Cardozo's death.

10. Some of the needs that scholars attempt to fulfill by attention to Supreme Court opinions are explored in Nagel, *On Complaining About the Burger Court*, book review, 84 Colum. L. Rev. 2068 (1984).

11. The difficulty of giving concrete meaning to such vague modern ideals as "personhood" and "public values" is self-evident. The complexities involved in serious efforts to accomplish the more traditional goals of deriving meaning from the framers' intentions or from the document's text are illustrated, respectively, in Tushnet, *Following the Rules Laid Down: A Critique of Interpretivism and Neutral Principles*, 96 Harv. L. Rev. 781, 786, and passim (1983); and in Laycock, *Taking Constitutions Seriously: A Theory of Judicial Review*, book review, 59 Tex. L. Rev. 343, 360, and passim (1981).

12. On teaching free speech, see, e.g., T. Emerson, THE SYSTEM OF FREEDOM OF EXPRESSION (New York: Random House, 1970). On mutual accommodation, see Burt, *The Burger Court and the Family*, in V. Blasi, ed., THE BURGER COURT: THE COUNTER-REVOLUTION THAT WASN'T 92, 107 (New Haven: Yale University Press, 1983). On moral philosophy, see, e.g., Dworkin, *The Forum of Principle*, 56 N.Y.U. L. Rev. 469 (1981); Fiss, *The Forms of Justice*, 93 Harv. L. Rev. 1 (1979). On prophesy, see M. Perry, THE CONSTITUTION, THE COURT, AND HUMAN RIGHTS (New Haven: Yale University Press, 1982). On voicing the spirit, see A. Cox, THE ROLE OF THE SUPREME COURT IN AMERICAN GOVERNMENT 117 (New York: Oxford University Press, 1976). On aesthetic principles, see P. Bobbitt, supra note 8, at 185.

13. For example, in places Philip Bobbitt writes as if the "expressive" function of the Court were independent of what it actually says in its opinions. See P. Bobbitt, supra note 8. Michael Perry refers almost exclusively to outcomes when making his claim that the Court helps society achieve moral progress. See, e.g., Perry, *Noninterpretive Review in Human Rights Cases: A Functional Justification*, 56 N.Y.U. L. Rev. 278, 314–15 (1981) [hereinafter cited as Perry, *Noninterpretive Review*]. See also Fiss, supra note 12, at 30 (arguing that adjudication gives "meaning to our public values" by enforcing or creating norms); Perry, *The Authority of Text, Tradition, and Reason: A Theory of Constitutional "Interpretation,"* 58 S. Cal. L. Rev. 551, 577 (1985) (claiming that case outcomes demonstrate that the Court builds the traditions of political community). Even Mark Tushnet, who emphasizes that constitutional interpretation is derivative from shared understandings within the community, shows little interest in the possibility that judicial review may be destructive of "shared system[s] of meanings." See Tushnet, supra note 11, at 824–27; Tushnet, *A Note on the Revival of Textualism in Constitutional Theory*, 58 S. Cal. L. Rev. 683, 683–92 (1985).

14. J. White, WHEN WORDS LOSE THEIR MEANING 273 (Chicago: University of Chicago Press, 1984). See also B. Barber, STRONG DEMOCRACY: PARTICIPATORY POLITICS FOR A NEW AGE 152–85 (Berkeley and Los Angeles: University of California Press, 1984); Cover, *Nomos and Narrative*, 97 Harv. L. Rev. 4 (1983).

15. J. White, supra note 14, at 245.

16. Justice Black titled his book A CONSTITUTIONAL FAITH (New York: Knopf, 1968). For general discussions of religiosity, see Lerner, *Constitution and Courts as Symbols*, 46 Yale L.J. 1290, 1294–95 (1937); Levinson, *"The Constitution" in American Civil Religion*, 1979 Sup. Ct. Rev. 123.

17. B. Jordan and S. Hearon, BARBARA JORDAN: A SELF-PORTRAIT 187 (Garden City, N.Y.: Doubleday, 1979) (recounting her address to

the House Judiciary Committee during consideration of articles of impeachment against President Nixon).

18. Fiss, *Objectivity and Interpretation*, 34 Stan. L. Rev. 739, 763
(1982).

19. E.g., Parker, *The Past of Constitutional Theory—And Its Future*, 42
Ohio St. L.J. 223, 223–24, 257–59 (1981); Tushnet, *Darkness on the
Edge of Town: The Contributions of John Hart Ely to Constitutional Theory*,
89 Yale L.J. 1037, 1058–60 (1980).

20. This phenomenon is given amusing treatment in Kaus, *Constitutional Boo-Boos*, Am. Law., March 1982, at 51. An example is art. II, § 2,
cl. 2, which provides: "The President . . . may require the Opinion, in
writing, of the principal Officer in each of the executive Departments,
upon any Subject relating to the Duties of their respective Offices." Many
serious people would judge the second amendment's right to keep and
bear arms as fundamentally misguided (at least if it were enforced). Early
experience with the requirement that the president seek "the advice and
consent" of the Senate was a failure and has been consistently ignored.
See H. Horwill, THE USAGES OF THE AMERICAN CONSTITUTION 104–5
(London: Oxford University Press, 1925). There is a venerable tradition
of criticizing the principle of separation of powers as a fundamental mistake. See, e.g., K. Loewenstein, POLITICAL POWER AND THE GOV-
ERNMENTAL PROCESS 244–50 (Chicago: University of Chicago Press,
1957); W. Wilson, CONGRESSIONAL GOVERNMENT: A STUDY IN AMER-
ICAN POLITICS (Boston: Houghton Mifflin, 1885). Jesse Choper, among
others, suggests that the principle of federalism has "outlived its usefulness" (JUDICIAL REVIEW AND THE NATIONAL POLITICAL PROCESS
255–56 [Chicago: University of Chicago Press, 1980]). Other examples
include the third amendment (prohibition against quartering soldiers)
and section 2 of the fourteenth amendment (number of representatives
apportioned by excluding "Indians not taxed").

For reprehensible provisions, see art. I, § 9, cl. 1:

> The Migration or Importation of such Persons as any of the States now exist-
> ing shall think proper to admit, shall not be prohibited by the Congress prior
> to the Year one thousand eight hundred and eight, but a Tax or duty may be
> imposed on such Importation, not exceeding ten dollars for each Person.

See also art. IV, § 2, cl. 3:

> No Person held to Service or Labor in one State, under the Laws thereof,
> escaping into another, shall, in Consequence of any Law or Regulation
> therein, be discharged from such Service or Labor, but shall be delivered up
> on Claim of the Party to whom such Service or Labor may be due.

21. The central example, of course, is school desegregation. See, e.g.,
Bickel, *The Original Understanding and the Segregation Decision*, 69 Harv.

L. Rev. 1 (1955). But similar difficulties surround almost all the highly regarded decisions of the modern era. See Perry, *Interpretivism, Freedom of Expression, and Equal Protection*, 42 Ohio St. L.J. 261, 284–301 (1981) (arguing that virtually all human rights decisions in this century have neither textual nor historical justification).

22. This occurred, for example, with the "advice and consent" clause. See note 20 supra. It has been the general history of the tenth amendment since 1937. See Wechsler, *Toward Neutral Principles of Constitutional Law*, 73 Harv. L. Rev. 1, 23–24 (1959) (arguing that the Court had virtually abandoned limits on federal commerce power). See also *Garcia v. San Antonio Metropolitan Transit Auth.*, 105 S. Ct. 1005 (1985).

23. The principle of freedom of speech, for example, was largely ignored or resisted for more than a century. See note 2, chapter 3.

24. The Court viewed the issue as one of content discrimination against nudity. *Erznoznik v. City of Jacksonville*, 422 U.S. 205 (1975). Although in *Roe v. Wade*, 410 U.S. 113, 153 (1977), the Court pointed to a number of serious concerns that might motivate an abortion, its formulation protects the right during the first two trimesters no matter how frivolous or odious the woman's motives might be.

25. On right answers, see Perry, *Noninterpretive Review*, supra note 13, at 295. Although it is understandable that interest groups, such as journalists, would see disaster behind every interpretation they disapprove of (see, e.g., Nagel, supra note 7), self-interest cannot explain similar kinds of reactions by scholars. The distinguished professor Archibald Cox, for example, went before Congress to oppose the balanced budget amendment to the Constitution. He testified that the amendment threatened "the ancient framework of American government and constitutional liberties of citizens." *Constitutional Amendments Seeking to Balance the Budget and Limit Federal Spending: Hearings Before the Subcomm. on Monopolies and Commercial Law of the House Comm. on the Judiciary*, 97th Cong., 2d sess. 542, 545 (1982) (statement of Professor Archibald Cox, Chairman, Common Cause) (hereinafter cited as *Hearings on Amendments*). Similarly, he testified that the proposed "Human Life Bill," which would have deemed fetal life to be human life for limited purposes under the due process clause, was a "radical and dangerously unprincipled attack upon the foundations of our constitutionalism." *The Human Life Bill: Hearings on S.158 Before the Subcomm. on Separation of Powers of the Senate Comm. on the Judiciary*, 97th Cong., 1st sess., 331, 346 (1981) (statement of Professor Archibald Cox). The certitude that lies at the base of such fears was revealed in Cox's assertion that "the Constitution is confined to those enduring fundamentals upon the essence of which we are all agreed." *Hearings on Amendments*, supra, at 542.

26. *United States v. O'Brien*, 391 U.S. 367, 376–77 (1968).

27. *Hughes v. Oklahoma*, 441 U.S. 322, 336 (1979).

28. For a description of common characteristics of Legal English, see Danet, *Language in the Legal Process,* 14 Law & Soc'y Rev. 445, 469–82 (1980).

29. For another example, see note 72 infra and related text.

30. See Danet, supra note 28, at 450–52, 465–67 (noting the view that while Legal English may be valuable to the legal profession, it should be avoided when talking with clients).

31. For an arresting account of how Justice Brennan designed doctrine "like a diagram with footprints and arrows" to achieve long-term objectives, see Fiss, *Dombrowski,* 86 Yale L.J. 1103 (1977).

32. It has taken many opinions and years of reflection for the Court to decide whether in sex discrimination cases the government must show a justification that is "compelling" or "important" or (as it seems now to have decided) "exceedingly persuasive." Compare *Frontiero v. Richardson,* 411 U.S. 677, 688 (1973) (plurality opinion applying "strict scrutiny" standard) with *Craig v. Boren,* 429 U.S. 190, 197 (1976) (requiring that gender-based classifications serve "important" governmental objectives) and *Mississippi Univ. for Women v. Hogan,* 458 U.S. 718, 731 (1982) (requiring "exceedingly persuasive justification" to sustain state's gender-based classification). Or, to use a different kind of example, when the Court assesses state regulations that affect interstate commerce, the "appropriate analysis" requires a "strong presumption" of validity and a "sensitive consideration" of the local safety purpose in relation to the burden on interstate commerce. Much analysis now goes into accommodating "sensitive consideration" with "strong presumptions." See notes 100–102 infra and related text.

A debate flourished for a while about whether "strict scrutiny" should be extended to areas in which "fundamental" interests are affected by limitations on governmental expenditure programs. Compare *Shapiro v. Thompson,* 394 U.S. 618 (1969) (applying "strict scrutiny" to denial of welfare assistance to new state residents) with *Dandridge v. Williams,* 397 U.S. 471 (1970) (refusing to apply "strict scrutiny" to a statutory ceiling on welfare assistance). Gerald Gunther called this "The 'Fundamental Rights and Interests' Strand of Strict Scrutiny" (CONSTITUTIONAL LAW 787 [11th ed.; Mineola, N.Y.: Foundation Press, 1985]). Other well-known debates about the appropriate scope of "strict scrutiny" have involved discrimination on the basis of sex, alienage, and race when used for compensatory purposes. See notes 106–7 infra. Recently, the Court virtually abandoned any effort to limit the federal commerce power by tenth amendment principles because it was persuaded that the applicable tests were unworkable. *Garcia v. San Antonio Metropolitan Transit Auth.,* 105 S. Ct. 1005 (1985). Currently, there is considerable debate about whether the establishment clause tests are only "useful" guidelines that ought sometimes to be ignored or are a "settled" and obligatory method of analysis. Compare *Lynch v. Donnelly,* 465 U.S. 668, 674–75 (1984) (opinion by Burger, C.J., enunciating "unwillingness to be confined to any single test or criterion") with *Lynch,* 465 U.S. at 694–96 (Brennan, J., dissenting, treating the establishment clause tests as firmly settled).

Justice Sandra O'Connor has suggested that the political divisiveness subprong of "the excessive-entanglement prong of the *Lemon* test" should be dropped (*Lynch v. Donnelly,* 465 U.S. 668, 689 [1984] [O'Connor, J., concurring]). In *Oregon v. Bradshaw,* 462 U.S. 1039, 1045 (1983), Justice William Rehnquist argued against "melding" prongs, while Justice Lewis Powell argued against "bifurcating" prongs (*Bradshaw,* 462 U.S. at 1048–50).

Justice Thurgood Marshall once argued that the various equal protection tests actually represented a single, "sliding" scale principle (*Dandridge v. Williams,* 397 U.S. 471, 519–21 [1970] [Marshall, J., dissenting]). See also *City of Cleburne v. Cleburne Living Center,* 105 S. Ct. 3249, 3260–61 (1985) (Stevens, J., concurring); *Craig v. Boren,* 429 U.S. 190, 211–12 (1976) (Stevens, J., concurring). Two Justices debated whether the rationality standard has any meaning in *Trimble v. Gordon,* 430 U.S. 762, 766–67, 780–82 (1977) (opinions by Powell, J., and Rehnquist, J.).

33. The style associated with formalism is described in K. Llewellyn, THE COMMON LAW TRADITION 100 (Boston: Little, Brown, 1960). See also G. Gilmore, THE AGES OF AMERICAN LAW 62–63 (New Haven: Yale University Press, 1977). For an example, see infra notes 47–49 and related text.

34. Llewellyn said that decisions in the grand style tended to be written simply and with "pungency" (see K. Llewellyn, supra note 33, at 37); on the relationship between realism and instrumentalism, see R. Summers, INSTRUMENTALISM AND AMERICAN LEGAL THEORY 48, 277 (Ithaca: Cornell University Press, 1982).

35. With both great legal traditions—formalism and realism—having been found wanting, legal decisions are now made without any settled tradition or philosophical basis. For discussions, see G. Gilmore, supra note 33, ch. 4; Goetsch, *The Future of Legal Formalism,* 24 Am. J.L. Hist. 221, 256 (1980); Hutchinson, *From Cultural Construction to Historical Deconstruction,* book review, 94 Yale L.J. 209, 212 (1984). For a critique of the realists and a tentative prescription for refinement, see R. Summers, supra note 34.

36. Although some formulae are related to the Constitution in only the most superficial way (e.g., *Roe v. Wade,* 410 U.S. 113, 164 [1973]), and although formulae tend quickly to substitute themselves for external constitutional authority (see infra notes 54–59 and related text), the

Court still generally claims that its doctrines implement values found in the Constitution. See, e.g., *Lynch v. Donnelly,* 465 U.S. 668, 678–79 (1984) (relating three-part *Lemon* test to "real object" of the first amendment). In light of current intellectual ferment over the extent to which a document can impose constraints on interpretation, this is not as small a point as it might seem. See, e.g., *Essays on "The Politics of Legal Interpretation,"* in W. Mitchell, ed., THE POLITICS OF INTERPRETATION 249–320 (Chicago: University of Chicago Press, 1982); symposium, *Law and Literature,* 60 Tex. L. Rev. 373 passim (1982).

37. For example, the standard for evaluating "time, place, and manner" restrictions on speech involves a principle (content discrimination is prohibited), a utilitarian calculus (the restriction must serve a significant interest), and an instrumental rule (alternative channels of communications must be available). See supra note 4.

38. See supra note 37. Other examples include the requirement that obscenity lack "serious literary, artistic, political, or scientific value" (see supra note 4); the rule that statutes must not foster "excessive government entanglement" with religion (see supra note 4); and the calculus for procedural due process claims, which focuses attention on "the risk of erroneous deprivation of [the individual's] interest . . . and the probable value . . . of additional or substitute procedural safeguards . . . and the . . . burdens that the additional or substitute procedural requirement would entail" (see supra note 4).

39. I am using the term as Robert Bennett uses it in *Objectivity in Constitutional Law,* 132 U. Pa. L. Rev. 445 (1984).

40. Formulae are specific to resident aliens who are denied economic benefits, as opposed to those who are denied membership in the political community (*Cabell v. Chavez-Salido,* 454 U.S. 432 [1982]); to restrictions on "child pornography" as opposed to obscenity (see supra note 4); to restrictions on "commercial speech" (see supra note 4); and so on.

41. For a summary, see R. Summers, supra note 34, at 144–47.

42. "Doctrine" (in the general sense of reasoning from rules) has the effect, of course, of focusing attention on itself and thus, as Philip Bobbitt noted, can easily be "severed from the animating text" (P. Bobbitt, supra note 8, at 54–55).

43. Although the phrasing is repeated frequently, no one thinks that inhibiting a religion can cause its establishment. See Laycock, *Towards a General Theory of the Religion Clauses: The Case of Church Labor Relations and the Right to Church Autonomy,* 81 Colum. L. Rev. 1373, 1380 (1981). Such phrases have much in common with the general phenomenon of "doublets" (the combination of words like "break and enter" or "rules and regulations"). See Danet, supra note 28, at 469. Doublets originally repeated a thought with a word of a different linguistic origin so that the phrase could be understood in cultures with multiple lan-

guages (id.). The combinations found in modern formulae, whatever their derivation, serve a roughly similar purpose; they are an attempt to assure understanding by repetition.

44. For example, the Court has removed the possibility of any real significance from the fourth prong of the test for assessing state taxes on natural resources (that the tax be "fairly related to the services provided by the State"). See Williams, *Severance Taxes and Federalism: The Role of the Supreme Court in Preserving a National Common Market for Energy Supplies*, 53 U. Colo. L. Rev. 281, 287–89 (1981). It still is carried as part of the formula and has a nice ring to it.

45. See, e.g., the "two-part test" for defining the "political function exception" (to the "strict scrutiny" standard for assessing discrimination against aliens). *Cabell v. Chavez-Salido*, 454 U.S. 432, 440–41 (1982). See also the "two requirements" used to implement a part of the middle level of review used in illegitimacy cases. *Mills v. Habluetzel*, 456 U.S. 91, 99–100 (1982). There is also a formula used to define "excessive sentence," a phrase that is itself part of a doctrine used to define "cruel and unusual punishment." *Solem v. Helm*, 463 U.S. 277, 290–92 (1983).

46. *Clark v. Community for Creative Non-Violence*, 104 S. Ct. 3065, 3079 (1984) (Marshall, J., dissenting).

47. *United States v. Butler*, 297 U.S. 1, 62 (1936).

48. 297 U.S. 1 (1936).

49. 297 U.S. at 62–63.

50. 17 U.S. (4 Wheat.) 316 (1819). For a related, but quite different, view of the decision, see J. White, supra note 14, at 263.

51. 17 U.S. (4 Wheat.) at 413–14.

52. 17 U.S. (4 Wheat.) at 415–19.

53. 17 U.S. (4 Wheat.) at 421.

54. 426 U.S. 833 (1976), overruled in *Garcia v. San Antonio Metropolitan Transit Auth.*, 105 S. Ct. 1005 (1985). The issues raised by these cases are discussed in chapter 4, supra.

55. 426 U.S. at 843, quoting *Fry v. United States*, 421 U.S. 542, 547 n.7 (1975).

56. *Hodel v. Virginia Surface Mining Reclamation Ass'n*, 452 U.S. 264, 287–88 (1981) (citations omitted) (emphasis in original). See also *EEOC v. Wyoming*, 460 U.S. 226 (1983); *FERC v. Mississippi*, 456 U.S. 742 (1982).

57. 426 U.S. at 845, citing *Coyle v. Oklahoma*, 221 U.S. 559, 565 (1911).

58. This is a position similar to one that Chief Justice Marshall once considered reading into the Constitution itself, although at a time when the commerce power seemed more confined (*Gibbons v. Ogden*, 22 U.S. [9 Wheat.] 1 [1824]).

59. See supra note 56 and cases therein. In the Federalists' theory,

general regulatory power was essential to a state's capacity to act as a governmental "counterpoise" to the national government. See text related to notes 89–100, 107–13, chapter 4.

60. See, e.g., the discussion of *Lynch v. Donnelly* in note 32 supra. See also *Solem v. Helm*, 463 U.S. 277, 291 (1983) (factors "may be helpful" or "useful").

61. For example, several formulae have been established for sex discrimination cases. Compare *Reed v. Reed*, 404 U.S. 71 (1971) ("rational relationship" standard for gender classifications) with note 32 supra and cases cited therein ("strict scrutiny" and "intermediate scrutiny" applied to gender-based classifications in different cases). On the abandonment of constitutional inquiry, see *Garcia v. San Antonio Metropolitan Transit Auth.*, 105 S. Ct. 1005 (1985). See also supra note 4.

62. See Danet, supra note 28, at 508–9.

63. At one time an effort was made to link creativity in the common law to custom and popular consent. See M. Horwitz, THE TRANSFORMATION OF AMERICAN LAW, 1780–1860, 18–23 (Cambridge: Harvard University Press, 1977). Formalism was often pictured as obscure, nonintuitive, elitist, and pseudoscientific. Under this view, "laymen's reasoning [is separated] from professional reasoning" in order to hide the connection between law and politics (id. at 256–59). Today, however, there is strong reason to identify reformers and realists as those who rely on a scientific overlay to protect their power. See G. Gilmore, supra note 33, ch. 4 (1977), suggesting this connection. See also B. Ackerman, RECONSTRUCTING AMERICAN LAW (Cambridge: Harvard University Press, 1984), illustrating the connection. At any rate, Philip Bobbitt is surely right that literalistic arguments "rest on a sort of ongoing social contract, whose terms are given their contemporary meanings continually" (P. Bobbitt, supra note 8, at 26). He notes that two great textualists, Justices Hugo Black and Joseph Story, believed that common understandings, rather than recondite meanings or superior learning, should control textual interpretations.

64. 298 U.S. 238, 307 (1936).

65. *United States v. Butler*, 297 U.S. 1, 72–74 (1936).

66. *Stafford v. Wallace*, 258 U.S. 495, 516 (1922). *Swift & Co. v. United States*, 196 U.S. 375, 399 (1905).

67. See supra notes 50–53 and related text. This theme is fully developed in J. White, supra note 14, at 247–63.

68. Holmes wrote:

But the character of every act depends upon the circumstances in which it is done. The most stringent protection of free speech would not protect a man in falsely shouting fire in a theatre and causing a panic. . . . The question in every case is whether the words used are used in such circumstances and are of such a nature as to create a clear and present danger. (*Schenck v. United States*, 249 U.S. 47, 52 [1919] [citation omitted])

69. In *Whitney v. California*, Brandeis wrote:

Those who won our independence believed that the final end of the State was to make men free to develop their faculties; and that in its government the deliberative forces should prevail over the arbitrary. They valued liberty both as an end and as a means. They believed liberty to be the secret of happiness and courage to be the secret of liberty. (274 U.S. 357, 375 [1927] [Brandeis, J., concurring] [overruled by *Brandenburg v. Ohio*, 395 U.S. 444 (1969)]; cf. L. Levy, FREEDOM OF SPEECH AND PRESS IN EARLY AMERICAN HISTORY: LEGACY OF SUPPRESSION [New York: Harper & Row, 1963])

70. 347 U.S. 483, 494 (1954). The Court also referred to social science evidence concerning detrimental educational effects, thus illustrating the unfortunate modern compulsion to rely on *something* other than common experience and understanding. It is this compulsion that finds its current expression in the artificial language of the formulaic style.

71. On state sovereignty, see supra note 56 and related text. It is almost indisputable that states should continue to exist. But see Tushnet, supra note 11, at 800 n.54. On furthering a state's interest, see note 26 supra and related text. In *United States v. O'Brien* itself the Court described the prohibition against burning draft cards as essential to certain governmental interests (391 U.S. 367, 381–82 [1968]), but these interests might have been satisfied as well by a requirement that draft boards be notified promptly upon destruction and that a self-addressed, stamped envelope be enclosed to assure prompt replacement.

72. 421 U.S. 349, 363–66 (1975).

73. The Court found that a city's crèche served the secular functions of celebrating the Christmas holiday and depicting its origins (*Lynch v. Donnelly*, 465 U.S. 668, 681 [1984]). As to the possibility that the city might have had other purposes, the Court commented that "all that *Lemon* requires" is that there be "a secular purpose" (465 U.S. at 681 n.6 [citation omitted]). Thus, only a wholly religious purpose would violate the "secular purpose" test.

74. See *Mueller v. Allen*, 463 U.S. 388, 396 n.6 (1983), distinguishing *Committee for Pub. Educ. & Religious Liberty v. Nyquist*, 413 U.S. 756 (1973). For a fuller discussion, see supra note 72 and related text.

75. For a criticism, see *Lynch v. Donnelly*, 465 U.S. 668, 687–89 (1984) (O'Connor, J., concurring).

76. A point made forthrightly by Justice O'Connor in *City of Akron v. Akron Center for Reproductive Health*, 462 U.S. 416, 459–61 (1983) (dissenting opinion).

77. See *Commonwealth Edison Co. v. Montana*, 453 U.S. 609, 625–26 (1981). For an insightful discussion, see Williams, supra note 44, at 287–89.

78. See supra note 27 and related text.

79. See supra note 26 and related text.

80. Examples, of course, are legion, but this one serves to illustrate the point: In a dissenting opinion, Justice Rehnquist argued that an alienage classification was not "suspect" and should be tested only by the rationality standard. Under this standard, the state's purpose was "surely" legitimate and the classification's rationality "evident" (*Toll v. Moreno,* 458 U.S. 1, 39, 47 [1982]). In a concurring opinion, Justice Blackmun labeled Justice Rehnquist's argument on suspect classifications "simplistic to the point of caricature" and "preposterous" (458 U.S. at 20, 23). Justice Blackmun thought that all alienage cases had been decided consistently with a single principle (458 U.S. at 21).

81. *U.S. v. Butler,* 297 U.S. 1, 62 (1936). See supra note 49 and related text.

82. Although an extreme example, here is an entire discussion of whether an ad valorem personal property tax on imported goods being stored for shipment violated the "dormant" commerce clause:

> Nor do I find merit in appellant's constitutional arguments. Appellees' taxes do not violate the Commerce Clause, as they are "applied to an activity with a substantial nexus with the taxing State, [are] fairly apportioned, [do] not discriminate against interstate commerce, and [are] fairly related to the services provided by the State." Complete Auto Transit, Inc. v. Brady, 430 U.S. 274, 279 (1977). (*Xerox Corp. v. County of Harris, Tex.,* 459 U.S. 145, 157 [1982] [Powell, J., dissenting])

83. The phrases are from *Larkin v. Grendel's Den,* 459 U.S. 116, 123 (1982); *Committee for Pub. Educ. & Religious Liberty v. Nyquist,* 413 U.S. 756, 780 (1973); *Committee for Pub. Educ. & Religious Liberty v. Nyquist,* 413 U.S. 756, 785 (1973); *EEOC v. Wyoming,* 460 U.S. 226, 258 (1983) (Burger, C.J., dissenting); and *EEOC v. Wyoming,* 460 U.S. 226, 236 (1983).

84. See supra note 32. "Yield" is from *Central Hudson Gas & Elec. v. Public Serv. Comm'n,* 447 U.S. 557, 566 (1980).

85. See, e.g., Bennett, supra note 39; Dworkin, *Law as Interpretation and My Reply to Stanley Fish (and Walter Benn Michaels): Please Don't Talk About Objectivity Any More,* in W. Mitchell, ed., THE POLITICS OF INTERPRETATION, supra note 36, at 249, 289. Fiss, supra note 18.

86. Bennett, supra note 39, at 447; Fiss, supra note 18, at 773.

87. Bennett, supra note 39, at 458; Dworkin, supra note 85, at 304; Fiss, supra note 18, at 744.

88. *McCulloch v. Maryland,* 17 U.S. (4 Wheat.) 316, 426 (1819).

89. 365 U.S. 715 (1961).

90. 365 U.S. at 725.

91. 365 U.S. at 725–26.

92. E.g., Lewis, *Burton v. Wilmington Parking Authority—A Case Without Precedent,* 61 Colum. L. Rev. 1458 (1961).

93. 365 U.S. at 726.

94. See *Jackson v. Metropolitan Edison Co.*, 419 U.S. 345, 366 (1974); *Gilmore v. City of Montgomery*, 417 U.S. 556, 564 (1974); *Moose Lodge No. 107 v. Irvis*, 407 U.S. 163 (1972); *United States v. Price*, 383 U.S. 787, 794 (1966); *Evans v. Newton*, 382 U.S. 296, 299 (1966); *Griffin v. Maryland*, 378 U.S. 130, 137 (1964) (Clark, J., concurring); *Lombard v. Louisiana*, 373 U.S. 267, 274 (1963) (Douglas, J., concurring); *Peterson v. City of Greenville*, 373 U.S. 244, 247 (1963); *Turner v. City of Memphis*, 369 U.S. 350, 353 (1962); *Griggs v. Allegheny County*, 369 U.S. 84, 89 (1962).

95. 365 U.S. at 724–25.

96. See supra note 56 and related text. "Must show" is from *In re Griffiths*, 413 U.S. 717, 721–22 (1973).

97. *Mississippi Univ. for Women v. Hogan*, 458 U.S. 718, 724 (1982) (emphasis added), quoting *Wengler v. Druggists Mut. Ins. Co.*, 446 U.S. 142, 150 (1980).

98. E.g., *Lynch v. Donnelly*, 465 U.S. 668, 679 (1984) ("useful" but the court will not "be confined to any single test or criterion"); *Solem v. Helm*, 463 U.S. 279, 291 (1983) ("may be helpful," "may find it useful"); *Meek v. Pittenger*, 421 U.S. 349, 359 (1975) ("not . . . precise limits . . . but . . . only . . . guidelines").

99. For a description of one example of redundancy, see Williams, supra note 44, at 288.

100. *Kassel v. Consolidated Freightways Corp.*, 450 U.S. 662, 670–71 (1981).

101. 450 U.S. at 671.

102. 450 U.S. at 675–76.

103. 450 U.S. at 671 (emphasis added).

104. E.g., *Meek v. Pittenger*, 421 U.S. 349 (1975).

105. Compare *Meek v. Pittenger*, 421 U.S. 349, 363 (1975) (Court accepts "legislative findings that the welfare of the Commonwealth requires that present and future generations of schoolchildren be assured ample opportunity to develop their intellectual capacities" and that the statute was intended to extend "the benefits of free educational aids to every schoolchild") with *Meek*, 421 U.S. at 365–66 ("massive aid provided the church-related nonpublic schools . . . is neither indirect nor incidental . . . [and] inescapably results in the direct and substantial advancement of religious activity").

106. The modern Court's effort to design the proper test for sex discrimination cases dates from 1971, and significant refinements were still being made in 1982. Compare *Reed v. Reed*, 404 U.S. 71 (1971), with *Mississippi Univ. for Women v. Hogan*, 458 U.S. 718 (1982). See supra notes 32, 61. Similar time has been devoted to alienage. Compare *Graham v. Richardson*, 403 U.S. 365 (1971), with *Bernal v. Fainter*, 467

U.S. 216 (1984). Nearly a decade was spent defining state sovereignty, and renewed efforts are likely. Compare *National League of Cities v. Usery,* 426 U.S. 833 (1976), with *Garcia v. San Antonio Metro. Transit Auth.,* 105 S. Ct. 1005 (1985). The tinkering with the tests for obscenity went on between 1957 and 1973. Compare *Roth v. United States,* 354 U.S. 476 (1957), with *Miller v. California,* 413 U.S. 15 (1973); *Paris Adult Theatre v. Slaton,* 413 U.S. 49, 73 (1973) (Brennan, J., dissenting).

107. The Court needed thirteen years to decide what standard of review should govern alienage discrimination cases. Then in *Bernal v. Fainter* (a case involving discrimination against aliens in laws governing notary publics) the Court spent more than four pages on doctrine selection and less than a single page—in fact, one paragraph—in applying the doctrine to the case (467 U.S. 216 [1984]). Only a few years earlier, in a similar case, the Court had spent almost nine pages on doctrine selection and a half page in application (*Ambach v. Norwick,* 441 U.S. 68 [1979]). After decades of reliance on the "minimum rationality" test, the Court in 1977 spent more than six pages on the test and less than a page in applying it (*Trimble v. Gordon,* 430 U.S. 762 [1977]). For other examples, see *Rostker v. Goldberg,* 453 U.S. 57 (1981); *Regents of the Univ. of Cal. v. Bakke,* 438 U.S. 265, 324–79 (1978) (Brennan, J., concurring); *Frontiero v. Richardson,* 411 U.S. 677 (1973); *San Antonio Indep. School Dist. v. Rodriguez,* 411 U.S. 1 (1973).

108. On judges as observers, see supra notes 82–84 and related text. On responsibility for formulae, see supra note 32 and related text.

109. See, e.g., *Wood v. Georgia,* 370 U.S. 375 (1962); *Dennis v. United States,* 341 U.S. 494 (1951); *Debs v. United States,* 249 U.S. 211 (1919); *Schenck v. United States,* 249 U.S. 47 (1919).

110. See generally E. Levi, An Introduction to Legal Reasoning (Chicago: University of Chicago Press, 1949).

111. See supra notes 90–95 and related text.

112. 411 U.S. 677, 682 (footnotes omitted) (1973).

113. 411 U.S. at 684–86.

114. E.g., *Mississippi Univ. for Women v. Hogan,* 458 U.S. 718 (1982) (exclusion of men from a state nursing school); *Michael M. v. Superior Court,* 450 U.S. 464 (1981) (statutory rape law that punished only males); *Craig v. Boren,* 429 U.S. 190 (1976) (statute allowing women to drink beer at an earlier age).

115. The long and unsuccessful effort to add the equal rights amendment to the Constitution is some evidence that, despite the plurality's certitude, a substantial part of the population prefers to view its history in a more benign or, perhaps, a more complicated way. For academic considerations of related issues, see J. Elshtain, Public Man, Private

WOMAN (Princeton: Princeton University Press, 1981); C. McMillan, WOMEN, REASON AND NATURE (Princeton: Princeton University Press, 1982).

116. See B. Barber, supra note 14, at 177.

117. The phrases are from B. Barber, supra note 14, at 177–78, who quotes William James, PRAGMATISM AND THE MEANING OF THE TRUTH 32 (Cambridge: Harvard University Press, 1978) (emphasis deleted).

118. On church and state, see, e.g., *Lynch v. Donnelly*, 465 U.S. 668 (1984). On probable cause, see, e.g., *Illinois v. Gates*, 462 U.S. 213 (1983). On state sovereignty, see, e.g., *Garcia v. San Antonio Metro. Transit. Auth.*, 105 S. Ct. 1005 (1985).

On abortion regulation, Justice Sandra O'Connor said:

> Neither sound constitutional theory nor our need to decide cases based on the application of neutral principles can accommodate an analytical framework that varies according to the "stages" of pregnancy, where those stages, and their concomitant standards of review, differ according to the level of medical technology available when a particular challenge to state regulation occurs. . . . Our recent cases indicate that a regulation imposed on "a lawful abortion 'is not unconstitutional unless it unduly burdens the right to seek an abortion.'" In my view, this "unduly burdensome" standard should be applied to the challenged regulations throughout the entire pregnancy without reference to the particular "stage" of pregnancy involved. (*City of Akron v. Akron Center for Reproductive Health*, 462 U.S. 416, 452–53 [1983] [O'Connor, J., dissenting] [citations omitted])

119. *Regents of the Univ. of Cal. v. Bakke*, 438 U.S. 265, 359–61 (1978) (Brennan, J., concurring).

120. 438 U.S. at 362, quoting Gunther, *In Search of Evolving Doctrine on a Changing Court: A Model for a Newer Equal Protection*, 86 Harv. L. Rev. 1, 8 (1972).

121. 438 U.S. at 356–58.

122. 438 U.S. at 365–66.

123. It is possible, for example, that discrimination by whites hurts both whites and minorities, so that a nondiscriminatory history could have improved Bakke's qualifications. Cf. G. Becker, THE ECONOMICS OF DISCRIMINATION ch. 2 (Chicago: University of Chicago Press, 1971) (discrimination results in decrease in net income of both blacks and whites). Under certain circumstances, it is possible that disfavored groups might respond to forms of discrimination in ways that improve their economic and social standing. See T. Sowell, ETHNIC AMERICA: A HISTORY 273 and passim (New York: Basic Books, 1981). It is not inconceivable that favored groups might in some instances respond to their circumstances by losing skills and, accordingly, status: "The extent to

which one group's poverty [and, it might be added, social or professional standing] is caused by another group's bigotry is a causal question, not a foregone conclusion because of the moral repugnancy of bigotry" (T. Sowell, supra, at 273–74).

124. 438 U.S. at 357–58.

125. B. Barber, supra note 14, at 183.

Index

227

Compositor: G&S Typesetters, Inc.
Text: 10/13 Galliard
Display: Galliard
Printer: Maple-Vail Book Mfg. Group
Binder: Maple-Vail Book Mfg. Group